Financial management for
the public services

MANAGING THE PUBLIC SERVICES

Series editor: Dr Alan Lawton, Open University
Business School

Financial management for the public services

Edited by
John Wilson

Open University Press
Buckingham · Philadelphia

Open University Press
Celtic Court
22 Ballmoor
Buckingham
MK18 1XW

email: enquiries@openup.co.uk
world wide web: http://www.openup.co.uk

and
325 Chestnut Street
Philadelphia, PA 19106, USA

First Published 1998

A catalogue record of this book is available from the British Library

ISBN 0 335 19845 7 (pb)   0 335 19846 5 (hb)

Library of Congress Cataloging-in-Publication Data
Financial management for the public services / edited by John Wilson.
    p.   cm. — (Managing the public services)
   Includes bibliographical references and index.
   ISBN 0–335–19846–5 (hardcover). — ISBN 0–335–19845–7 (pbk.)
   1. Finance, Public—Great Britain. 2. Public welfare—Great
Britain—Finance. 3. National Health Service (Great Britain)—
Finance. 4. Government spending policy—Great Britain—
History—20th century. 5. Local finance—Great Britain.
I. Wilson, John. 1958– . II. Series.
HJ1023.F537 1998
336.41—DC21   98–9195
                                   CIP

Typeset by Graphicraft Limited, Hong Kong
Printed in Great Britain by Biddles Limited, Guildford and Kings Lynn

This book is dedicated to my mum, Anne, to the loving memory of my dad, Jack, and to Eileen, Maura, Frank, Sheila and Phil

Contents

The editor and contributors

Anita Carroll lectures at the University of Salford, having previously worked at Liverpool John Moores University and as a practising accountant in the National Health Service. She is a qualified member of the Chartered Institute of Public Finance and Accountancy (CIPFA) and an associate member of the Chartered Institute of Marketing. Her main research interests are in the area of public service financial management.

Alan Doig is Professor of Public Service Management and Head of the Unit for the Study of White Collar Crime, Liverpool Business School. He was previously Sub-Dean of the Faculty of Social and Environmental Studies and Fellow of the Institute of Public Administration and Management, University of Liverpool. His main research interests concern corruption and fraud in the public sector, on which he has published extensively. He is the author of *Corruption and Misconduct in Contemporary British Politics* (1994, Harmondsworth: Penguin) and *Westminster Babylon: Sex, Scandal and Money in British Politics* (1990, London: Allison & Busby). He has also co-edited (with F. F. Ridley) *Sleaze: Politicians, Private Interests and Public Reaction* (1996, Oxford: Oxford University Press).

George Foster lectures at Liverpool Business School. He is a professionally qualified member of CIPFA and joined the Business School in 1994 after gaining over twenty years experience as a practitioner in the National Health Service, the last eight of which were at Director of Finance level.

David Gardner lectures at Liverpool Business School. He is a qualified member of CIPFA with an academic background in economics. His main research interests are in the area of public service performance measurement, with a specific interest in the finance and economics of local government. He currently acts as an academic adviser to CIPFA.

Bob Hopkins is a Senior Consultant with Price Waterhouse, having previously lectured at Liverpool Business School. He is a qualified member of CIPFA. Prior to joining the Business School he worked in senior positions in both accountancy and audit in a number of local authorities. His main research interests concern audit expectations, quality and the expectations gap, on which he has undertaken extensive research into public service organizations in collaboration with CIPFA.

Christopher J. Pyke lectures at Liverpool Business School. He is a qualified member of CIPFA and specializes in local authority accounting and auditing. Prior to joining the Business School he held senior positions with Cheshire County Council. His main research interests are in the areas of local authority budgeting and financial accounting.

John Williams formerly lectured at Liverpool Business School. He is a qualified member of the Chartered Institute of Management Accountants (CIMA) and acts in an advisory capacity for CIMA. He previously held senior financial management positions in a variety of private sector multinational organizations and has developed a research interest in the applicability of private sector financial management techniques to the management of public services.

John Wilson is Head of the Centre for Public Service Management and Assistant Director for Postgraduate and Professional Programmes, Liverpool Business School. He is a qualified member of CIPFA with an academic background in politics and economics. His main research interests concern the management and economics of public service provision. He has co-edited (with P. Hinton) *Public Services and the 1990s: Issues in Public Service Finance and Management* (1993, Eastham: Tudor) and edited *Managing Public Services: Dealing With Dogma* (1995, Eastham: Tudor) and *Current Issues in Accounting and Auditing* (1996, Eastham: Tudor). He currently acts as an academic adviser to CIPFA.

Series editor's preface

Managing the public services is, increasingly, a complex activity where a range of different types of organization are involved in the delivery of public services. Public services managers have had to develop new skills and adopt new perspectives as the boundaries between public, private and voluntary sector organizations become blurred. The management task becomes one of managing ambiguity in an ever-changing world. At the same time, however, there is a certain timeliness to any debate concerning the management of public policies and managers will need to acknowledge the continuing relevance of traditions and the enduring nature of the themes of accountability, responsibility, acting in the public interest, integrity, probity, and responding to citizens, clients and customers.

This series addresses key issues in managing public services and contributes to the debates concerning the appropriate role for managers in the public services located within a contested governance arena. Through the use of original research, case studies and commentaries on theoretical models, the books in the series will be of relevance to practitioners and to academics and their students. An underlying theme of the series is the inescapable intertwining of theory and practice such that theory will be tested out in practice and practice will be grounded in theory. Theoretical concepts and models need to be made relevant for the practitioner but at the same time good practice will need to be analysed, tested against theoretical models and disseminated. In this way the series will fulfil its commitments to both an academic and a practitioner audience.

Alan Lawton

Preface

Public service provision is one of the most important issues confronting any economy. In the United Kingdom (UK), the nature and scale of public service activity have been at the centre of political and economic debate for over two decades. The belief in the merits of public sector expansion, which characterized much of the period since the Second World War, was replaced, particularly throughout the 1980s and 1990s, by a belief in the need to reverse the process of public sector growth in order to free resources for the private sector.

It became fashionable to believe that the public sector was inherently inefficient and needed to be coerced into efficiency by: transferring activities into the private sector where appropriate; exposing to competition activities which remain in the public sector; and revolutionizing public sector management so that it approximated more closely to the private sector model.

The above policies all led to ever-greater pressures and constraints on public sector personnel and placed the issue of financial management at the centre of public service provision.

This book addresses the key issue of financial management in the public services, with in-depth chapters on the National Health Service (NHS) and local government. The meaning and importance of financial management are considered within the wider economic and management context of public service delivery. The text is written by public service specialists of Liverpool Business School, the University of Salford and Price Waterhouse.

Written for new and existing managers, students and lecturers in the public services, the text explores the meaning and significance of financial management in the public services, in a way which combines both theoretical arguments and practical applications. Written for the non-specialist, it:

- examines the economics of public services provision;
- considers the extent to which the management of public services has actually changed in practice;
- explains the meaning and applicability of financial management tools including those relating to budgets and capital investment;
- presents original work on the issue of audit expectations;
- presents case studies on the problems which can arise when traditional concerns on probity and stewardship are neglected;
- considers the benefits and problems of measuring performance in the public services;
- examines in-depth financial management in the NHS and local government.

The text comprises eleven chapters, structured into five key sections, each of which addresses different aspects of financial management. Chapter 1 examines the nature and scale of public service provision and public expenditure in the UK and contains comparative information. The chapter evaluates the overall approach to public expenditure pursued by successive Conservative governments and the Labour government. In so doing, it considers the debate as to the most appropriate level of public expenditure.

Chapter 2 analyses the significant changes that have occurred in the management of public services. The reasons for and nature of the changes are analysed within the context of the New Right critique of traditional public sector service delivery.

Chapter 3 considers the importance of budgeting and budgetary control for management of resources within public services and explains the various techniques adopted.

Chapter 4 considers the significance and complexities of costing public service activity and its implications for competitiveness and pricing of services.

Chapter 5 examines the significance of the appraisal of capital projects and the merits and demerits of different techniques in deciding how scarce resources are to be allocated. It also considers the applicability to public services of techniques conventionally applied to private sector projects.

Chapter 6 considers the role of audit in public services, with particular reference to its role in the achievement of quality in service provision.

Chapter 7 considers the implications of inadequate management of financial resources, focusing on the issues of mismanagement and fraud within the NHS, considered within the context of the changes which have been introduced in the management of public services.

Chapter 8 examines the importance of measuring performance in the public services, focusing on the problems of output and effectiveness measurement and the limitations of comparative information.

Chapter 9 considers financial management in local government, including financial accounting, financial reporting and budgeting.

Chapter 10 considers financial management within the NHS and, in doing so, highlights the key issues confronting the NHS today.

Chapter 11 draws common themes and conclusions from the preceding chapters and considers likely future developments in the management of financial resources within the public services.

Each chapter contains learning objectives and, as appropriate, rationale and critique of existing practice and case studies for illustration and discussion. References for further reading are also included. The text is intended for use at final year undergraduate level and postgraduate and MBA public service courses and options. It will also be of use on professional courses, e.g. with the Chartered Institute of Public Finance and Accountancy (CIPFA), and, as such, is intended to be accessible to practitioners and students alike.

Acknowledgements

I am extremely grateful to all my colleagues who have contributed to this text, not least for their patient and constructive responses to all my deadlines and suggested amendments. I am also grateful to colleagues, both academics and practitioners, who have commented on earlier drafts of the chapters, particularly Dr Alan Lawton. Thanks are also due to Denise Quinn for her invaluable assistance in preparing the final manuscript. Needless to say, responsibility for errors and omissions is entirely mine. Finally, and above all, I am grateful to Chris and Hannah for their tolerance and understanding.

John Wilson, January 1998

Abbreviations

ABC activity-based costing
AHA area health authority
ASB Accounting Standards Board
CCT compulsory competitive tendering
CFO chief financial officer
CHC community health council
CIM *Capital Investment Manual*
CIMA Chartered Institute of Management Accountants
CIP cost improvement programme
CIPFA Chartered Institute of Public Finance and Accountancy
DHA district health authority
DLO direct labour organization
DoH Department of Health
DSO direct service organization
EFL external financing limit
EMU economic and monetary union
FBC full business case
FHS family health services
FHSA family health service authority
FMI financial management initiative
FPC family practitioner committee
FRS Financial Reporting Statement
GDP gross domestic product
GGE general government expenditure
GGR general government receipts
GP general practitioner
HCHS hospitals and community health services
HRG healthcare resource group

IFS Institute for Fiscal Studies
IMF International Monetary Fund
IR/IT Inland Revenue Information Technology Services
IRR internal rate of return
LASAAC Local Authority (Scotland) Accounts Advisory Committee
NAO National Audit Office
NDPB non-departmental public body
NHSE NHS Executive
NHSME NHS Management Executive
NNDR national non-domestic rates
NPM new public management
NPV net present value
OBC outline business case
OECD Organization for Economic Cooperation and Development
PESC Public Expenditure Survey Committee
PFI private finance initiative
PPBS planning programming budgeting systems
PSBR public sector borrowing requirement
PSO public service organization
RAWP Resource Allocation Working Party
RHA regional health authority
ROCE return on capital employed
ROI return on investment
RPI retail price index
RSG revenue support grant
SLA service level agreement
SORP Statement of Recommended Practice
SSA standard spending assessment
SSAP Statement of Standard Accounting Practice
VFM value for money
WHO World Health Organization
ZBB zero-based budgeting

part one

Public service environment

one

Economics of public service provision

John Wilson

Key learning objectives

After reading this chapter you should be able to:

1 Understand the distinction between public and private sector activity and appreciate the scale of public sector activity in the United Kingdom.
2 Discern trends in public expenditure.
3 Evaluate critically the nature and validity of public expenditure policy from mid-1970s to the present.
4 Place into a wider political and economic context the environment within which public service managers operate.

Introduction

The scale and nature of public sector activity have been key subjects of political and economic debate, internationally and domestically, throughout the twentieth century. Particularly since the mid-1970s, however, the essence of the debate has changed. Consensual support for expansion of public sector activity was replaced, not least within the United Kingdom (UK), by demands for contraction relative to the private sector. Although the election of a Labour government, in May 1997, after 18 years of Conservative rule, brought to an end central government's ideological hostility to the public sector, the allocation of resources to the public sector must still be justified and their efficient and effective utilization demonstrated.

In this new environment, public service managers in general and financial managers in particular must increasingly adopt commercial, even entrepreneurial, attitudes and techniques as they strive to provide services within ever-tighter resource constraints.

This chapter considers the economic environment within which public service managers operate and is divided into five sections: the distinction between the economic objectives of private and public sector organizations (considered in more detail in Chapter 2); scale of UK public sector activity; trends in UK public expenditure; an evaluation of the rationale of governmental economic policy towards the public sector, including international comparisons as appropriate; and, finally, conclusions.

UK economy: private and public sectors

The UK is a mixed economy; it can be divided into two main categories or sectors, a private sector and a public sector. The private sector, though containing a myriad number of different types of organizations providing a vast range of products and services, constitutes a discrete sector in terms of ownership and purpose.

With regard to ownership, all private sector activity is privately owned, either individually (e.g. the self-employed) or collectively (e.g. families or shareholders); as for purpose, the overriding objective is to ensure that the activity which is being undertaken earns a profit for the owners. Profit is the return on effort, risk and capital and provides, directly or indirectly, the capital for future innovation and growth. It is an indicator not only of organizational efficiency but also, more fundamentally, of society's demand for the product or service which is being supplied. For example, in the case of falling demand, this may be the result of seasonal factors, temporary dissatisfaction with the quality of a product, or fundamental concern as to its safety (e.g. beef). It may, however, also indicate the beginning of a long term and irreversible shift in consumer preferences, leading, for instance, to the decline of certain industries (e.g. coal, textiles, shipbuilding) and the growth of others, producing goods perhaps previously regarded as luxuries. This may be because of economic growth, leading to a generally wealthier society, or through technological advance, itself contributing to economic growth, which enables goods to be produced more cheaply (e.g. cars, televisions, microwaves, video recorders, etc.). Technological advance will also render certain products obsolete.

These short term, long term and interrelated changes in supply and demand make domestic and international markets highly competitive and dynamic, thereby imposing fierce disciplines on private sector managers as they seek to earn profits for their owners. Profit, therefore, can be seen as an indicator of both macroeconomic and microeconomic trends, from relative organizational efficiency in the use of resources to shifts in consumer behaviour, and facilitates comparisons with competitors. The private sector owner or manager has a relatively clear lodestar: the pursuit of profit.

This view of profit is, however, misleading. Viewed from an accountancy perspective, whether a company is reported to have made a profit or a loss will in part depend upon the accountancy treatment of various items. Profit – or loss – is not a single and unique figure, one to which all arithmetic roads lead, awaiting discovery by objective means; rather, it is a figure which emerges from, and varies with, a particular application of accounting principles. Similarly, from an economic perspective, profit may, for instance, simply be the result of exploitation of consumers by a monopoly provider. In short, the reporting of a profit or loss is not in itself sufficient to draw definitive conclusions as to inherent efficiency or consumer preferences, even if it is often presented in this way (though this does not mean that profit is meaningless). On the contrary, the pursuit of it is a defining feature of a market economy in general and private sector activity in particular.

The situation in the public sector, however, is not so straightforward. Comprising central government, local government and public corporations, it, too, is characterized by diversity but it differs from the private sector in that the overriding objective is to provide a service rather than earn a profit. There are and have been exceptions to this non-profit objective. Certain former nationalized industries, for instance, were meant to be commercial entities (e.g. steel, shipbuilding), though they often suffered from political interference which constrained managers' ability to make decisions on commercial grounds. Similarly, other activities are ostensibly provided on a commercial basis. Local authorities, for instance, provide markets, car parks, certain leisure facilities etc. though commercial considerations may coexist with economic or social ones (e.g. reduced leisure fees for the unemployed; notional car park charges to attract consumers into town or, alternatively, very high car park fees to encourage use of public transport etc.). In addition, a number of services are, or were, also provided in competition with private sector organizations (e.g. railways competed with road haulage), and the degree of competition has increased since 1979 following the election of the first Thatcher government.

However, for much of the period up to 1979, commercial considerations were not, generally, evident in public sector activity, not least because they were not applicable and the nature of the activity was not easily quantifiable. Defence, education, health, law and order, and social services, for instance, do not exist in order to make a profit but because, as a society, we believe they should be provided for our individual and collective benefit. Consequently, the state assumes responsibility to ensure the provision of services from which society generally benefits and which would not

	Excludable	Non-excludable
Rivalrous	Pure private goods, such as food and clothing.	Common goods, such as public parks or nature reserves.
Non-rivalrous	Mixed goods, such as roads where tolls can be imposed to reduce traffic.	Pure public goods such as defence or law and order.

Figure 1.1 Characteristics of public markets

have been provided on the same basis or at all had provision been dependent upon market forces. Such state intervention in economic activity is designed to correct market failure, which may occur because of, for instance, the existence of externalities and public goods.

With regard to externalities, these may occur when, for instance, the consumption or production activity of one party affects the welfare of others in a way which is not reflected in market prices. For example, an externality, or social cost, arises from a factory chimney belching smoke into the atmosphere which affects those who involuntarily consume the pollution. In the same way, external or social benefits may also occur. Externalities, therefore, generate costs or benefits that are not included in market prices. Governments can intervene to correct such market failure by, for instance, imposing pollution taxes or emission standards.

A further dimension to externalities is the existence of public goods which yield benefits from which people cannot be excluded, for example, defence, law and order, and street lighting. These goods are non-excludable, in that, in contrast to private goods such as food or clothing from which people can be excluded unless they pay, it is not possible to deny the benefits of these goods to those who, for instance, refuse to pay their taxes or to meet their full tax liability. Because of their non-excludable nature, there is no real incentive for a private sector firm to provide the goods, so the state does so for the benefit of society.

Pure public goods are also non-rivalrous. This means that the addition of another consumer will not lead to a subtraction from any other individual's consumption of that good (e.g. defence, broadcasting). Where goods are rivalrous, for example, land, the government may intervene to limit the use of the resource so as to preserve it for the common good. Characteristics of public markets are represented in Figure 1.1.

A government may, therefore, intervene in economic activity in order to influence or regulate production and consumption, or to produce certain goods and services directly. In doing so, its motive is generally not to make a 'profit' but, rather, to provide a service from which society benefits. However, the non-existence of a public sector equivalent of profit, the 'bottom line', makes the provision and management of public sector organizations highly problematic, for a range of reasons including the difficulty in discerning trends in societal preferences in the long term and measuring the relative efficiency of public sector managers in the short term. More fundamentally, determining the optimum macroeconomic scale of public sector activity is as important as it is difficult, given that, first, resources are finite and their allocation to the public sector means they are denied to the private sector and, second, public sector activity must be financed either through taxation or borrowing, both of which may impede enterprise and private sector growth.

The distinction in the *raison d'être* of public and private sector organizations has, however, since 1979, become less clear-cut (see Chapter 2). In an effort to address the perceived problems of inexorable public sector expansion exacerbated by inherent inefficiency, successive Conservative governments sought to reduce the size of the public sector ('roll back the frontiers of the state'), and therefore the level of public expenditure, mainly through the policy of privatization, and to expose to competition many of the activities which remain in the public sector. The justification for doing so has, it would seem, been accepted rather than challenged by Labour.

Scale of UK public service activity

Unlike the private sector, the goods and services that the public sector produces are not sold in the marketplace. This means that public sector output cannot be measured at market prices, so its scale must be measured by the volume of its input. Two measures are available: employment levels, and the cost of service provision, i.e. the level of public expenditure.

Table 1.1 provides details of employment levels; figures for 1979 have been included for comparative purposes and to indicate the considerable impact that privatization has had on manpower levels within the public sector, particularly within the civil service (mainly shown as 'Other' under 'Central government') and public corporations. The figures also reveal a significant increase in personnel in the police service and health and social services. The scale of activity, as represented in employment levels, is further reflected in the figures for public expenditure. This is the second measure of the volume of inputs.

Definitions of public expenditure are subject to change but, providing appropriate adjustments are made for such changes, its level represents the cost of public sector provision of certain goods and services. In planning public expenditure, the government annually announces a control total and, in June 1995, a new definition of spending was announced, GGE (general government expenditure) (X). GGE (X) excludes expenditure paid out of the National Lottery distribution fund and deducts interest and dividend receipts from central government debt interest payments. The scale of public expenditure is then expressed as a percentage of gross

Table 1.1 Public sector manpower 1979–92 (thousands)

	1979	1992	Variation (%)
Central government			
HM Forces	314	290	−7.7
National Health Service including NHS Trusts	1,152	1,233	+7.0
Other	921	800	−13.1
Sub-total	2,387	2,323	−2.7
Local authorities:			
Education	1,539	1,392	−9.6
Health & social services	344	410	+19.2
Construction	156	97	−37.8
Police & civilians	176	204	+15.9
Other	782	798	+2.0
Sub-total	2,997	2,901	−3.2
Public corporations			
Nationalized industries including Post Office	1,849	477	−74.2
Other	216	94	−56.5
Sub-total	2,065	571	−72.3
Total	7,449	5,795	−22.2

Source: Economic Trends Annual Supplement 1995, Table 3.4, pp. 168–9.

domestic product (GDP), i.e. the annual value of goods and services produced by UK residents. It is important to note that the previous Conservative government's objective with regard to public expenditure was to reduce it to below 40 per cent of GDP (discussed below), as announced by the Chancellor, Kenneth Clarke, in the 1996–7 budget statement on 28 November 1995. The Labour government has no such intention but is none the less committed to controlling public expenditure. For instance, in an interview given by Tony Blair, when leader of the opposition, to the *Financial Times*, 16 January 1997, Blair was reported to have no ambition to raise the share of national income consumed by public spending. To reinforce the point he remarked that Clement Attlee, the Labour prime minister under whose premiership the welfare state was established immediately after the Second World War, presided over a much smaller share of national income than that which prevails today and that in 1950, a year before Attlee left office, the ratio of state spending to national income was around 30 per cent (see '*Public expenditure policy: evaluation of rationale*', page 18).

The objective announced by the former Conservative chancellor follows previously abandoned ones. Initially, the intention was to reduce expenditure in real terms; this was then changed to holding it constant in real terms, then to reducing it as a percentage of GDP and, finally, to reducing it to below 40 per cent of GDP (see page 21).

The new Labour Chancellor, Gordon Brown, announced in his first budget (2 July 1997), that GGE (X) was forecast to be £315.3bn in 1997–8, representing 39.5 per cent of GDP. The control total for 1997–8 represented a reduction of £5.72bn from that announced in the 1995–6 Budget (29 November 1994). An obvious reason for the squeeze on spending plans was that the government had less money available than was initially forecast to finance expenditure. The reason for this was the shortfall in estimated taxation revenues:

Estimated general government receipts (GGR) 1997–8 as per:

	£bn
Nov 1994 budget	316.0
Nov 1995 budget	304.0
Nov 1996 budget	299.4
Variation	−16.6

A shortfall in tax receipts leads to higher levels of borrowing and a greater squeeze on public expenditure. To some extent this was addressed by Brown in that taxation increases were announced in July 1997 (the November 1996 and July 1997 estimates of 1997–8 receipts were £299.4bn and £308.3bn respectively) but, inevitably, the tight expenditure plans have consequences for public sector managers and users of public services. The overall forecast for 1997–8 is as follows:

	£bn
GGE	319.4
GGR	308.3
General government borowing requirement	11.1
Public corporations' market and overseas borrowing	−0.2
Public sector borrowing requirement (PSBR)	10.9

Tables 1.2 and 1.3 provide details of 1997–8 expenditure plans and illustrate the relative magnitudes of expenditure on various functions. Note particularly the significance of social security expenditure as a proportion of the total. Table 1.4 provides details of how the expenditure is to be financed (note: totals may not add due to roundings).

Please note that the figures in Tables 1.2, 1.3 and 1.4 are drawn from the November 1996 and July 1997 budget statements, the reason being that Labour had, prior to the general election of 1997, committed itself to the departmental spending plans, i.e. the control total, for 1997–8 and 1998–9 announced by the Conservatives in November 1996. For this reason,

Table 1.2 Public expenditure forecasts 1997–8

	£bn (rounded)
Control total	**266.4**
Welfare to work	0.2
Local authority spending under the capital receipts initiative	0.2
Cyclical social security	13.7
CG net debt interest	24.6
Accounting adjustments	10.1
GGE (X)	**315.3**
Privatization proceeds	–2.0
Other adjustments	6.2
GGE	**319.4**
GGE (X) as a % of GDP	**39.5**

Source: HM Treasury (1997), Table 2.4, p. 43.

the Chancellor made no changes in July 1997 to the departmental ceilings within the control total for 1997–8, though changes were announced regarding the means by which expenditure was to be financed, notably involving the introduction of a windfall tax on the privatized utilities. However, with regard to expenditure, in addition to undertaking a comprehensive spending review, changes were announced in respect of 1998–9, primarily involving increased resources to the NHS (an extra £1.2bn) and schools (an extra £1bn) from the government's contingency reserve. In the case of education, the increase will be supplemented by further increases, totalling £1.3bn, spread over the lifetime of the parliament, resulting from the imposition of a windfall tax in 1997–8 and 1998–9.

Trends in UK public expenditure

It is not particularly easy to make sense of public expenditure figures, not least because claims and counterclaims are made by politicians to convince the voters that they, unlike their opponents, can be trusted to devote increased resources to public services while simultaneously securing improved efficiency, promoting enterprise and minimizing the tax burden. This political crossfire makes it difficult to establish an accurate picture of expenditure levels and trends but, in attempting to do this, it is useful to place the figures into a historical context.

Table 1.5 shows that the proportion of expenditure to GDP is expected to be below 40 per cent, the target of the previous government, in 1997–

Table 1.3 Public expenditure 1997–8 by department and function

Department	£bn
Social security (excluding cyclical)	79.7
Health	34.9
Dept of environment – local government	31.4
Dept of environment – other	7.6
Scotland, Wales and N. Ireland	29.5
Defence	21.8
Education and employment	14.0
Home Office	6.8
Transport	5.2
Other departments	19.5
Local authority self-financed expenditure	13.7
Reserve	2.5
Control total	**266.5**
Welfare to work	0.2
Local authority spending under the capital receipts initiative	0.2
Cyclical social security	13.7
CG net debt interest	24.6
Accounting adjustments	10.1
GGE (X)	**315.3**

Function	£bn
Social security	100
Health and personal social services	53
Education	38
Defence	22
Law and order	17
Housing, heritage and environment	15
Industry, agriculture and employment	13
Transport	9
Other	23
Debt interest	25
GGE (X)	**315**

Source: HM Treasury (1996), Table 1.3, p. 11, and Chart 1.2, p. 10; HM Treasury (1997), Table 2.4, p. 43.

8. In only 10 of the 34 years included in Table 1.5 is public expenditure shown to be below 40 per cent. It can also be seen that expenditure grew significantly between the mid-1960s and mid-1970s and it was against this background that increasing numbers of economists and politicians

Table 1.4 Financing of GGE 1997–8

	£bn
Inland Revenue	
Income tax	76.5
Corporation tax	30.1
Windfall tax	2.6
Petroleum revenue tax	1.3
Capital gains tax	1.3
Inheritance tax	1.6
Stamp duties	3.3
Sub-total	116.7
Customs and Excise	
Value added tax	50.0
Fuel duties	19.2
Tobacco duties	8.5
Spirits duties	1.5
Wine duties	1.4
Beer and cider duties	2.9
Betting and gaming duties	1.5
Air passenger duty	0.5
Insurance premium tax	1.1
Landfill tax	0.4
Customs duties	2.1
Sub-total	89.2
Vehicle excise duties	4.4
Oil royalties	0.6
Business rates	14.5
Social security contributions	49.5
Council tax	10.6
Other taxes and royalties	7.5
Total taxes and social security contributions	**293.0**
Interest and dividends	5.0
Gross trading surpluses and rent	4.9
Other receipts	5.4
General Government Receipts (GGR)	**308.3**
Borrowing	11.1
Total	**319.4**

Source: HM Treasury (1997), Table 4A.1, p. 113 and Table 4.2, p. 96.

Table 1.5 Historical series: Public expenditure and general government receipts

Year	Control total		GGE (X)			GGR
	£bn	Real terms £bn	£bn	Real terms £bn	% of GDP	% of GDP
1964–65			11.8	128.7	35	
1965–66			13.1	136.3	36.5	35.25
1966–67			14.5	144.6	38	36.25
1967–68			16.8	163.2	41.5	38
1968–69			17.5	161.8	40	40.75
1969–70			18.5	162.7	39.25	41.75
1970–71			20.7	167.9	39.5	40.25
1971–72			23.3	173.1	40	39.75
1972–73			26.4	181.5	39.75	38
1973–74			30.5	196.3	41.5	38.5
1974–75			41.0	220.7	46.75	40.5
1975–76			51.6	221.3	47.25	40.25
1976–77			57.0	215.5	44.75	41
1977–78			61.7	205.1	41.5	39.75
1978–79			72.0	215.5	42.25	38.75
1979–80			87.0	222.9	42.5	38.75
1980–81			104.8	227	44.75	40.75
1981–82			116.3	229.8	45.5	43.75
1982–83			127.8	235.7	45.5	43.75
1983–84			136.5	240.8	44.75	43
1984–85	126.0	211.4	147.9	247.8	45.25	43.5
1985–86	129.5	206	154.9	246.4	43.25	42.25
1986–87	136.0	210	163.3	252.1	42.25	41.5
1987–88	148.6	217.8	172.9	253.5	40.5	41
1988–89	156	214.4	180.7	248.3	38	40.25
1989–90	175.1	224.9	198.0	254.4	38.25	40.25
1990–91	193.5	230.2	217.2	258.4	39	39.25
1991–92	213.2	238.3	238.5	266.7	41	38.25
1992–93	231.7	248.5	263.5	282.6	43.5	36.75
1993–94	240.7	251	277	288.8	43.25	36
1994–95	247.9	254	288.3	295.3	42.75	37
1995–96	255.2	255.2	299.7	299.7	41.25	38
1996–97	260.6	254.3	307.4	289.9	41	38
1997–98	266.4		315.3		39.5	38.75

Notes: Figures for control total are only available on a consistent basis for years shown. Cash figures adjusted to price levels of 1995–6 except for 1997–8.

Source: HM Treasury (1996), Table 5A.1, p. 120 and HM Treasury (1997), Table 4A.7, p. 119.

questioned the economic efficacy and social desirability of state activity, with some regarding state expansion as almost sinister and constituting a threat to individual liberty. Between 1979 and 1997, the prevailing orthodoxy was to reduce expenditure, though the track record of the Conservative governments was largely inconsistent with the rhetoric.

In considering the statistics, however, it is important to remember that the changing ratios may actually be the result of changes in GDP as presently compiled rather than fluctuating spending levels. The mid-1970s, for instance, was a period of economic recession caused by dramatic increases in the price of oil. Such exogenous occurrences are likely adversely to affect the rate of growth of GDP while simultaneously, perhaps, increasing public expenditure (e.g. increased heating costs of public sector buildings and fuel costs for public sector vehicles) and can lead to erroneous conclusions concerning government expenditure.

Similarly, the impact of transfer payments is particularly important. These are redistributions of cash from one section of the community to another, including pensions, child benefit, social security benefits etc. – transfers effected by the state acting as an intermediary. These payments are largely demand-led and inevitably fluctuate with economic activity (e.g. benefits to the unemployed) and demographic trends (e.g. pensions and child benefit). Their significance is apparent in Table 1.3 which shows estimated expenditure on social security in 1997–8 as £100bn, accounting for approximately one-third of total public expenditure. This represents an increase from 10 per cent of GDP in 1978–9 to approximately 12.5 per cent in 1997–8. Sir Geoffrey Holland, formerly permanent secretary at the education department, has said that the overriding priority of every spending round was to settle the DSS (Department of Social Security) budget. 'Every other public expenditure programme – housing, defence, law and order . . . and education – is a residue. Each is fighting, as it were, for the scraps from the social security table' (see Adonis 1996).

However, it must also be pointed out that the proportion of GDP accounted for by social security spending is low by international standards. Hutton (1995) reveals that, on the basis of 1994 figures, of the seven leading industrialized countries (USA, Japan, Germany, France, Italy, Canada, and the UK) only Japan spent less than the UK, i.e. 12.8 per cent, compared with 13.9 per cent of GDP. Even the USA, with expenditure equivalent to 14.2 per cent of GDP, ranks above the UK. In Europe, only Iceland spends less. This is contrary to the view which is fashionable within the Conservative shadow Cabinet – notably expressed by Peter Lilley and John Redwood – that social security spending is unsustainable. Bill Robinson, for instance, former director of the Institute for Fiscal Studies (IFS) and adviser to Norman Lamont for the period when he was Chancellor, has described the social security budget as 'an uncontrollable monster' (Robinson 1993). Hutton's view, however, is consistent with an earlier report published by the Joseph Rowntree Foundation (1993). This points out that, though welfare spending has risen sharply, particularly since 1990, it has remained stable as a share of national income over the medium term and is low by European standards (see also Glennerster and Hills 1998).

None the less, in the UK, the significant increase in the social security budget – partly resulting from increased numbers of unemployed but also substantial increases in, for instance, invalidity benefit and housing benefit payments – contributed to the Conservatives' inability to reduce expenditure in the way they initially intended. Their task was made more difficult by promises, at the outset, actually to increase certain aspects of expenditure, including commitments to honour the recommendations of a public sector pay review body and to devote more resources to certain programmes, viz. defence and law and order. Since then, despite the rhetoric concerning the need to reduce public expenditure, significant increases have occurred, particularly prior to the 1992 general election, contributing to a sharp deterioration in public finances, notably between 1990–1 and 1993–4 when a forecast budget surplus of £7bn was transformed into a forecast deficit of £50bn (respectively 1.5 per cent and 8 per cent of GDP).

This sharp swing had inevitable consequences as the Conservatives sought to regain control of public finances. Though a less stringent fiscal stance was deliberately adopted in the run-up to the 1992 general election, and the deterioration in public finances was partly cyclical in nature reflecting the depth and the duration of the recession of the late 1980s and early 1990s, and partly actually reflected highly inaccurate forecasts, the Conservative response was to introduce an increase in taxation which was unprecedented in peacetime. Norman Lamont's last budget (March 1993) and Kenneth Clarke's first budget (November 1993) involved substantial, and phased, increases in direct and indirect taxation (totalling £16.4bn between 1995–6 and 1996–7). It was, of course, ironic that the Conservatives, given all they had said about the need for sound finances and reduced taxation, should preside over such wildly erratic fiscal policy (i.e. the manipulation of levels of expenditure, taxation and borrowing for the purposes of economic management) and levels of debt and taxation unprecedented in peacetime in the UK. None the less, they never altered their public commitment to reduce public sector activity *vis-à-vis* the private sector.

Despite this unswerving commitment, their record is mixed. In 1978–9, the last full financial year prior to their election, the ratio of expenditure to GDP was 42.25 per cent; the forecast for 1996–7 was 40.5 per cent. During this period, however, there have been significant fluctuations. Overall, expenditure has grown by approximately 35 per cent in real terms during the period 1978–9 to 1996–7 (see Table 1.5). However, as can be seen from Table 1.6, this increase disguises considerable variations in different spending programmes. There is prima facie evidence to show favourable treatment of certain services (e.g. law and order, health) and unfavourable treatment

Table 1.6 General government expenditure by function in real terms[1]

Function	1978–9 outturn £bn	1994–5 estimated outturn £bn	Variation (%)	1978–9 % of GDP	1994–5 estimated % of GDP
Defence	21.8	21.7	−0.46	4.5	3.3
Overseas services	3.0	3.7	+23.3	0.6	0.6
Agriculture, fisheries & food	3.0	3.9	+30	0.6	0.6
Trade, industry, energy and employment	11.7	8.4	−28.2	2.4	1.3
of which, employment and training	*2.9*	*3.7*	*+27.6*	*0.6*	*0.6*
Transport	8.6	10.1	+17.4	1.8	1.5
Housing	12.9	5.4	−58.1	2.6	0.8
Other environmental services	7.6	9.4	+23.7	1.6	1.4
Law, order and protective services	7.3	15.1	+106.8	1.5	2.3
Education	26.2	34.4	+31.3	5.4	5.2
National heritage	2.1	2.7	+28.6	0.4	0.4
Health and personal social services	26.4	45.5	+72.3	5.4	6.9
of which, health	*22.4*	*37.2*	*+66.1*	*4.6*	*5.6*
Social security	48.8	88.8	+82	10.0	13.4
Miscellaneous	7.9	8.2	+3.8	1.6	1.2
Total expenditure on services	**187.3**	**257.3**	**+37.4**	**38.3**	**38.7**

1 Cash figures adjusted to 1993–4 price levels.

Source: HM Treasury (1995), Table 1.3, p. 9 and Table 1.4, p. 10.

of others (e.g. housing). However, the figures require further investigation as there are several important reasons for exercising extreme care when interpreting the statistics.

Public expenditure is generally presented in cash terms (current prices) and conversion into real terms is problematic. Real terms figures are calculated by adjusting the initial data so as to take account of inflation and this is achieved by using the GDP deflator – an index which allows money values caused by price changes to be isolated from those caused by physical changes in output. However, the real terms figures do not precisely reveal the volume of goods and services which the cash buys. The absence of accurate information concerning volume makes it extremely difficult to establish what is actually happening to the level of service provision. This is illustrated by Wilson (1993: 14). Suppose £35bn is spent on health, of which £25bn relates to salaries and wages and the following happens:

Expenditure	£35bn
Government announced increase	£2.45bn
% increase	7.0
Inflation forecast – % increase	4.0
Real terms % increase	3.0
Actual pay award – % increase	10.0
Cost of pay award	£2.5bn

In this example, the cost of the pay settlement has exceeded the increased allocation, resulting in less money being available to spend on beds, equipment, etc. The result is that only £9.95bn (i.e. £37.45bn minus £27.5bn) is available for non-pay expenditure when £10.4bn is actually needed just to maintain the same level of service. This means a reduction in volume of service in excess of 4 per cent even though the government has announced a cash increase of 7 per cent and a 'real terms' increase of 3 per cent.

Such anomalies are particularly likely to arise where the rate of inflation in a particular service is greater than that as indicated by the GDP deflator, thereby requiring deflation of cash figures by a dedicated index. The difference between a specific index or deflator and the GDP deflator is known as the 'relative price effect', which may be positive or negative (Johnson 1991: Ch. 3). However, the Treasury prohibits any detailed focus on changes in inputs; it also prohibits the publication of any assumptions about future price movements, particularly pay (Gillie 1995: 3–4).

Such constraints increase the difficulty of establishing precisely the impact on services of annual expenditure announcements. This was illustrated after the July 1997 budget when the Liberal Democrats accused the Chancellor of hiding a £5bn real-terms cut in public spending, more than offsetting the extra £2.2bn of spending on health and education which the Chancellor announced would be financed from the contingency reserve (see 'Scale of UK public service activity', page 7). The Liberal Democrats claimed the Chancellor had 'scaled up' tax revenue forecasts to reflect higher inflation without increasing the spending totals; as a result, real public spending will be £3bn lower in 1997–8 and £5.3bn lower in 1998–9 than under the previous government's plans. These claims were given apparent support by Andrew Dilnot of the IFS (see *Financial Times*, 7 July 1997).

The difficulties of measuring the impact on services are exacerbated by wider social and economic developments, not least demographic and technological changes, both of which are of particular significance to the health service. Technological advances combined with the increased proportion of the population accounted for by the elderly lead to increased pressures upon the health service as demand for treatment increases. Both variables need to be analysed when assessing the real increase or decrease in the level of resources devoted to the NHS (see Chapter 10).

A final reason for caution when interpreting real-terms increases is that often no distinction is made between capital and revenue expenditure. It may be the case that, in an era of severe financial constraints, capital schemes are postponed or eliminated in order to devote resources to maintain existing levels of service and employment: 'Such action is likely to have long-term implications and any assessment of expenditure must isolate capital and current components in order to ascertain more accurately and realistically the present situation in the context of past and anticipated trends' (Wilson 1993: 17).

An important innovation in this respect, however, is the private finance initiative (PFI), announced by then Chancellor Norman Lamont in the autumn statement, November 1992 (Terry 1996). The policy is designed to enable the government to control expenditure by increasing the involvement of the private sector in the financing and management of public sector capital projects.

There is a need, therefore, to be cautious about political claims concerning expenditure on any particular service and how this may have increased, or reduced, over time. However, more fundamentally, there is also a need to consider the rationale underpinning policy towards the public sector generally.

Public expenditure policy: evaluation of rationale

The commitment of the Conservatives when in office to reduce the scale of public-sector activity reflected the change in the politico-economic environment since the mid-1970s, which is generally interpreted as having its roots in the gradual disillusionment with the political and economic consensus which was forged during, and emerged after, the Second World War. It was after the Second World War and the measures for economic and social reform introduced by the 1945–51 Labour governments, designed in part to meet ever-increasing public expectations, that governmental expenditure began to grow rapidly.

The post-war consensus essentially involved a commitment to the creation of the welfare state, itself constructed on the Beveridge Report (Cm. 6404 1942) and Keynesian economics (i.e. the work of John Maynard Keynes). The latter involved a rejection of classical economic orthodoxy and advocated state intervention to manage demand in the economy, particularly for the purposes of achieving a 'high and stable' level of employment, the phrase used in the 1944 White Paper *Employment Policy* but which came to be known as 'full employment'. Public expenditure was now used as an instrument of economic management (a key part of fiscal policy). Keynesianism became the new economic paradigm and led to general political and economic agreement as to the desirability and attainability of a number of macroeconomic objectives.

By the end of the 1960s, however, increasing numbers of politicians and economists were questioning the efficacy of Keynesianism. Against a background of acute industrial unrest and high levels of both unemployment and inflation (a phenomenon known as stagflation), a new consensus began to grow against Keynesian demand management. It was seen not only as inappropriate to the modern era but in fact as a contributor to the seemingly intractable problems with which it was beset. Keynesian economics, it was said, was the product of the 1930s and as such was concerned almost exclusively with unemployment; the work and ideas of Keynes were not simply irrelevant to the 1970s, particularly in addressing price and wage inflation, but their implementation actually exacerbated the problems with which they were meant to deal. The policy of demand management, involving the manipulation of levels of expenditure, taxation and borrowing to sustain 'full employment', was regarded as being inflationary in that it led to an excessive growth in the money supply and temporarily and artificially pushed unemployment below levels which would otherwise prevail if left to market forces, thereby perpetuating uncompetitiveness and creating demand unmatched by increases in output. The governmental commitment to 'full employment' also encouraged irresponsible behaviour from the labour force, particularly the large proportion represented by powerful trade unions. They could be confident of protection from the risk of unemployment even though pay awards were often gained without being justified on the basis of increased productivity.

Added to this was the expansion of the welfare state. This, it was said, created a 'dependency culture' which was both personally reprehensible and economically harmful. It discouraged enterprise, demotivated those in work whose remuneration was not much greater or possibly less than it would be if they were unemployed, and discouraged those who were unemployed from seeking employment. It also added to the sustained growth in public expenditure, which needed to be financed by those in work but ultimately could only be financed by taxation of the wealth-creating private sector. For many, Keynesianism and post-war socioeconomic policies were discredited.

The theoretical lacuna resulting from the rejection of Keynesianism was most importantly, but temporarily, filled by monetarism (Smith 1987) and a rediscovery of the merits of a *laissez-faire* economy (i.e. one driven by market forces). The intellectual attack on Keynesianism was mainly and variously rooted in the work of Friedrich von Hayek (1944, 1960), Milton Friedman (1962) and a body of mainly American literature which became known as public choice theory.

Public choice theory is the application of economic methods of analysis to the study of political decision making. It adopts a number of assumptions similar to those of neo-classical market economics. These are summarized by Sloman (1994: 450–1):

- Voters are seen as customers and politicians as business people. Politicians produce decisions and outcomes which are 'sold' to the voters.
- The 'money' for which these political decisions are sold is votes. If people want, say a ring-road built, they will vote for the politician or party who will support it. The more actively and successfully the politician or party supports it, the more votes they are likely to get.
- Voters and politicians (and state bureaucrats too) are assumed to be rational utility maximisers aiming for their own personal gain. Everyone weighs up his or her own personal marginal costs and benefits when deciding between alternatives: voters when deciding how to vote; politicians when deciding which policies to pursue.
- In the simplest public choice models it is assumed that politicians' utility is achieved through winning votes. They are thus vote maximisers.

The role of the bureaucrat needs to be stressed as, in public choice theory, the bureaucrat is, like everyone else, a utility maximizer which, for the bureaucrat, means budget maximizer (Niskanen 1971).

In essence, public choice theory postulates that politicians, bureaucrats, interest groups and individuals are motivated by self-interest and act accordingly. To a certain extent the self-interest may be reconciled in that, for instance, politicians may continue to be elected by incurring expenditure on projects which are electorally popular. In the same way, bureaucrats may seek to enlarge their own empire, and in so doing enjoy greater prestige and power, by persuading politicians to devote more resources to their own particular departments on the grounds that the electorate demands it. However, although interests may, to a degree, be reconciled, everyone's utility cannot be maximized. By definition, resources are finite and the opportunity cost of devoting resources to one bureaucrat, interest group or public expenditure project is the utility forgone by those associated with an alternative allocation. None the less, although utility cannot be universally maximized, because of resource constraints, the central relevant point made by public choice theorists is that certain individuals and groups have a vested interest in the growth of public expenditure and, because of that, 'The whole system of public spending and public services is therefore geared to expansion' (Flynn 1990: 12). Unless countervailing policies are adopted (as they have been in the UK and USA), designed to reduce public expenditure, the 'inherent bias of representative democracy to over-produce public services' (Hood 1995: 5) results in an allocation of resources which is economically damaging in that it diverts resources from the private sector. The situation is exacerbated by the apparent irreversibility of the expansion and the propensity for service providers to become detached from service recipients.

Public choice arguments are hardly conclusive. The assumptions upon which the case is based are suspect (Dunleavy 1986), particularly those concerning rational behaviour generally and the behaviour of bureaucrats in particular. However, the literature (e.g. Downs 1957, 1967; Niskanen 1971, 1973; Tullock 1974), became increasingly influential in the late 1970s and throughout the 1980s and, combined with the work, in particular, of Hayek and Friedman, provided a powerful intellectual legitimization for reducing the scale of the public sector. Collectively, it constituted what has become known as a New Right agenda.

The New Right shaped political and economic thinking. Also influential in the mid-1970s was the work of Bacon and Eltis (1976; see also Bacon and Eltis 1996) which put forward a 'crowding out' hypothesis whereby public sector expansion, requiring ever-greater allocations of finite resources, crowded out private sector investment which meant that, in essence, the unproductive sector grew at the expense of the productive one, with obvious economic harm.

Margaret Thatcher, in particular, was influenced by these attacks on post-war conventional wisdom. Her views were restated in January 1996 in a Keith Joseph Memorial Lecture (Thatcher 1996): 'What marks out our Conservative vision is the insight that the state – government – only underpins the conditions for a prosperous and fulfilling life. It does not generate them. Moreover, the very existence of this state, with its huge capacity for evil, is a potential threat to all the moral, cultural, social and economic benefits of freedom'.

Though perhaps it would not be as extremely expressed, this view appears still to be shared by many Conservatives. Their previous commitment to reduce the scale of state activity stemmed from their belief that, beyond a certain point, it is inherently harmful, politically and economically. At what point, however, does it cease to be necessary and beneficial and become harmful? On the basis of Conservative policy when in office, the answer would appear to be 40 per cent of GDP or somewhere below it. Though this allows expenditure to be increased once the desired level has been achieved, as long as the rate of increase is less than the rate of growth in GDP, the policy tells us nothing about the desired level below 40 per cent nor was the 40 per cent figure ever explained.

In analysing any policy which seeks to contain expenditure at a given percentage of GDP, a number of points need to be borne in mind. The first is that measurement of public expenditure and GDP in an economy the size of the UK is predictably difficult and figures are continually being revised. The margin of error involved in statistical compilation should influence policy formulation, not least because economic experiments are not conducted in laboratories; decisions which are taken have a real impact on people's lives. A clear example of the dangers of placing too much reliance on economic forecasts occurred in 1976 when there was a general view that the economy was in crisis and Labour had to seek a loan from the International Monetary Fund (IMF). It was subsequently shown that the expenditure and borrowing forecasts were significantly wrong and the loan was never taken up.

Similarly, quantifying GDP is hardly characterized by precision nor is GDP necessarily an accurate measure of economic and social progress. For instance, it excludes the impact of environmental degradation and, by so doing, falsifies the true nature of any growth which is being recorded. In addition, and related to the first point, it does not measure the quality of life, i.e. the underlying economic and social health of a nation, such as life expectancy, crime, social stability, educational attainment, distribution of income, etc. (see Boulton 1996; Eisner 1996).

Conversely, it could be reasonably assumed that GDP is, in two key ways, perhaps significantly undervalued, and, consequently, the expenditure to GDP ratio overstated. First, and particularly problematic, is the size of the shadow economy. This refers to the value of work undertaken for which payment is received but which is unrecorded (e.g. payments in cash). In fact Eurostat, the European Commission's statistical service, is preparing revised statistics to take account of the problem and has estimated that the Belgian, Greek and Portuguese economies are about 20 per cent bigger than the current figures suggest (Norman 1996). It is reasonable to assume that UK GDP is also undervalued, even if not to that extent. Second, GDP excludes the value of unpaid work done at home, as housework does not normally involve a financial transaction. Were unpaid activities to be given a monetary value, the total level of GDP would be dramatically increased.

This is not to argue that all economies should revalue their GDP, though a precedent was created by Italy when it revised the size of its economy upwards by 17 per cent in the 1980s, with the approval of the OECD (Organization for Economic Cooperation and Development). It is simply to point out the fact that the statistics on which policy is formulated are not precise. An important practical significance of this, it could be argued, is that current attempts across the European Union to achieve borrowing targets as a prerequisite for economic and monetary union (EMU) are excessively stringent, leading to unnecessary levels of unemployment.

However, even supposing there was consensus as to how GDP should be measured and complete confidence in its statistical accuracy, was it, or is it, sensible to pursue an expenditure-GDP ratio target of less than 40 per cent? Even within the former Conservative Cabinet, there appeared to be disagreement. For instance, in an interview in the *Financial Times* (see Chote and Peston 1996) Kenneth Clarke stated: 'My personal judgment was that 40 per cent is the maximum [cut] that should be aimed at. I'd be very surprised if you got a developed western economy much below 40 per cent'. Prior to this, William Waldegrave, speaking as chief secretary to the Treasury at a fringe meeting at the Conservative Party conference, October 1995 (see Blitz 1995) insisted on the need to reduce spending, and stated: 'Overall, the further into the 30s in percentage terms of GDP taken by government you can get, the safer and more stable your country is likely to be in the long-term'.

Again, this view can, at best, charitably be described as unproven. Later, in an interview with the *Financial Times* (see Chote 1996) William Waldegrave said that, in framing a long-term strategy for public spending, it was unrealistic to aim for the low government shares of national income achieved in some Asia-Pacific countries – averaging perhaps 20 per cent – and that nations such as the USA, New Zealand and Switzerland were better role models, implying a government share of national income of 35 per cent or 36 per cent, a target also favoured by the former Prime Minister, John Major. The difference of opinion between Major and Clarke led to the Treasury 'furiously briefing the media' (Peston and Tett 1996) that there was no real difference between them.

Despite the view expressed by William Waldegrave, Chris Patten, speaking at the time as Governor of Hong Kong and as a former Cabinet minister, implied, in an interview with the *Guardian* (see Brummer 1996), that very real lessons could be learned from the Asia-Pacific countries:

> Can I, an intelligent man, sit here and look at the balance between tax and spending in Asia and tax and spending in Europe and not believe in some lessons for Europe? Particularly, can I believe that there is no connection between sluggish growth in Europe, high levels of unemployment in Europe and public spending and tax? I am not in favour of a slash and burn approach to public spending but I do believe that we have to reduce the role of the state in the economy in the medium- and long-term.

A counter-argument to this, however, is that east Asian governments have not generally been known for their *laissez-faire* approach, an example being their mandatory pension schemes, and that 'Ironically enough, the most relevant lesson for Europe of east Asia's growth miracle may in fact be the need for more rather than less state involvement in the functioning of certain parts of the economy' (Flanders 1995). In addition, it may be contended that the low public spending ratios of countries such as Hong Kong, Singapore, South Korea and Taiwan is the result, rather than the cause, of economic success, but that this will change in the long-term:

> it is far easier to keep government expenditure rising in line with GDP when the denominator is going through the roof . . . In the long-run, though, it is one of the best-established relationships in economics – Wagner's law, named after Adolph Heinrich Wagner, a nineteenth-century

German economist – that the ratio will rise as a country grows richer. This is because publicly-provided services, such as education and health, are 'superior goods': a 1 per cent increase in income triggers a more than 1 per cent rise in demand. Over the years, every industrialised country has tended to confirm Wagner's prediction.

(Flanders 1995)

A further counter-argument to Patten's view is that the problems which have been experienced in Europe, and particularly the UK, may perhaps be attributable to macroeconomic mismanagement and an overemphasis on price stability at the expense of employment. In the past, the related policies of over-valued currencies (particularly sterling), excessive interest rates (monetary policy, i.e. the manipulation of interest rates and the money supply for the purposes of economic management) and overly restrictive fiscal policy, in part aimed at achieving equally arbitrary targets for government borrowing as prerequisites for EMU, have combined to lock European economies into a sustained period of deflation largely of their own making. There appears to be little recognition that price stability is neither central to nor essential for economic growth, nor does it appear to be generally accepted that the most effective way to reduce government expenditure and borrowing, and to increase income (through increased direct and indirect tax revenues), is to reduce unemployment. There have been welcome signs of change in this regard, partly the election of Labour to government but, more significantly, the emphasis placed upon employment by the French Premier, Lionel Jospin, following the elections in France in June 1997. However, a general inability to change the prevalent macroeconomic mindset is a legacy of the paradigmatic shift which occurred in the 1970s. It could be argued that a central criticism of Keynesianism – that it exacerbated the problems with which it was meant to deal – was unjustified and should in fact be levelled at the macroeconomic orthodoxy which supplanted it.

Internationally, particularly from the mid-1970s, there was general concern in the countries of the OECD over rising levels of public expenditure and government borrowing. This concern was most evident in the USA, with the election of Ronald Reagan in 1980, and in the UK with the election of the Conservatives in 1979. In both cases, particularly the USA, the anti-public expenditure rhetoric was not justified on the basis of international comparisons. The UK expenditure to GDP ratio was not exceptional, though it could be said that the ratio in the USA was actually exceptionally low. Table 1.7 provides details of a sample of OECD countries for four of the years in the period 1979–94.

In 1979, of the seven major economies in the OECD, three had expenditure-GDP ratios greater than the UK and three (USA, Japan and Canada) had ratios which were smaller. By 1994, only the USA and Japan were

Table 1.7 General government total outlays (% of nominal GDP)

	1979	1985	1990	1994
United States	29.9	33.2	33.3	33.5
Japan	31.1	31.6	31.7	35.8
Germany	47.2	47.0	45.1	49.1
France	45.0	52.1	49.8	54.8
Italy	41.6	50.9	53.2	54.1
United Kingdom	40.9	44.0	39.9	43.2
Canada	37.3	45.3	46.0	47.1
Australia	31.4	36.4	34.9	37.4
Austria	48.2	50.9	48.6	52.2
Belgium	57.7	61.9	55.0	56.1
Denmark	53.2	59.3	58.6	63.3
Finland	38.4	43.8	45.4	59.2
Greece	30.2	43.6	46.4	48.0
Ireland	45.1	52.4	41.2	43.5
Netherlands	53.7	57.1	54.1	53.1
Norway	45.2	40.9	49.2	49.3
Portugal	34.4	41.2	41.8	44.0
Spain	30.1	41.2	42.0	46.1
Sweden	60.0	63.3	59.1	68.8
Total of above OECD countries	35.9	39.7	39.2	41.4

Source: OECD (1995), Annex Table 28, p. A31.

below the UK; Canada's ratio had risen significantly from 37.3 per cent to 47.1 per cent between 1979 and 1994. In the same period, the UK ratio had grown from 40.9 per cent to 43.2 per cent, with considerable fluctuations in between. The figures show that the UK ratio is remarkably low by European standards. They also illustrate the enormous differences between economies, with the extremes represented by the 'free market' United States and social democratic Sweden. However, there have been international attempts to reduce public expenditure, particularly on welfare spending and public borrowing. This is certainly the case in the European Union which has established criteria to enable monetary union to be achieved, as part of the prevailing orthodoxy that emphasizes the importance of competition and public sector contraction. This new orthodoxy, strongly advocated and pursued by successive Conservative governments in the UK, initially showed little sign of being jettisoned. On the contrary, in April 1996, the IMF (1996; see also Ryle, 1996) warned of the dangers inherent in current international levels of government expenditure and borrowing and advocated reductions in expenditure rather than increases in taxation. This is the policy to which the former Conservative government was committed and which, it would seem, the Labour Party favours. However, as stated above, the new French and UK governments are increasingly emphasizing the importance of reducing unemployment.

Previous Conservative governments, however, did not have much success in terms of reducing expenditure or the overall tax burden (see Table 1.5, page 13), but it is certainly true that they implemented policies which have resulted in expenditure being lower than it would otherwise have been. Three key ones, in addition to privatization, can be identified.

First, in 1982 it was announced that public expenditure was to be planned in cash terms rather than volume. This was a major shift in policy, though it built upon the introduction of cash limits introduced by the Labour government in 1976, which in turn supplemented the PESC (Public Expenditure Survey Committee) system for planning and controlling public expenditure introduced in 1961 following publication of the Plowden Report. Now, instead of planning on the basis of the increased physical inputs each department would require to meet its objectives, a cash limit, determined within the context of the government's overall macroeconomic policy, was imposed on departments from above. This supposedly gave departmental managers an incentive to improve efficiency and value for money in order to attain programme objectives. From the government's viewpoint, it enabled expenditure to be more rigorously controlled, as previously it was difficult to ascertain the degree to which expenditure in excess of budget was attributable to inflation or volume limits being exceeded.

The second key policy change was the decision, taken in the early 1980s, to link pensions and other benefits to price inflation rather than earnings. Given that earnings tend to increase by more than price inflation, indexing pensions and benefits to prices rather than earnings has helped reduce the growth in governmental expenditure, at the expense of the elderly who have experienced an ever-widening gap between the level of their income and that of those in work.

The third change was the introduction of an incomes policy, in November 1992, for the public sector; a policy completely at odds with all previous statements as to the ineffectiveness of incomes policies and the importance of non-intervention. All three policies have, of course, had wider economic and social consequences, but they represent important features of Conservative policy on public expenditure.

Their overall lack of success, however, has led to more demands for spending and tax reductions. Bosanquet (1995) argues against the 'illusion' that public spending is under control and believes that, in the next recession, the public spending ratio could easily rise to 45 per cent. He also points to specific policies which actually create pressures for spending to rise, including *The Citizen's Charter* (Cabinet Office 1991), by increasing public demand, particularly on health and education. Numerous politicians, led in the main by John Redwood, strongly advocate cuts in public expenditure. Others, however, believe that spending and borrowing should increase, particularly to address the problems caused by previous reductions in capital expenditure (e.g. Corry and Holtham 1995). It is, however, ironic that the lack of success can, in part, be attributed to the actions of former Conservative ministers themselves, as Jenkins (1995: 248–9) states:

> The single overwhelming fact of public expenditure in Britain since 1979 is that the greatest indiscipline lay not with sub-national administration – local government, nationalized industries and quangos [non-departmental public bodies] – but with programmes directly under the control of ministers. Throughout [this] period, the fastest rising items were health, law and order, social security, agricultural and (initially) defence. All were areas in which ministers felt vulnerable and found themselves drawn into spending commitments. Items not the direct concern of ministers tended to lag, such as education, housing and public transport . . . [P]ay rises were highest for those closest to the politics of the cabinet. Nurses, policemen, soldiers, senior civil servants did better than, say, teachers, lecturers or local government officers.

A more fundamental point can be made, however, about the context within which such ministerial lack of resolve has been displayed. It could be argued that macroeconomic policy between 1979 and 1997, including all economic U-turns (e.g. monetarism, incomes policies, exchange rate policy, public expenditure objectives), actually militated against the achievement of the objective of reducing public expenditure to below 40 per cent of GDP. In addition to expensive policy errors (e.g. ranging from the community charge, poll tax, to the likely cost of culling cattle to restore confidence in British beef), there has been the expenditure associated with sustained mass unemployment. The desired expenditure-GDP ratio was more likely to be achieved, and tax revenues increased and borrowing lowered, if an expansionist policy had been pursued designed to reduce, significantly, existing levels of unemployment. This argument, it must be said, applies across the European Union.

In the meantime – not least given the points made earlier as to the reliability and appropriateness of the measurement of GDP, the inaccuracy of economic forecasts and the redefinitions of expenditure – economic policy was, and perhaps remains, overly restrictive and designed to achieve an arbitrary and unsubstantiated balance between two extremely large variables. Such a policy may be said to be suspect statistically, counterproductive economically, subjective politically and risky socially.

Conclusions

Between 1979–97, successive Conservative governments emphasized the need strictly to control public expenditure and to reduce public sector activity relative to that of the private sector. These emphases were, and, in part, still are, key features of the prevailing domestic and international orthodoxy. Under Labour, the need to control expenditure is frequently reiterated but it remains to be seen whether they will similarly emphasize the need to reduce the ratio of public-private sector activity. In large part, however, the economic priorities which were established in the 1970s, at a time when inflation was a real problem, remain unchanged and have out-lived the adoption of the doctrine which gave them a theoretical frame-work (i.e. monetarism). New Right thinking appears still to influence significantly political and economic debate. This is true in many countries, but particularly so in the USA and the UK. Indeed, the American influence on Labour is remarkable, as reflected in the priorities and language adopted by Gordon Brown in the budget of July 1997 (e.g.: five year 'deficit reduc-tion programme'; 'new deal' on welfare-to-work) in addition to measures announced prior to the budget, notably the granting of operational inde-pendence to the Bank of England and creating a new institution to regulate the City of London (both initiatives modelled on the Federal Reserve and the Securities and Exchange Commission in the USA). As Hutton (1997) states: 'The Government's emerging strategy is to get as close to the US model as possible while taking limited measures to ameliorate the social costs within the bounds of fiscal "prudence" and a conservative consensus it hesitates to challenge'.

Perhaps Hutton understates the case, however. It is true that the Labour government has been radical in a number of respects since the general election, but Labour's unwillingness to challenge the New Right assump-tions is not due to 'hesitancy' but rather to an acceptance of them. For as long as this continues to be the case, the environment for public service managers will remain unfavourable. The need to work within tight re-source constraints will continue for the foreseeable future. It is right to expect public service managers to demonstrate economy, efficiency and effectiveness in the use of resources (see, in particular, Chapters 2 and 8) and, where appropriate, to learn lessons from the private sector. It is, however, legitimate to question the economic and social validity of macro-economic policy and the assumptions which have, for the last two decades, fashioned the environment in which public service managers must operate.

References

Adonis, A. (1996) Welfare for the millennium, *Financial Times*, 24 January.
Bacon, R. and Eltis, W. (1976) *Britain's Economic Problem: Too Few Producers*. London: Macmillan.
Bacon, R. and Eltis, W. (1996) *Britain's Economic Problem Revisited*. London: Macmillan.

Blitz, J. (1995) Waldegrave takes tough line on spending, *Financial Times*, 11 October.

Bosanquet, N. (1995) *Public Spending into the Millennium*. London: Social Market Foundation.

Boulton, L. (1996) Statisticians link economy to environment, *Financial Times*, 30 September.

Brummer, A. (1996) Still the governor, *Guardian*, 8 March.

Cabinet Office (1991) *The Citizen's Charter: Raising the Standard*, Cm. 1599. London: HMSO.

Chote, R. (1996) Waldegrave resolves to start early, *Financial Times*, 2 January.

Chote, R. and Peston, R. (1996) A one nation Tory adrift in a two-party government, *Financial Times*, 31 January.

Cm. 6404 (1942) *Social Insurance and Allied Services*. London: HMSO.

Corry, D. and Holtham, G. (1995) *Growth with Stability: Progressive Macroeconomic Policy*. London: Institute for Public Policy Research.

Downs, A. (1957) *An Economic Theory of Democracy*. New York: Harper and Row.

Downs, A. (1967) *Inside Bureaucracy*. Boston: Little, Brown.

Dunleavy, P. (1986) Explaining the privatization boom: Public choice versus radical approaches. *Public Administration*, 64: 13–34.

Eisner, R. (1996) The point of using GDP. *New Economy*, 3 (1): 2–5.

Flanders, S. (1995) Why states must grow, *Financial Times*, 6 November.

Flynn, N. (1990) *Public Sector Management*. Hemel Hempstead: Harvester Wheatsheaf.

Friedman, M. (1962) *Capitalism and Freedom*. Chicago: University of Chicago Press.

Gillie, A. (1995) Reporting government expenditure, in A. Gillie (ed.) *The Big Spenders: A Review of the Government's Departmental and Major Spending Programmes, 1995–96*, pp. 1–12. London: Public Finance Foundation.

Glennerster, H. and Hills, J. (eds) (1998) *The State of Welfare: The Economics of Social Spending*, (2nd edn). Oxford: Oxford University Press.

Hayek, F. (1944) *The Road to Serfdom*. London: Routledge.

Hayek, F. (1960) *The Constitution of Liberty*. London: Routledge.

HM Treasury (1995) *Public Expenditure: Statistical Supplement to the Financial Statement and Budget Report 1995–96*. London: HMSO.

HM Treasury (1996) *Financial Statement and Budget Report 1996–97*. London: HMSO.

HM Treasury (1997) *Financial Statement and Budget Report July 1997*. London: The Stationery Office.

Hood, C. (1995) Controlling public management. Public Finance Foundation *Review*, 7: 3–6.

Hutton, W. (1995) Forget austerity era – Britain's rich, *Guardian*, 16 October.

Hutton, W. (1997) Break the locks on Labour's war chest, *Observer*, 6 July.

IMF (International Monetary Fund) (1996) *World Economic Outlook*. Washington DC: IMF.

Jenkins, S. (1995) *Accountable to None: The Tory Nationalization of Britain*. Harmondsworth: Penguin.

Johnson, C. (1991) *The Economy Under Mrs Thatcher 1979–1990*. Harmondsworth: Penguin.

Joseph Rowntree Foundation (1993) *The Future of Welfare: A Guide to the Debate.* New York: Joseph Rowntree Foundation.

Niskanen, W. (1971) *Bureaucracy and Representative Government.* Chicago: Aldine-Atherton.

Niskanen, W. (1973) *Bureaucracy: Servant or Master?.* London: Institute of Economic Affairs.

Norman, P. (1996) Shadow economy could help EMU fly, *Financial Times,* 10 June.

OECD (Organization for Economic Cooperation and Development) (1995) *Economic Outlook,* 58, December.

Peston, R. and Tett, G. (1996) Clarke rejects demands for deep spending cuts, *Financial Times,* 7 February.

Robinson, W. (1993) Don't pay the rich to be ill, *Financial Times,* 3 August.

Ryle, S. (1996) IMF calls for painful cuts in public services, *Guardian,* 18 April.

Sloman, J. (1994) *Economics* (2nd edn). Hemel Hempstead: Harvester Wheatsheaf.

Smith, D. (1987) *The Rise and Fall of Monetarism: The Theory and Politics of an Economic Experiment.* Harmondsworth: Pelican.

Terry, F. (1996) The private finance initiative – overdue reform or policy breakthrough? *Public Money & Management,* 16 (1): 9–16.

Thatcher, M. (1996) The common ground, *Guardian,* 12 January.

Tullock, G. (1974) Dynamic hypotheses on bureaucracy. *Public Choice,* 17 (2): 128–32.

Wilson, J. (1993) Public services in the UK, in J. Wilson and P. Hinton (eds) *Public Services and the 1990s: Issues in Public Service Finance and Management,* pp. 1–21. Eastham: Tudor.

Further reading

A good way of keeping abreast of developments in economic policy is to read the economic commentaries in newspapers such as the *Financial Times* and the *Guardian,* both of which provide comprehensive and understandable supplements following the annual budget, and journals, particularly *The Economist.* The government's expenditure and taxation plans, currently brought together in a unified budget, are published annually, in the *Financial Statement and Budget Report* (the 'Red Book'). A very good annual publication is the *Public Services Yearbook* (London: Public Finance Foundation) which contains excellent overviews on economic policy, prospects, public expenditure, and taxation measures. There are also chapters on topical issues and individual departmental expenditure programmes. Other texts have useful chapters on the rationale of state intervention and theoretical explanations for and scale of public expenditure growth, including: Bailey, S. J. (1995) *Public Sector Economics: Theory, Policy and Practice* (London: Macmillan); Brown, C. V. and Jackson, P. M. (1990) *Public Sector Economics* (4th edn) (Oxford: Blackwell); Curwen, P. (ed.) (1994) *Understanding the UK Economy* (3rd edn) (London: Macmillan); Sandford, C. (1992) *Economics of Public Finance: An Economic Analysis of Government Expenditure and Revenue in the United Kingdom* (4th edn) (Oxford: Pergamon Press). Still of use, though inevitably dated in some respects, is

Likierman, A. (1988) *Public Expenditure: Who Really Controls it and How* (London: Penguin). An excellent set of discussions on public expenditure can be found in Corry, D. (1997) *Public Expenditure: Effective Management and Control* (London: The Dryden Press). For the broader background to the meaning of and shift from Keynesianism, see Curwen, P. (1994) op.cit., Chapter 1. Also recommended is Skidelsky, R. (1996) *Keynes* (Oxford: Oxford University Press). Finally, an interesting article on economic policy has been written by the Permanent Secretary to the Treasury, Sir Terry Burns (1996), 'Managing the nation's economy: The conduct of monetary and fiscal policy'. This appears in *Economic Trends*, 509: 21–6.

two

The new management of public services

John Wilson

Key learning objectives

After reading this chapter you should be able to:

1 Understand the differences and similarities between public and private sector management.
2 Evaluate the validity of the criticisms of traditional public administration.
3 Understand the nature and rationale of Conservative policy 1979–97 towards the public sector.
4 Evaluate the nature and appropriateness of new public management and its relevance to financial management.

Introduction

The changed environment outlined in Chapter 1 has resulted in significant structural, organizational and managerial changes to the public sector in the UK. This chapter discusses these changes and, in so doing, places the issue of financial management into the broader context of public sector change. It is vital to stress at the outset the pivotal importance of financial management in delivering public services. Resource constraints, for macroeconomic and microeconomic reasons, are becoming more intense. Simultaneously, increased emphasis is placed on managerial accountability, largely through performance measurement, in an ever more competitive environment. The need effectively to manage financial resources in the public sector has perhaps never been more obvious.

Box 2.1 Public and private sector attributes

Dissimilarities:

1 Public sector organizations are not exposed to the competitive world of the market and hence have no incentives to reduce costs or operate efficiently.
2 Objectives are usually ill-defined and expressed in vague terms such as serving the public, maintaining law and order, reducing inequality, removing poverty or improving health.
3 Strategic planning is more difficult because of the short-term considerations of politicians.
4 The public sector organization is susceptible to greater and more open account-ability with politicians, pressure groups, taxpayers and voters all having an interest in the performance of the public sector.
5 The functions of the public sector are limited by statute.
6 The public sector is funded by taxation and not by charging for its services.
7 Certain goods have to be provided by the state. Defence, law and order and street lighting are enjoyed collectively and are, in theory, equally available to all. The provision of such 'public goods' cannot be left to the vagaries of the market.

Similarities:

1 Increasingly, the public sector charges for some of its services, for example through increased prescription charges or charges for leisure facilities.
2 The private sector also operates within a political environment as decisions made by politicians to, for example, keep interest rates high, will have a pro-found effect upon the very existence of some firms faced with high borrowing costs and reduced sales.
3 The activities of the private sector are also constrained by statute as firms are regulated over unfair trading practices, health and safety at work or environ-mental pollution.
4 Public and private partnerships have developed over urban redevelopment, promoting private sector involvement at all levels.

Source: Lawton and Rose (1994: 6–7).

Public sector administration

The changing nature of the public sector and the increased emphasis on private sector techniques has inevitably led to certain tensions, particularly between those who believe the public sector is unique, and should not have private sector culture and practices imposed upon it, and those who do not. Lawton and Rose (1994: 6–7) summarize the arguments put forward to indicate the uniqueness of the public sector and also those which sum-marize the similarities with the private sector; see Box 2.1.

Viewed collectively, the arguments provide a useful indication of sim-ilarities and dissimilarities in general, but, in the main, are more applicable to the situation in 1979 rather than today and, considered in isolation, some of them are misleading. For example, under dissimilarities, Point 1 ignores the fact that British Rail traditionally competed with private sector companies for haulage business. Also, both public and private sector organizations today strive to reduce costs and operate efficiently, though, again, it could perhaps be argued that they always did seek to achieve this. Point 6 is incorrect in so far as it does not reflect the fact that the public has always been charged for certain services, including gas, electricity, water, postal services and railway journeys. With regard to Point 7, there are also local public goods (an example of which is actually street lighting). To this list can be added the provision of 'merit goods', notably health and education, which perhaps are also too important to be left to the market. These are goods (or 'bads') that society thinks everyone ought to have (or ought not to have) regardless of whether they are wanted by each individual (merit bads are products such as cigarettes) (see Begg *et al.* 1987: 343–4).

With regard to similarities, Point 4 can be illustrated by the private finance initiative (PFI) announced by the then Chancellor, Norman Lamont, in the 1992 autumn statement. The initiative was designed to attract private sector funds to finance public sector capital schemes (Bailey 1995: 136–43; Terry 1996).

Despite the diversity of the public sector, however, and the arguments concerning its actual or imagined uniqueness, between 1979 and 1997, successive Conservative governments sought, to some extent, to impose uniformity in that they stressed the importance of economy, efficiency and effectiveness (the '3 Es') and the 'supremacy' of private sector values. In other words, they believed there was no fundamental distinction between the sectors. Essentially, both exist for the purposes of serving their 'customers' and both must demonstrate efficiency in the use of finite resources within a competitive framework across and within the sectors. The problem, however, the Conservatives believed, was that not only was the public sector incapable of satisfactorily fulfilling these roles, given its traditional inherently bureaucratic and monopolistic nature, but its inexorable growth also impeded the private sector from fulfilling the same roles, and from growing as it otherwise naturally would, for the reasons suggested by the New Right theorists as outlined in Chapter 1.

The belief that the public sector was incapable of emulating the private sector in terms of efficiency and competitiveness led to a critique of conventional public administration and to the development of what has become known as new public management (NPM).

Public administration: a critique

Public sector structure and practices were, particularly from the late 1970s onwards, seen as impediments to economic efficiency and militated against the development of a customer awareness culture. The traditional bureaucratic model, largely based on principles codified by Max Weber (1864–1920), was too rigid and mechanistic. The virtues by which it was characterized, for half a century, include machine-like efficiency achieved through stability, predictability, continuity, adherence to rules and regulations, and a system of recruitment, selection and training which ensured the values were inculcated and perpetuated – all epitomized by the UK civil service. These virtues, combined with the factors which contribute to the uniqueness of the public sector (see Box 2.1) collectively constitute the traditional public administration model, but, equally, they were seen as handicaps in the modern era: 'In attempting to control virtually everything, we became so obsessed with dictating *how* things should be done – regulating the process, controlling the inputs – that we ignored the outcomes, the *results*. The product was government with a distinct ethos: slow, inefficient, impersonal' (Osborne and Gaebler 1992: 14, original emphasis).

The criticisms of traditional public administration led to the emergence of an alternative paradigm which emphasized management rather than administration and which was much more able to cope with the dynamic – as opposed to a 'steady state' – environment with which it was confronted. Osborne and Gaebler writing about American private as well as public bureaucracies, describe the nature of the changing world which, it can be said, is particularly affecting the public sector in all advanced economies:

the bureaucratic model developed in conditions very different from those we experience today. It developed in a slower-paced society, when change proceeded at a leisurely gait. It developed in an age of hierarchy, when only those at the top of the pyramid had enough information to make informed decisions. It developed in a society of people who worked with their hands, not their minds. It developed in times of mass markets, when most Americans had similar wants and needs. And it developed when we had strong geographic communities . . .

Today all that has been swept away. We live in an era of breathtaking change. We live in a global market place, which puts enormous competitive pressures on our economic institutions. We live in an information society, in which people get access to information almost as fast as their leaders do. We live in a knowledge-based economy, in which educated workers bridle at commands and demand autonomy. We live in an age of niche markets, in which customers have become accustomed to high quality and extensive choice. In this environment, bureaucratic institutions developed during the industrial era – public *and* private – increasingly fail us.

Today's environment demands institutions that are extremely flexible and adaptable . . . [and which] deliver high-quality goods and services

...It demands institutions that are responsive to their customers, offering choices of nonstandardised services; that lead by persuasion and incentives rather than commands; that give their employees a sense of meaning and control, even ownership. It demands institutions that *empower* citizens rather than simply *serving* them.

(Osborne and Gaebler 1992: 15, original emphasis)

Osborne and Gaebler proceed to identify ten 'threads' (pp. 19–20) which entrepreneurial public organizations have in common. They:

1 promote competition between service providers;
2 empower citizens by pushing control out of the bureaucracy;
3 focus on outcomes not inputs;
4 are driven by goals and not by rules and regulations;
5 redefine clients as customers and offer them choices;
6 prevent problems before they emerge rather than simply offering services afterwards;
7 earn money not spend it;
8 decentralize authority and embrace participatory management;
9 prefer market mechanisms to bureaucratic mechanisms;
10 catalyse public, private and voluntary agencies to solve community problems.

These threads are, for Osborne and Gaebler, the principles on which all public organizations should be based and, although their work can be criticized for being long on description and short on analysis (see Jordan 1994), it none the less exerted influence, not least in the UK, given its timing. Butler (1994: 64) says that 'every set of ideas has to have a seedbed in which they [*sic*] can germinate and grow' and identifies three pressures which made the environment much more favourable for Osborne and Gaebler's ideas to grow:

1 the growing demand for public services;
2 the growing potential scope and range but also cost of those services which advancing technology brought about, not least in defence and health;
3 the stage of resistance reached in developing countries to paying higher taxes.

The third point can, however, be said to apply to industrialized just as much as developing countries.

Faced with these irresistible developments, reflected in and reinforced by the changes in the politico-economic environment (see Chapter 1), the acceptance of the obsolescence of the traditional public administration model was assured. Increasingly, the private sector was seen to be the model to emulate, both structurally and culturally. More precisely, the

---

Box 2.2 Features of organizations indicating corporate excellence

Feature:	Involving:
A bias for action	Flexibility, experimentation, getting things done
Closeness to the customer	Being customer-focused
Autonomy and entrepreneurship	Encouragement of individual initiatives, not slavish adherence to the 'rulebook'
Productivity through people	Emphasis on service quality through innovations rather than cost reductions
Hands-on, value drive	Sharing of values and commitment to organizational goals, all focused through the customer
'Stick to the knitting'	Concentrating on what the organization is good at; for the public sector this could mean retaining core activities and contracting out others
Simple form and lean staff	Retaining only the minimum staff and hierarchical tiers required
Simultaneous 'tight-loose' properties	A balance between central direction and local direction

---

attributes associated with excellence in the modern world were identified by Peters and Waterman (1982). On the basis of their research and available empirical evidence, they suggested a number of features exhibited by organizations to indicate corporate excellence, shown in Box 2.2.

Despite the questions that may be asked about certain features and the usefulness of the analysis, it can none the less be seen that traditional public sector organizations did not approximate to the 'excellence' model. It was characterized, for instance, as being rigid rather than flexible, focused on inputs rather than outputs, officer-driven rather than customer-focused, hierarchical rather than flat, overstaffed rather than streamlined. Similarly, in a later work, Peters (1989: 27) says that:

Take all the evidence together, and a clear picture of the successful firm in the 1990s and beyond emerges. It will be:

- flatter (have fewer layers of organisation structure)
- populated by more autonomous units (have fewer central-staff second guessers, more local authority to introduce and price products)
- oriented towards differentiation, producing high value-added goods and services, creating niche markets

- quality-conscious
- service conscious
- more responsive
- much faster at innovation
- a user of highly-trained, flexible people as the principal means of adding value

Taking an overview of the work of Osborne and Gaebler (1992), Peters and Waterman (1982) and Peters (1989), the following key themes can be identified:

- Competition.
- Decentralization (involving freedom to manage).
- Customer-focus.
- Performance measurement ('more for less').

These themes define the emphasis which has been placed on public service management over the last two decades. Within the context of the New Right hegemony, domestically and internationally, and the shift in economic and organizational paradigms, a new model emerged, with its emphasis on the above themes, which is generally referred to as NPM (sometimes the word 'managerialism' is used).

Conservative policy and NPM

Conservative policy 1979–97

The NPM model was a function of a wider paradigmatic shift, the nature of which was essentially anti-public sector. Domestically, a central feature of this shift was the range of policies pursued by successive Conservative governments from 1979. Stewart and Walsh (1992) identify the main features of the wider programme and state that: 'The emphasis in the restructuring of the management of public services has been increasingly placed, both by the government and opposition, on strengthening the position of the public as customer or as citizen in public services' (p. 501).

These changes have affected the civil service, the health service and local government. With regard to the civil service, a series of scrutiny programmes were undertaken, beginning in the early 1980s, under Sir Derek Rayner which, though designed to improve efficiency, were also intended to have a longer-term impact on the management of the civil service generally (see Metcalfe and Richards 1990: 1–21). The goal was one of sustained improvement in civil service management to prevent any slide back into inefficiency. To this end, the financial management initiative (FMI) was introduced in May 1982, designed to:

Promote in each department an organisation and a system in which managers at all levels have:

(a) a clear view of their objectives and means to assess and, wherever possible, measure outputs and performance in relation to those objectives;
(b) well-defined responsibility for making the best use of their resources, including a critical scrutiny of output and value for money; and
(c) the information (particularly about costs), the training and the access to expert advice that they need to exercise their responsibilities effectively.

(Metcalfe and Richards 1990: 183)

The FMI was concerned with the delegation of budgets, creation of cost centres to hold managers accountable for expenditure, delegation of decision making, decentralization of various functions (e.g. finance, personnel) and the regrouping of these functions into 'businesses'. It had limited success, and departments displayed varying levels of commitment and enthusiasm. It was followed by a more radical programme, the 'next steps' initiative, which was heralded as the biggest attempt at civil service reform this century. It entailed the transfer of the executive functions of central government to agencies charged with specific tasks. It also involved a key distinction between policy formulation and policy implementation, though this distinction is hardly clear-cut in practice and raises fundamental questions concerning ministerial accountability (O'Toole 1995; Foster and Plowden 1996; see also Stewart 1996 for a particularly robust criticism of this distinction).

Another part of the wider programme of the former Conservative governments which has affected the civil service is that of market testing, referred to as compulsory competitive tendering (CCT) in the case of local government and health. This involved exposing public service activity to competition and has resulted, *inter alia*, in certain work being contracted-out to the private sector. Such an approach, which is not confined to the UK but has been pursued internationally, is based on the assumption that competition leads to improved efficiency and greater awareness of customer needs and preferences whatever the outcome of the tendering process (see Wilson 1995).

The impact of this wider programme can be gauged by referring to Tables 2.1, 2.2, 2.3 and 2.4. With regard to central government, *The Citizen's Charter Second Report* (Cm. 2540 1994: 93) stated that, by the end of 1993, approximately £1.1bn (see Table 2.1) of work covering 25,000 posts, out of an intended programme of £1.5bn and involving 44,000 posts, had been exposed to competition. A total of 389 individual market tests had been completed. The private sector was awarded over £855m of this

Table 2.1 Savings from market testing

	Pre-test value of activities (£000)	Savings (£000)
Departments	594,148	135,575
AWE and IR/IT	525,000	Not available
Total	**1,119,148**	

Source: Cm. 2540 (1994), Table 3, p. 101.

work. Of this, £768m was contracted-out with no in-house bid, and of this £525m was accounted for by two reviews – the Atomic Weapons Establishment (AWE) in the Ministry of Defence and the Inland Revenue Information Technology Services (IR/IT).

Overall, the process resulted in savings of over 25 per cent where comparisons were possible and an overall average gross saving of over 22 per cent (approximately 20 per cent net). The report confirmed the former government's commitment to complete the first programme and to carry out a new programme of £830m involving 35,000 posts. Of the 389 market tests:

- 25 resulted in a decision to abolish all or a substantial part of the activity;
- three activities were privatised;
- 113 activities were contracted out as a result of a strategic decision to employ an outside supplier. No in-house bid was permitted in these cases;
- where there was an in-house bid 82 activities were contracted out and 147 were awarded to the in-house team;
- six activities were restructured without a formal test;
- 13 tests were withdrawn and efficiency gains made internally.

. . . In-house teams won 68% of the work where they competed, amounting to £189m in value before testing.

(Cm. 2540 1994: 93)

Of the 25,000 posts covered by the programme to the end of 1993, departments reported a reduction of 14,587 posts (see Table 2.2). The programme, however, was not without its critics. The Treasury and Civil Service Committee (1994) stated it had not been conducted effectively by the former government and had not won the broad support of the civil service. The committee expressed its astonishment at the small number of in-house bids which had been permitted (see *Financial Times*, 25 November 1994). The Defence Committee (1995) highlighted the pitfalls of contracting out when it reported the damage to RAF Tornado fighters caused by outside contractors, probably costing more than £100m to repair (see

Table 2.2 Summary of results of 1992–3, competing for quality programme

Results of test	Pre-test value of activities (£m)	No. of tests	Pre-test no. of civil-service posts	Reduction in posts
Abolished	22.8	25	753	397
Contracted out (no in-house bid)	767.9	113	14,722	10,801
In-house win	189.3	147	7,086	1,713
Contracted out (with in-house bid)	87.4	82	1,591	1,054
Privatized	24.9	3	441	436
Untied[1]	11.7	6	144	33
Withdrawn (with efficiency gains)	15.2	13	409	153
Total	**1,119.2**	**389**	**25,146**	**14,587**

1 Untied means the activity has been restructured without a formal test.

Source: Cm. 2540 (1994), Table 2, p. 101.

the *Guardian*, 15 November 1995). The Labour Party, when in opposition, criticized the expenditure involved on consultants who advise on privatization and market testing, amounting to over £318m between 1979–95 according to official figures, but this was just the 'tip of the iceberg' as many departments refused to make public their consultancy costs (see the *Guardian*, 18 September 1995). Similarly, Flemming and Oppenheimer (1996) queried the extent to which contracting-out had resulted in savings and claimed that the policy had led to questionable efficiency gains and may have reduced quality in some services.

One reason for the scepticism, and a key consideration in introducing market mechanisms to the delivery of public services, is that of transaction costs. Williamson (1975, 1985), focusing on both public and private sector organizations, analysed in-house or direct provision in order to establish why some services are provided by the market (externally) and others hierarchically (internally). The most advantageous form of provision is dependent on the level of transaction costs:

> In everyday language, transaction costs include risk factors relating to the viability and trustworthiness of the contractor, the chances and potential costs of service disruption, the feasibility and cost of the information requirements necessary for contract monitoring, the feasibility and effectiveness of penalties for non-compliance and the availability of alternative sources of supply.
>
> (Bailey 1995: 372)

Where these are high, reflecting a complicated service, hierarchical organizations may be most efficient:

> However, low transaction costs do not automatically mean that a service should become subject to a contracting regime. This would only be appropriate if it promoted service objectives, whether in terms of cost reductions or in securing wider benefits. Hence transaction cost theory does not provide a mechanistic cost-based formula from which to derive definitive rules and decisions. There is a large element of subjective assessment and discretion in reaching decisions.
>
> (Bailey 1995: 372)

Key factors relating to transaction costs include bounded rationality (most commonly associated with Simon 1947), uncertainty, opportunism, asset specificity and the 'small numbers problem' (see Nichols 1995 for a practical application of these concepts).

The problem of bounded rationality refers to the limited ability of individuals to receive, assimilate and communicate information. Uncertainty reflects the fact that decisions have to be made about the future on limited information. Contracts cannot be written to cover all eventualities. Opportunism involves 'interest seeking with guile', and the practice of 'loss leading' is consistent with this concept (i.e. individuals are selfish and will pursue their own interests at the expense of others). In the context of a contract, a private contractor, for instance, may deliberately fail to comply with a specification, or act outside the spirit of a loosely-defined specification, in order to increase profit margins. Asset specificity involves the acquisition of specialist resources – including human – in order to undertake the work relating to a particular service. The specialist resources cannot easily be transferred to other activities and, by virtue of their specialist nature, few alternative suppliers will exist and quasi-monopoly advantages accrue to the contractor who has made the investment. The practical consequence of this is that once a contractor has been selected, it is relatively expensive to terminate and re-tender a contract. This is linked to the small numbers problem, whereby only a few actors participate in the exchange: 'Even though a small numbers condition does not obtain at the outset, this condition tends to evolve as the contractual partners invest in *transaction-specific capital* and acquire *transaction-specific skills*. This process makes maintenance of the contractual relation all the more important for the parties to the contract, as the consequences of termination become severe' (Lane 1993: 181, original emphasis).

These key factors help in determining whether a service should be provided in-house or not. Most blue-collar services have relatively low transaction costs and, given a high level of competition between alternative suppliers, the services can be provided by private contractors. This is not necessarily the case, however, with professional services given the difficulties

involved in identifying, measuring and evaluating the quality of their outputs. These difficulties may invite opportunistic behaviour by private companies, though it must also be recognized that 'it is an act of faith to assume
that public servants are completely devoid of self-serving behaviour' (Bailey
1995: 373). (See also the arguments of public choice theorists, viz. utility-
maximizing behaviour as suggested by Niskanen 1971.)

Williamson (1975, as summarized in Ascher 1987: 254–5) has identified
five situations where internal provision has advantages over contracting in
the market:

1 Where flexible sequential decision-making is needed to cope with uncertainties in the environment.
2 Where only a small number of competitors are present and there is a
  likelihood of opportunistic and predatory behaviour.
3 Where a divergence of expectations is likely to occur between the internal purchaser and the external seller.
4 Where operational or technological information gained from experience is likely to give one external supplier a strategic advantage over all
  others, thereby reducing competition.
5 Where a transaction-specific 'calculative-relation' between parties is inappropriate and 'quasi-moral involvement' between those supplying and
  organizing the service is necessary to effective provision.

Williamson believes that the existence of one or more of these conditions
may result in a preference for internal provision even if it is less cost-
effective than contracting-out, or 'outsourcing', as it is often referred to
when a private sector organization externalizes work. This is because it
involves greater flexibility and less risk in the longer-term in terms of
quality and security of supply.

The validity of Williamson's argument will partly depend upon the
nature of the market. The threat of entry to a market by potential rivals
reduces the possibility of anti-competitive behaviour. It should also help
eliminate concerns over the security and quality of provision. In addition,
reliance on in-house provision can lead to what Leibenstein (1976) has
called 'X-inefficiency' which occurs where firms do not maximize efficiency
in the use of factors of production, i.e. inputs to create outputs. This again
is largely the result of the absence of competition.

Williamson also identified four specific 'biases' associated with internal
provision (see also Flynn 1990: 78–9). The biases are:

1 Internal procurement bias (reluctant to undertake cost comparisons with
  external providers).
2 Internal expansion bias (inherently expansionist tendencies of bureaucracies, largely the result of ambitions of bureaucrats).
3 Programme persistence bias (unjustified continuation of existing services).

4 Imperfect communication bias (use of imperfect or inappropriate information for decison making).

These biases, though they relate to both public and private sector organizations, reinforce the New Right anti-bureaucratic viewpoint which stresses
the inherent microeconomic merits of competition. As a result:

> A variety of market mechanisms have been proposed and adopted for
> the reform of state bureaucracy, apart from outright privatisation.
> The first is the introduction of pricing and charging for public ser-
> vices . . . There have been attempts to give the users of public services
> the ability to act as customers with choices through the use of vouchers.
> There has been extensive development of pricing and charging within
> public service organisations, involving a move from 'hierarchies' to
> 'hierarchies with markets'. There is a process of internal privatisation.
> The second and most fundamental mechanism for changing public
> service management is the development of contract . . . The public ser-
> vice is becoming a 'nexus of contracts', rather than a bureaucratic
> hierarchy.
>
> (Walsh 1995: xvii–iii)

The emphasis on market mechanisms and contractual frameworks may
result in increased efficiency in the longer term but there is evidence that it
may also lead to increased costs. A clear example of this was provided by
the Audit Commission (1996) report into general practitioner (GP) fundholding. It stated that the scheme had resulted in efficiency savings of £206m
but these were more than offset by the £232m increase in management and
transaction costs. Similarly, the quasi-contractual nature of service delivery
in local government, increasingly characterized by CCT (though this is to
be abolished by the Labour government), and service level agreements (see
Chapter 9), may result in significant transaction costs and the creation of
a different form of bureaucracy. None the less, the Conservatives were
convinced of the merits of the changes, a key one of which was CCT.

Competitive tendering and contracting-out take place in numerous countries around the world, but only in the UK was systematic compulsion
introduced. The policy reflected the previous government's frustration at
the minimal level of contracting-out in the UK, in contrast with other
countries, and its ideological commitment to reducing the scale of public
sector activity.

Ideology is also a factor in Europe. Digings (1991) refers to the ideological commitment of both right- and left-wing governing parties to use
contracting and tendering to achieve their aims. Digings points out, for
instance, that in The Netherlands throughout the 1980s the government
was committed to reducing public expenditure and promoting privatization, while the socialists in Spain 'have used private contractors to achieve

Table 2.3 Cost savings from competitive contracting: international evidence

Country	Activity	Reported savings
Australia	Water supply	Estimated potential cost savings of 15%
Canada	Refuse collection	Public collection up to 50% more costly
Denmark	Fire services	Public provision almost three times more expensive than private contractors
Germany (West)	Office cleaning	Public sector provision 44–66% more costly
Japan	Refuse collection	Municipal collection 124% more costly
Sweden	Road and park maintenance, water supply, sewerage	Cost reductions of 10–19% in several municipalities
	Waste collection	Average cost reductions of 25%
	Leisure activities	Cost reductions of 13–15%
	Child care	Cost reductions of 9–15% in nurseries
Switzerland	Refuse collection	Costs of private contracts 20% cheaper
USA	Refuse collection	Savings of 29–37%
	Street cleaning	Savings of up to 43%
	Office cleaning	Savings of up to 73%
	Federal government	Cost savings of up to 35% with an average saving of around 20%
	Mass transit	Potential savings of 20–50%

Source: Bailey (1995), Table 15.1, p. 370.

political ends of a very different kind: the most rapid possible extension of public services to the shanty towns ignored by Franco' (p. 16). However: '. . . in the majority of cases contracts tend to be let to private contractors for purely pragmatic reasons with no ideological undertones. The degree of privatisation might ebb and flow slightly with changes in administration, but it generally remains a fundamentally unpoliticised issue' (p. 16).

With regard to specific countries, excluding the UK, obtaining accurate data is very difficult but certain evidence, summarized by Bailey (1995) and drawn from OECD (1993) and Parker (1990), is presented in Table 2.3.

Domestically, there is evidence that savings have occurred in blue-collar services, particularly refuse collection, as a result of CCT, though evidence concerning the impact on quality is mixed. The Local Government Chronicle (supplement, 6 July 1990, summarized in Walsh 1991: 123) provides

Table 2.4 *Local Government Chronicle* survey of competition

Service	Total contract value (£m)	Total net saving (£m)	Saving (%)
Refuse collection	410.9	42.6	40.4
Street cleaning	46.2	1.41	3.1
Building cleaning	94.4	14.2	15.0
Catering	297.0	0.5	0.2
Vehicle maintenance	127.1	6.62	5.2
Grounds maintenance	278.2	8.2	2.9
Other cleaning	64.6	0.9	1.4
Total	**1318.4**	**74.4**	**5.6**

Source: Local Government Chronicle supplement, 6 July 1990, as summarized in Walsh (1991), Table 13.1, p. 123.

information on 476 contracts let after the Local Government Act 1988. The results of the survey are given in Table 2.4.

The savings achieved through market testing and CCT confirmed the previous Conservative government's belief in the efficacy of competition and the scope for improved efficiency in public service provision. Similarly, its belief in the wider benefits of competition were evident in the restructuring of central government, the National Health Service (NHS) (involving the introduction of an internal market and a distinction between purchasers and providers; see Chapter 10) and local government (where CCT was extended to white-collar services; see Chapter 9). Local government has also had to cope with various changes based upon the introduction of the market mechanism (affecting education, community care, housing management, urban renewal, etc.) which, in turn, has influenced the structure of local authorities. Within all these changes, Stewart and Walsh (1992: 504–8) identify a number of key themes in the 'transformation of public service management' (p. 504), summarized here:

- Separation of the purchaser role from the provider role.
- Growth of contractual or semi-contractual arrangements.
- Accountability for performance.
- Flexibility of pay and conditions.
- Separation of the political process from the management process.
- Creation of markets or quasi-markets.
- Emphasis on the public as customer.
- Reconsideration of the regulatory role.
- A change of culture.

It may, however, be said that two strands run through most of the above themes: competition and a focus on the customer (identified in the list as a separate theme). To these themes can be added, as mentioned earlier, the emphasis on performance measurement (identified above by Stewart and Walsh (1992: 504) as 'accountability for performance') and decentralization, involving freedom to manage (which, in part, is implicit in some of the points made by Stewart and Walsh). These strands contributed directly to and subsequently reflected the development of the NPM.

NPM

Jackson (1996) identifies two distinct tendencies which gave rise to NPM. First, the libertarian ideology of the New Right; second, a contribution from the Left in that they, combined with the general public, demanded that professional monopoly suppliers of public services be held more accountable. 'Taken together, these sentiments amounted to a growing demand for greater efficiency in the use of public finance and enhanced value for money' (Jackson 1996: 1).

However, although NPM may, in part, have developed for political reasons, this does not negate the managerial validity of some of its prescriptions. Hood (1991: 4–5) states there are seven main 'doctrinal components' to NPM, summarized as follows:

1 Hands-on professional management.
2 Explicit standards and measures of performance (involving greater managerial accountability).
3 Greater emphasis on output controls (the need to stress results rather than procedures).
4 Disaggregation of units.
5 Greater competition (involving the move to term contracts and public tendering procedures), designed to reduce costs and improve standards.
6 Adoption of private-sector styles of management.
7 Greater discipline and 'parsimony' in resource use (involving cutting costs, reducing demands for more resources and the need to do more with less).

Clark (1996) summarizes what he considers to be the three main components of NPM: marketization, disaggregation, and incentivization (see Box 2.3) (see also Farnham and Horton 1993: 47; Hughes 1994: 69–73). NPM can be seen to be consistent in many respects with the analyses of Peters and Waterman (1982) and Osborne and Gaebler (1992). This is unsurprising given that a fundamental objective, as stated above, was to import private sector culture and practices into the public sector.

Overall, Conservative policy between 1979 and 1997 was to decentralize and, in so doing, devolve managerial and financial responsibility and, where possible, to rationalize procedures and levels of employment. Examples

---

Box 2.3 The three main components of NPM

Marketization
Introducing market competition into public services production:

- Separating out purchaser/regulatory and provider roles.
- Creating quasi-markets among public agencies, firms and not-for-profit organizations in health care, education, the personal social services and social housing.
- Compulsory competitive tendering and market testing.

Disaggregation
Strengthening central strategic capacity by decoupling policy and executive functions:

- Tighter central control over the definition of policy and resource frameworks.
- Decentralizing responsibility for discrete blocks of executive activity to devolved service units.
- A shift from process to output in control and accountability mechanisms.

Incentivization
Linking incentives to performance in order to foster greater entrepreneurialism and closer attention to cost cutting and organizational efficiency:

- Increased differentiation in pay at an individual level, and revenue-maximizing incentives at an organizational level.
- Quantitative methods of performance and efficiency measurement.
- Human resource management strategies.
- The deprivileging of professionals and public sector workers.

Source: Clark (1996), Figure 2, p. 24.

---

of financial devolution included the granting of budgets and recruitment decisions to individual schools and hospitals and the hiving-off of civil servants from Whitehall into quasi-autonomous agencies under the 'next steps' initiative. This decentralization led to a fragmentation of procedures for pay determination, and the increased use of performance-related pay and flexible working practices. The citizen is now recognized as a consumer entitled to a given standard and variety of service. The traditional model for public service delivery, whereby bureaucrats sought to ensure equitable treatment for taxpayers through the provision of uniform services, has been jettisoned. Competition, responsiveness and choice prevent the standardization of services in the private sector and should do so in the public sector. The need to apply to public service delivery the economic principle of consumer sovereignty is accepted by the Conservative Party and, it may be argued, the Labour government. Adonis (1991) correctly observed: 'Choice, standards and quality are the catchwords; flexibility, performance and local management the tools; the private sector the model'. In short, traditional public service management and delivery mechanisms were to be transformed.

It is important, however, not to exaggerate the extent of the transformation. There has clearly been significant change across the public sector and this has affected structure, service delivery, power relationships (e.g. between a GP and a local hospital; between a central finance department and a front-line service), and culture. In addition, for the financial manager, the traditional emphasis on stewardship and probity has been replaced by an increased emphasis on costing and value for money. However, the transition from 'administration' to 'management' is easy to overstate. The principle of consumer sovereignty, for instance, as a key feature of the changed public sector environment, is more stated than observed. An illustration of this is the widespread apathy to *The Citizen's Charter* (Cm. 1599 1991) initiative (see below and Wilson 1996). Similarly, even if the consumer was 'sovereign', the freedom of managers to respond is considerably constrained by: statutory requirements to provide particular services to a specific level; political pressures, locally and nationally (e.g. the police, in reality, must prioritize in favour of nationally- and politically-determined performance targets which may or may not correspond to local priorities); ongoing commitments, reflecting decisions previously made and which have a recurrent impact on resources; and finally by an overall lack of resources. There are also examples where, rather than allocating additional resources, the withdrawal of a particular service is justified, operationally and financially (such as the entire or partial closure of a hospital), but is impossible to implement because of local 'consumer' resistance and, resulting from this, a lack of political support.

It is legitimate, therefore, to question the extent to which 'freedom to manage' has been enhanced. The actual discretion public managers have over their budgets remains very limited, particularly in local government, not least because they have little influence over budget size, growth or allocation. The majority of expenditure from one year to the next is committed on the basis of previous years' decisions and the proportion of the budget on which discretion can be exercised is, in practice, small (see, for example, Lawton and McKevitt 1995).

However, it is also true to say that constraints act as an incentive to managers to be resourceful in their response to pressures. Jones (1995: 15) lists these pressures in relation to local government, but they are of wider applicability:

- The possibility of developing and operating a 'one-line budget'.
- Tight controls on both revenue and capital expenditure and heavy pressure to conform or even to work well within imposed limits.
- A pressure for economy and efficiency, i.e. productivity in both personnel and cash terms. Fewer people, paid less overall if possible, should do the same or more work.
- A pressure for effectiveness – quality of service delivery whether the service is delivered internally or externally to the authority.

- A clear understanding that developments can usually only be financed from savings and that managers have to make their own space.
- Time pressures due to compulsory competitive tendering which have meant little breathing space for managers over the past few years.

The extent of the above pressures has also led to an increased emphasis on performance measurement (see also Chapter 8).

Performance measurement

In measuring performance, the Conservatives placed considerable importance on *The Citizen's Charter* initiative, and this also is to continue under Labour. The *Charter* represents a systematic attempt to focus on four main objectives across the public services: quality, choice, standards, and value. According to Cm. 1599 (1991: 4–5) these are to be achieved through:

- Privatization.
- Competition.
- Contracting-out.
- Performance-related pay.
- Published performance targets.
- Comprehensive publication of information.
- Effective complaints procedures.
- Tougher and more independent inspectorates.
- Better redress for the citizen.

However, the new managerialism in general and the *Charter*'s emphasis on performance measurement in particular are problematic for the public services. A key aspect of performance measurement is the use of performance indicators, but there are inherent difficulties in their compilation. In the private sector the overriding indicator is that of profitability, but for the majority of public service activity there is no equivalent 'bottom line' and, because of this, 'performance measures need to be developed in public service agencies as surrogates of profit and loss' (Rouse 1993: 66). This point is reinforced by Stewart and Walsh (1994: 46) who state that in the private sector: 'profit . . . is the measure of final output . . . there are universally accepted, abstract, performance measures, such as return on capital available. Such simple, unequivocal measures are neither available nor appropriate in the public service. A range of measures is needed to cope with the multi-dimensional nature of public service'.

This is true but, broadly, there are two main types of performance indicator: financial (or cost-related, viz. unit costs), and non-financial (or quality-related) (see Chapter 8). The latter can include such indicators as:

- Percentage of trains arriving on time.
- Percentage of patients receiving treatment within 10 minutes of arriving at a hospital accident and emergency unit.
- Number of complaints about the refuse collection service.
- Proportion of children in a school achieving a specified number of GCSEs.

The former can include such indicators as:

- Cost per passenger journey.
- Cost per patient day.
- Cost per dustbin emptied.
- Cost per pupil per week.

The use of such indicators is designed to help measure and improve economy, efficiency and effectiveness but they are not new; they have not been introduced as a direct result of NPM. Similarly, the public sector has always been concerned to demonstrate that finite resources have been allocated and utilized efficiently, through the use of unit costing and investment appraisal techniques, including cost benefit analysis. However, they are now increasingly emphasized, not least by the Audit Commission, established in 1982 to promote value for money in local government, and now also in the NHS. In addition, increasingly within the public services, private sector measures of performance are being adopted. Though they are not new to the public sector (current and former nationalized industries and aspects of local authority blue-collar work have been subject to commercial accounting measures, notably that of 'return on capital employed'), they are becoming more widespread as competition increases and 'profit' is measured.

This, in itself, poses problems in that private sector techniques and measures are not necessarily appropriate for the public sector (see next section). Measuring 'returns' in the context of a school, hospital or motorway is just as problematic now as it was when, for instance, cost benefit analysis was fashionable. This is not to argue against attempts to measure public service performance – on the contrary, measurement is to be encouraged – but the problems of so doing need to be borne in mind before conclusions are drawn.

Applicability of the private sector model

The complexities of performance measurement illustrate the difficulties of seeking universally to apply private sector techniques to public service management:

> The danger for the development of public service management is that it is based on the private sector model, because most management thinking in this country has developed in or for the private sector.

Public services can learn from the private sector *as the private sector can learn from the public services.* Specific techniques are and should be transferable. What is not transferable is the private sector model of the role and nature of management, because that assumes the purposes, conditions and tasks of the private sector not those of the public domain. There is a tendency for thinking on public service management to take as its starting point private sector management . . . If the private sector model is taken as the basis for management in the public domain it can mean neglect of key issues . . . There can be arguments for or against the present scale of the public services, *but services are placed in or retained in the public sector because the private sector does not provide an adequate means for delivery* . . .

(Stewart 1989: 12–13, my emphasis)

The public service context is different (see Box 2.1, page 33) and needs to be managed differently. Though the uniqueness of the public sector may be seldom recognized, there is even less recognition that it has anything to teach the private sector, despite the point made by Stewart above.

Similarly, the view of Stewart that services are placed or remain in the public sector because the private sector does not provide an adequate means of delivery was being questioned in 1989 and is perhaps even more open to question today. The Conservatives were convinced of the 'supremacy' of the private sector and the need for the public sector to import private sector techniques, and in many ways these are beliefs which have not been challenged by Labour. None the less, the dangers of applying such beliefs remain, as highlighted by Stewart and Walsh (1992: 512):

One of the dangers of emerging patterns of public management is that approaches that have value in particular situations are assumed to have universal application. Public organizations carry out a wide range of activities subject to very different conditions. If in the past there were dangers in the universal assumption of direct provision of services in organizations structured by hierarchical control, there may, equally, be danger in the new assumptions that are replacing it, if universally applied.

However, perhaps a more fundamental point can be made concerning private and public sector models. Although it is perfectly legitimate and sensible to question the applicability and relevance of the private sector model to the public sector, it is also legitimate to question the validity of the private sector model *per se*, though this is not often evident in the literature. Some commentators, such as Hutton (1996), point to fundamental weaknesses in the political, economic and financial institutions of the UK as contributors to relative economic decline. For Hutton, endemic short-termism and a propensity for damaging take-overs characterize the

UK and show no sign of changing. Short-termism is exacerbated by, for instance, inadequate investment, inadequate training, and lack of competitiveness. Hutton's work has its critics (e.g. Wolf 1996) but his analysis is one which appears to have considerable support. It at least forces questions to be asked about the private sector model and reinforces the reservations concerning its public sector manifestation, i.e. NPM.

None the less, the application of NPM continues and the merits of competition and customer-focus, with concomitant emphases on restructuring, measuring performance, etc. are stressed as key characteristics of the new public service environment. Thomson (1992) points out that:

> Some of the characteristics of a market have been simulated (with competitive tendering in local authorities, and in central government with the introduction of market testing)... This has had the effect not only of introducing external competition into the provision of services, but also of altering the relationship between groupings of employees in what were formerly unitary bodies. The *political* objective has ostensibly been to reduce costs and often to increase customer choice. The effects in *management* terms are to necessitate the accurate costing of activities... to arrive at unit costs that form the basis of service pricing, and to enhance the general efficiency and effectiveness of the function in order that it can compete effectively. The new management processes include the specifying of a service, management of the contract and monitoring of performance.
>
> (Thomson 1992: 35, original emphasis)

In making the above statement, Thomson (1992) highlights the importance of financial management in delivering public services, the key aspects of which are discussed in subsequent chapters within the context of the central themes – competition, decentralization, customer-focus and performance measurement – as given on page 38.

Conclusion

The management of public services has undergone significant change, particularly since 1979. Private sector values and techniques have been imported as change has been imposed. Bureaucratic and monopolistic provision of services, and the alleged concomitant indifference to the consumer, have been replaced by a sharper focus on customer care and efficiency, delivered largely by means of restructuring, market forces and an emphasis on performance measurement. This managerial revolution, though perhaps overstated, had its origins in the political and economic ascendancy of the New Right and has had fundamental implications, not least for those who work in the public sector. Effective resource management must be demonstrated and, in this, the role of financial management is central, embracing issues as diverse as budgeting, costing, investment appraisal, audit and performance measurement. These issues are now considered in the following chapters, followed by a more in-depth consideration of financial management within local government and the NHS.

References

Adonis, A. (1991) The leviathan limbers up, *Financial Times*, 26 July.

Ascher, K. (1987) *The Politics of Privatisation: Contracting out Public Services*. Basingstoke: Macmillan.

Audit Commission (1996) *What the Doctor Ordered? A Study of GP Fundholders in England and Wales*. London: HMSO.

Bailey, S. J. (1995) *Public Sector Economics: Theory, Policy and Practice*. London: Macmillan.

Begg, D., Fischer, S. and Dornbusch, R. (1987) *Economics*, (2nd edn). Maidenhead: McGraw Hill.

Butler, R. (1994) Reinventing British government. *Public Administration*, 72 (Summer): 263–70.

Clark, D. (1996) Open government in Britain: discourse and practice. *Public Money & Management*, 16 (1): 23–30.

Cm. 1599 (1991) *The Citizen's Charter: Raising the Standard*. London: HMSO.

Cm. 2540 (1994) *The Citizen's Charter: Second Report*. London: HMSO.

Defence Committee (1995) *Market Testing And Contracting Out Of Defence Support Functions*. London: HMSO.

Digings, L. (1991) *Competitive Tendering and the European Communities: Public Procurement, CCT and Local Services*. London: Association of Metropolitan Authorities.

Farnham, D. and Horton, S. (eds) (1993) *Managing the New Public Services*. Basingstoke: Macmillan.

Flemming, J. and Oppenheimer, P. (1996) Are Government spending and taxes too high (or too low)? *National Institute Economic Review*, 3: 58–76.

Flynn, N. (1990) *Public Sector Management*. Hemel Hempstead: Harvester Wheatsheaf.

Foster, C. and Plowden, F. (1996) *The State Under Stress: Can the Hollow State be Good Government?* Buckingham: Open University Press.

Hood, C. (1991) A public management for all seasons? *Public Administration*, 69 (1): 3–19.

Hughes, O. E. (1994) *Public Management and Administration: An Introduction*. Basingstoke: Macmillan.

Hutton, W. (1996) *The State We're In* (2nd edn). London: Vintage.

Jackson, P. (1996) Public sector management: beyond the hype. Public Finance Foundation *Review*, 10: 1–6.

Jones, B. M. (1995) *Local Government Financial Management*. Hemel Hempstead: ICSA Publishing.

Jordan, G. (1994) Reinventing government: but will it work? *Public Administration*, 72, Summer: 271–9.

Lane, J. (1993) *The Public Sector: Concepts, Models and Approaches*. London: Newbury.

Lawton, A. and McKevitt, D. (1995) Strategic change in local government: comparative case studies. *Local Government Studies*, 21 (1): 46–64.

Lawton, A. and Rose, A. (1994) *Organisation & Management in the Public Sector* (2nd edn). London: Pitman.

Leibenstein, H. (1976) *Beyond Economic Man*. Cambridge, MA: Harvard University Press.

Metcalfe, L. and Richards, S. (1990) *Improving Public Management* (2nd edn). London: Sage.

Nichols, G. (1995) Contract specification in leisure management. *Local Government Studies*, 21 (2): 248–62.

Niskanen, W. (1971) *Bureaucracy and Representative Government*. Chicago: Aldine-Atherton.

OECD (Organization for Economic Cooperation and Development) (1993) Some measures to improve the quality of government spending. *Economic Outlook*, 54: 34–42.

Osborne, D. and Gaebler, T. (1992) *Reinventing Government: How the Entrepreneurial Spirit is Transforming the Public Sector*. Reading, MA: Addison Wesley.

O'Toole, B. J. (1995) Accountability, in J. Wilson (ed.) (1995) *Managing Public Services: Dealing With Dogma*, pp. 58–70. Eastham: Tudor.

Parker, D. (1990) The 1988 Local Government Act and compulsory competitive tendering. *Urban Studies*, 27 (5): 653–68.

Peters, T. (1989) *Thriving on Chaos: Handbook for a Management Revolution*. London: Pan.

Peters, T. J. and Waterman, R. H. (1982) *In Search of Excellence*. New York: Harper & Row.

Rouse, J. (1993) Resource and performance management in public service organisations, in K. Isaac-Henry, C. Painter and C. Barnes (eds) (1993) *Management in the Public Sector: Challenge and Change*, pp. 59–76. London: Chapman & Hall.

Simon, H. A. (1947) *Administrative Behavior*. New York: Macmillan.

Stewart, J. (1989) Management in the public domain. *Local Government Studies*, September/October: 9–15.

Stewart, J. (1996) A dogma of our times – the separation of policy-making and implementation. *Public Money & Management*, 16 (3): 33–40.

Stewart, J. and Walsh, K. (1992) Change in the management of public services. *Public Administration*, 70, winter: 499–518.

Stewart, J. and Walsh, K. (1994) Performance measurement: when performance can never be finally defined. *Public Money & Management*, 14 (2): 45–9.

Terry, F. (1996) The private finance initiative – overdue reform or policy breakthrough? *Public Money & Management*, 16 (1): 9–16.

Thomson, P. (1992) Public sector management in a period of radical change: 1979–1992. *Public Money & Management*, 12 (3): 33–41.

Treasury and Civil Service Committee (1994) *The Role Of The Civil Service*, vol. 1. London: HMSO.

Walsh, K. (1991) *Competitive Tendering for Local Authority Services: Initial Experiences*. London: HMSO.

Walsh, K. (1995) *Public Services and Market Mechanisms: Competition, Contracting and the New Public Management*. Basingstoke: Macmillan.

Williamson, O. E. (1975) *Markets and Hierarchies: Analysis and Antitrust Implications*. New York: Free Press.

Williamson, O. E. (1985) *The Economic Institutions of Capitalism*. New York: Free Press.

Wilson, J. (1995) Competition and public service provision, in J. Wilson (ed.) *Managing Public Services: Dealing With Dogma*, pp. 37–57. Eastham: Tudor.

Wilson, J. (1996) Citizen Major? The rationale and impact of The Citizen's Charter. *Public Policy and Administration*, 11 (1): 45–62.

Wolf, M. (1996) No answer in Germany, *Financial Times*, 16 April.

Further reading

Relevant articles can be found in a variety of journals but particularly relevant are *Public Administration*, *Public Policy and Administration* and *Public Money & Management*. It is also helpful to place developments in an international context, and Flynn, N. and Strehl, F. (1996) *Public Sector Management in Europe* (Hemel Hempstead: Prentice Hall), and Farnham, D., Horton, S., Barlow, J. and Hondeghem, A. (1996) *New Public Managers in Europe* (Basingstoke: Macmillan) are recommended. See also Pollitt, C. and Summa, H. (1997) 'Trajectories of reform: public management change in four countries', which appears in *Public Money & Management*, 17 (1): 7–18.

part two

Understanding finance

three

Budgeting and budgetary control

John Williams and Anita Carroll

Key learning objectives

After reading this chapter you should be able to:

1 Understand the aims of budgeting and budgetary control.
2 Appreciate the various approaches to preparing a budget and obtaining its approval.
3 Understand the process of budgetary control – using the budget to control operations and the limitations on the process.
4 Appreciate the special problems of budgeting for services and budgeting for large numbers of separate local units – problems which are particularly significant for the public sector.
5 Develop a critical approach to the advantages and limitations of using budgets to plan and control organizational action.

Introduction

Chapters 1 and 2 have, among other things, emphasized the importance of effective resource management in the provision of public services. In demonstrating effective resource management the role of the financial manager is pivotal. Financial management involves a variety of techniques and the main ones are considered here and in Chapters 4 and 5. The focus in this chapter is on budgeting and budgetary control.

Budgeting refers to the process of preparing, negotiating and agreeing a quantified and specific plan, i.e. a budget, for an organization, normally for a 12 month period. Budgetary control can similarly be described as the process of using the plan to facilitate the control of an organization's activities for the period covered by the budget.

Budgeting, though a familiar process, is one which is difficult to explain with any degree of certainty as practices and usage vary between organizations, between different parts of the same organization, and over time. There is also a problem in that the language of budgeting can be variously interpreted, even within the same organization (Samuelson 1986). These variations make it difficult to generalize. However, there is a need to understand the parts of budgeting that are common to virtually all organizations; generally the mechanical processes. There is also a need to understand the factors which can lead to the differences in practice. This chapter will consider these issues and place them within a public sector context.

The nature of budgeting

For reasons outlined in Chapters 1 and 2, the boundaries between public and private sectors have become less clear-cut. This has numerous implications, including those relating to financial management. With regard to budgeting, parts of the public sector, working under the discipline of markets or *quasi*-markets, work in very similar ways to the private sector. This also applies to certain not-for-profit organizations, such as charities, which compete in markets for donations.

In the private sector the discipline of the market is paramount. If a product or service does not sell there is no income and, regardless of the budget, there is nothing from which to pay expenses, including payments to staff. Success in the market, however, leads to the achievement of, at least, budgeted sales and profits and enables all internal services to be funded as planned. Significant success, probably as much against market expectations as the budget, facilitates expansion.

In the market sector all sub-organizational budgets depend on the achievement of the overall organizational budget, and performance against individual budgets must be assessed within this context. Assuming that the organizational budget reflects market expectations and requirements, achieving or exceeding budgeted performance may be used for short-term performance measurement at the organizational and sub-organizational levels (e.g. sections, divisions). This is an argument for divisional structures and local autonomy – that authority can be delegated and individuals motivated knowing that their achievement is additive. However, in a fast-moving market sector, a difficulty may arise in that market expectations move ahead of managerial ones, in which case the budget ceases to be a relevant yardstick. A supermarket chain, for instance, can achieve profits ahead of budget and ahead of the previous year but still disappoint City expectations compared with the market leader.

In the market sector the budget is dominated by the problem of forecasting sales and achieving the sales volume at prices that reflect minimum cost, though there are exceptions to this. For instance, in the case of firms operating in capital-intensive industries where there is a shortage of capacity, the critical factor is the volume that can be produced, as everything produced can be sold. In this instance, budgeting is dominated by the critical factor of feasible production.

Within the non-market sector the fundamental difference is that the income, when agreed by the ultimate authority (e.g. a council), is virtually certain, unlike the market sector, where income depends on the operation of the market, which is dynamic, and, therefore, any budget can only be conditional. This means that within the non-market sector an agreed budget can represent and be regarded as a more complete delegation of authority to act than is ever possible within the market sector.

The budget negotiation is also quite different in that those involved have the advantage of knowing that the budget, once agreed, will be a commitment for the whole year. This allows close monitoring of actual performance against the original budget. In the market sector, however, there is always the possibility of change; such change may be small in the case of a large corporation operating in a stable environment, but may be considerable in the case of smaller organizations. This difference is explained by Jonsson (1984: 129):

> ... resources are allocated to activities via the budget in the public sector. It is a fundamental difference between private and public sector organisations that the public organisation is related to its source of finance by a budget, while the finances of the private organisation are moderated by market forces. Therefore a great deal of attention is paid to budgeting in the public sector, while performance in the market place provides the equivalent focus for the private sector organisation. So, if you want to have resources in the public sector to carry out all the good things you want to do, you had better be good at budgeting! ... in the public sector the budget decision is built on the exclusive right to tax citizens which, in turn, makes it necessary to make visible the decisions on the tax rate and the appropriation of funds.

Budgeting in the public sector will inevitably be political and is often described in this way. Wildavsky (1975) describes it as an attempt to allocate financial resources through political processes to serve differing human purposes. This is not to say that political considerations are unknown or even unusual in the market sector, but they are much less important than market considerations.

An important part of budgeting in a public sector organization is the presentation of an image of control, policy and clear direction. The organization is seeking legitimacy, a justification for its use and continued receipt of public funds. Similarly, politicians seek to demonstrate that they have achieved something. Within limits, the appearance is at least as important as the reality. This can be illustrated by reference to hospital budgeting in a number of countries which describe changing systems but ineffectual control, the result of the enormous problem of reconciling clinical freedom with cost control and rational planning with largely unpredictable demand and rapidly changing technology. Examples of such studies include Brunsson (1995), Pettersen (1995) and Preston *et al.* (1992).

Budget preparation

The Chartered Institute of Management Accountants (CIMA) (1996: 43) defines a budget as: 'A quantitative statement, for a defined period in time, which may include planned revenues, expenses, assets, liabilities and cash flows. A budget provides a focus for the organization, aids the co-ordination of activities, and facilitates control'. The following terms used in the above definition are now considered:

- Quantitative
- Statement
- Defined period
- Plan
- Focus for the organization
- Coordination
- Control

Quantitative

Budgets are numerical statements, not statements of principle. They are not expressions of aspirations to sell more, or to provide more services; specific figures are included against which progress, or lack of it, can be measured. Budgets usually include physical and cash units for inputs and outputs and are designed in such a way as to ease comparison of actual results, period by period, with the budgeted figures, and enable causes and effects of differences (variances) to be analysed. The key extension to all budgets to ease this comparison is the preparation of a phased budget, i.e. a budget for each period of the year, as well as an overall budget for the year.

Statement

The budget is a formal statement formally made and agreed. Most organizations have developed systems of distinguishing budgets from estimates to emphasize commitment to achievement, the important difference being that all concerned know that comparison will continue to be made with the budget throughout the period in question. The budget cannot be instantly replaced by a new forecast every time circumstances change. Commitments cannot be forgotten when convenient.

Defined period

This is almost always a year. There are organizations who budget for longer periods and some smaller organizations in circumstances of rapid change who budget for shorter periods. For instance, two exceptions in the private sector are the fashion and construction industries. The former typically produces two collections of designs each year and budgets, for each collection, every six months. In the case of the latter, the basic budgeting unit is the contract, regardless of whether it is for six months or two or more years. However, the norm is the annual budget, and this is consistent with formal reporting on an annual basis to shareholders, electors or their representatives, directors, councillors or Members of Parliament.

Plan

Budgeting – dealing with the future – involves planning the organizational response to anticipated events. It assumes some overall strategy, even if a formal, structured, strategic planning process does not exist within the organization. Normally, the budget reflects the proportion of the plan which may be implemented in the defined timescale, given the constraints of resources and anticipated problems and events.

In small, flexible organizations, planning and budgeting are often combined; all envisaged changes can probably be achieved within the budget year. Within large organizations, however, in both public and private sectors, the development of the strategic plan is a major undertaking. While it is annually refined and developed, the main thrust of the strategy would normally remain unchanged for a considerable time. Change is slow and difficult, involving major investment, structural change and considerable change of personnel. Within the budget period, relatively small changes are all that can be achieved, and the budget is often best seen as a balance between moving towards strategic objectives (the envisaged route to maximum long-term profits) and maximizing short-term profit.

Most public sector organizations are quite large except for local units such as schools which have limited autonomy. In addition, there are also considerable difficulties relating to the availability of capital and revenue funds and changing personnel. There is often a severe limit to what can be achieved in one year.

Focus for the organization

Budgeting is for the whole organization: a budget for part of the organization's activity, ignoring other parts, or ignoring certain items, is ineffective. In many small organizations, the budget is the only formal statement of organizational purpose and of the results expected from managers. In more complex organizations, the problems arise of reconciling other more general statements of aims, mission, and strategy with a budget statement of what is regarded as achievable in a defined period.

Coordination

An important result of the process of formulating a budget for the whole organization is that it makes clear the links between its component parts. To the extent that budgeting is an open process, which is normal in the public sector, it communicates these interrelationships to all the managers involved. Within the private sector, there is less disclosure of overall budgets, sometimes because of the difficulties in making what the stock exchange would regard as a forecast of profits. In some large private companies, budgeting is regarded as highly confidential, but none the less it is still a means by which the top managers can see and understand how the component parts of an organization interrelate.

Control

Control has a number of meanings. Here it does not normally mean 'prevent' in that mechanisms which prevent a manager from committing or spending anything not authorized are rarely part of a budgeting system. Such mechanisms exist, typically in controls of organizational staff numbers (headcount) where personnel departments will not advertise for or appoint staff without there being an identified vacancy and appropriate authority for recruitment (public sector organizations in particular have been characterized by such control mechanisms).

Another preventative control system is that of comparing proposed commitments or purchase orders with budgets. Many managers operate private 'black book' systems for noting commitments and comparing the cumulative total with the budget, and regard this as far more useful than the budget report of the amount invoiced to date by suppliers. Increasingly, organizations are trying to replace these informal records with computer systems which are integrated with the financial accounting system, the formal purchasing system (official orders) and the control of stores. Most progress in this is being made in such industries as contracting and advertising but there is potential for this in the public sector.

Control in budgeting normally means regular (typically monthly) reporting of actual achievement and cost compared with budgeted, followed by management review and any necessary corrective action.

In addition to the above points, as taken from the CIMA (1996) definition, two further aspects of budgeting require further consideration: motivation and the authorization of expenditure. With regard to motivation, the formality of the procedures of budgeting is designed to ensure that managers feel obliged to make every effort to achieve the anticipated quantitative results. The approach generally recommended is to involve managers in all the discussions and to obtain their agreement that the budget is achievable and desirable and that all necessary efforts will be made. In reality, managers and subordinates may have different views on the process and the budgets eventually agreed.

There are differences in motivation between public and private sectors. For instance, in the private sector, a manager may be rewarded with a bonus for achieving – and a larger bonus for exceeding – the budgeted profit. The manager is motivated to maximum achievement with no budget 'ceiling'. If budgeted profit can be increased there is unlikely to be an expenditure ceiling, though there may be other constraints, such as those relating to funds employed or working capital. In the public sector, however, a manager responsible for delivering a set of services within an agreed budget must remain within the budget, in any other than quite exceptional circumstances, even if this leads to a reduction in the service level. This applies to even such extreme cases as running an emergency unit in a hospital.

A manager in the private sector, responsible for delivering services such as computing or accounting, to the organization but not responsible for profits, would initially appear to be in a similar position to a public sector manager, but in practice there are two important differences. First, if the overall budget for the profit centre is being exceeded as greater volumes are being sold, the priority for the cost centre manager is to support the greater volume of sales, increasing the cost as necessary, regardless of the original budget. There is widespread use of the concept of flexible budgeting, where many costs are regarded as strictly proportionate to volume. Second, the manager is likely to be rewarded not by a bonus on the achievement of his or her own cost centre budget, but by a bonus scheme based on achieving or exceeding the overall, organizational, budgeted profit. This places considerable emphasis on the importance of all managers working together towards a shared goal regardless of sub-organizational objectives.

A considerable amount of literature is available on motivational aspects of budgeting. For example, Argyris (1953) reports on the way supervisors react to the imposition of budgeting. Autocratically-imposed budgeting systems and targets produce feelings in supervisors of being under pressure and lead to defensive behaviour, such as the search for excuses or scape-goats, or the determination of budgets with built-in safety margins. The tensions are likely to be dysfunctional, leading to inefficiency and/or a breakdown in working relationships. A normal defensive reaction is the development of informal groups united by a suspicion of every move made by management to improve efficiency. As a solution, Argyris recommended participative budgeting and the training of budget staff in behavioural implications of control systems.

His study has been replicated a number of times with similar results but controversy remains over the link between the recommendations and the study. The recommendation of training is non-contentious, but there is a considerable political background to the recommendation for participative processes. This background includes arguments for industrial democracy and participation by all employees in decision making. However, there are a number of valid and interrelated arguments in favour of participative systems, including:

- Managerial motivation.
- Commitment to the achievement of the budget.
- Belief that the agreed target is achievable.
- Some form of obligation to the firm as the system is accepted as being considerate of individual views.
- Better information obtained through participation than in a top-down system of budgeting.

However, there will also be problems, the most notable being that full consultation takes a considerable time and these systems can easily lead to slower decision making. There is also scope for managers to build 'slack elements' into their estimates, not all of which will be detected by any review system.

The work of Hofstede (1968) showed that budgets only work as targets if they are accepted by the managers. This, in turn, requires their participation. However, there is empirical evidence that managers build in safety margins and that they spend exactly to target, rather than attempting to improve that target. This is particularly evident in the public sector as conventional accounting rules do not permit the carry-forward of any unspent moneys into the next financial year.

A good analysis of the literature concerning the behaviour of managers in relation to the imposition of budgetary constraints is provided in Brownell (1982) and Briers and Hirst (1990). See also Emmanuel *et al.* (1990) for a fuller treatment.

With regard to the authorization of expenditure, a key aspect of budgeting is that the agreement of a budget enables the delegation of authority to act within the budget. A manager with a budget can act within the scope of the resources budgeted and, subject to any other control procedures, achieve the budgeted aims of the department. In the absence of a budgeting system decisions concerning resources would continually need to be referred upwards.

Within the non-market parts of the public sector the budget authorization decision is all-important. Once it is taken, clear authority has been provided to act within the limits of the budget, in the way specified by the detail in the budget. The approval of the budget is in fact an instruction to spend the money in the way budgeted. Very little flexibility, technically known as virement, is allowed in moving funds from one budget head to another. The revenues of the non-market public sector are predictable coming, as they do, from taxation.

This does not apply in the market sectors, private or public. Here, the income is not certain, because it arises from trading in markets, not from taxation. Some markets are, of course, more certain than others: everyone at present 'buys' their water from the local water company; most people purchase gas from British Gas; most patients get sent by their general practitioner to the local district general hospital; and most children get sent by their parents to local schools. *Quasi*-markets, as in the National Health Service (NHS) and in education, are an uneasy mixture of uncertainties arising from the market and the changing system, and continuing support from taxation. However, despite these examples, no matter how stable the market and however careful the budgeting, the exact income is not known in advance in the way it is known when the income comes from taxation. The income depends on success in the markets, so any decisions on how the money is spent can only be conditional and subject to review throughout the year in line with market developments.

Current practice in public sector budgeting

Practice varies considerably across the public sector in terms of the way that budgets are prepared and used and the managerial processes involved. The mechanics, however, are progressively becoming more standardized. This is in part due to the influence of drives towards best practice by the Audit Commission, the National Audit Office, the professional accounting bodies and, importantly, central government. Coombs and Jenkins (1994) describe four paradigms:

1 The bid system.
2 Financial planning systems.
3 Planning programme budgeting system.
4 Zero-based budgeting.

The first two are examples of incremental/departmental budgeting, and the last two are examples of rational/corporate budgeting. Each is now considered in turn.

The bid system

This is the purest form of incremental budget. Each department prepares its own estimate of future requirements and plans. These are aggregated and compared with the resources it is possible to obtain from local taxation, charges for services, and/or government grants. Inevitably, total proposed expenditure will exceed forecast revenue and this leads to plans being cut so they can be accommodated within the likely level of resources. It is difficult for central management and policy makers, such as councillors, to manage this process for three main reasons:

1 Time constraints: by the time the estimates are available and a realistic forecast of possible revenue can be made, little time will remain in which to finalize estimates.
2 Internal politics: the bid system leads to 'winners' and 'losers' in that resources allocated to one department are, by definition, unavailable for any other department. See Chapter 1, Table 1.3 (page 11). If the departmental head is 'good at budgeting' the committee will think that the proposed increase in that department's budget is absolutely essential and other departments will inevitably, and not always justifiably, suffer as a result.
3 Absence of criteria for comparing estimates: in the private sector the key criterion is the contribution each department/service/product makes to ultimate profit. This test can be applied to requests for new machinery, increased advertising, better quality control and so on. In the public sector, however, it is not so clear-cut. A local council may be trying to balance street cleaning with expenditure on the arts and with a variety of other services to disparate groups within the community. There is no one simple question to ask. A value judgement has to be made and different people will naturally reach different conclusions. The problem is usually resolved by cutting each department back to a figure somewhere between current expenditure and proposed expenditure, often on a fairly arbitrary basis.

The weaknesses of the bid system are:

• The system works on the annual cycle of budgeting but many costs can only sensibly be planned over several years.
• While staff can react favourably at first to being asked to make their bids, the reaction will turn to cynicism if the bids are cut arbitrarily,

which is almost inevitable. In the next round, there will be a great temptation to overbid to allow for potential cuts.

- The system concentrates attention on the marginal items, the increases sought and the necessary cuts. There is little review of the base expenditure.
- There is little policy input to the process. Many decisions may be taken by default on the basis of the separate interpretations of policy by all the departmental managers.

Financial planning systems

These are attempts to meet the main criticisms of the bid system by providing central guidance at the start of the process and by looking at the medium-term at the same time as the budget year. The central guidance will try to indicate the year-on-year increase permissible, and, if all departments can work within this and no further changes are imposed by government, should eliminate the need for reworking and reconsideration. A normal feature of these systems is to be more specific about the nature of changes from year to year; instead of just looking at base expenditure plus increment, to look at:

Base expenditure	plus	inflation
	minus	reductions
	plus	committed growth
	plus	new growth

While financial planning systems permit a more rational analysis of changes, the weaknesses of the bid system largely remain, i.e.:

- There is little consideration of the base expenditure; the system is still incremental.
- The system is still departmental with little scope for imposing overall objectives.

However, financial planning systems normally work reasonably smoothly in conditions where no major change is required. Where, however, there is a need for major change, the techniques of planning programming budgeting systems and zero-based budgeting, considered below, are more appropriate.

Planning programming budgeting system (PPBS)

This, and the zero-based system (see below) were both originally developed in the USA. They can both be considered as rational systems which, in theory, address all the weaknesses of incremental systems. However, neither is easy to implement, and, consequently, neither is used to a significant extent. The basic PPBS approach is to:

- Identify objectives, i.e. analyse all programmes in terms of their objectives.
- Plan and analyse costs, budgeted and actual expenditure by area of activity and by purpose of expenditure over a series of years.
- Analyse alternative ways of achieving programme aims and objectives.

Put simply, the main advantage (and problem) with this approach is that it starts with the question of what ought to be done (see Bellamy and Kluvers 1995). The approach may work if a clear answer can be given and where reasonable stability is anticipated. However, the answer has to be expanded in detail because the aims have to be expanded to include all the things that the organization is compelled to do in providing services. Further detail is required because programmes will often consist of a range of services provided by different departments and different functional specialists. The problem is that a considerable level of detailed analysis is required which is difficult to prepare and difficult for policy-makers to assimilate.

Zero-based budgeting (ZBB)

This is a radical approach which can be likened to taking a clean sheet of paper and starting from scratch. All expenditure, current and proposed, has to be justified, building up alternative possible service levels or packages of services into decision packages – effective choices of the cost and service level combination affordable in view of the overall objectives. Nothing from the past is automatically rolled or brought forward.

This approach can work well, though it requires major efforts, particularly when used as a special review of a particular set of services, or as a consequence of a major policy change. It is of less use as an annual routine mainly because of its time-consuming nature. More fundamentally, however, if it is *required* as an annual routine, it is reasonable to conclude that it is not being done properly.

Budgeting in the private sector

While a great variety of budgetary practices are carried out in the private sector, most firms emphasize something parallel to the financial planning systems discussed above, in that broad outlines are discussed and guidance given before all the detailed work of departmental budgeting is started. The sales budget is usually agreed before other work begins, as it indicates production volumes and available resources. In the public sector, a starting point is likely to be continuation of service estimates, which may then be compared with available, or likely, resources.

There has been considerable interest in recent years in activity-based costing and budgeting. This involves analysing costs and budgeting for them on the basis of the activities causing (driving) those costs, such as the services provided, rather than by departmental responsibility (see Chapter 4). This is especially helpful where a service is provided by the joint efforts of several departments. In many ways, activity-based costing parallels PPBS systems described above, and it suffers from the same problems of needing a considerable effort in data collection and analysis. However, it is being used to some extent in NHS hospital cost analysis and budgeting.

Budgeting and financing

Budgeting methods have to be considered – whether in a local authority, a government-funded quango (quasi autonomous non-governmental organization), or part of central government – against their fit with:

- Local management and policy objectives.
- Declared government objectives.
- Methods of finance.

The first two of these are self-explanatory. With regard to financing, the main distinguishing feature of the public sector is that funds are, in the main, derived from taxation, not from the customer. This has a number of consequences (see Midwinter and Monaghan 1995), but key points to note are:

- Service growth and scope for service initiatives are constrained by central government's control of funding.
- Change can only be achieved by rethinking some existing services, which suggests some selective use of ZBB approaches.
- Financing can be affected by changing services. Financing is primarily incremental: past spending and grants, plus a small increment for inflation and planned changes. It may be disturbed by structural change. There is little point in making changes which reduce costs and grants at the same time. The effect of the standard spending assessment (SSA) (see Chapter 9), for instance, is to tie plans to central policy and further weaken local control. The effect of the financing constraints can be to tie organizations even more closely to an incremental approach to avoid the risks of change that could disturb existing financing.

Budgetary control

Once formulated, budgets need to be controlled. This involves regular comparisons between actual results and the budget. These comparisons remind all concerned of the original planning process and objectives. Where there are differences between the original plan and actual achievement, variances need to be explained. Reporting actual progress against budget (budgetary control) influences the restart of the budgeting process, i.e. discussing the next budget for the next financial year.

In the market sector these processes become a system of encouraging managers to achieve what they originally considered feasible, and to maximize profit. In the non-market sector the system highlights overspending and acts as a control mechanism against it. Performance measurement is separate from expenditure control. In the market sector the achievement against budget is the most important measurement of performance. In the non-market sector it is essential not to overspend but performance is not measured so narrowly (see Chapter 8).

It was previously explained that 'control' in a budgetary sense means, primarily, evaluation of performance after the event, not preventative control. The basic control process in a budgetary system is feedback, comparing actual expenditure with the budget, and subsequent correction. This is usually done by using the cybernetic control model, otherwise known as the thermostat mechanism or feedback loop. The model requires:

- An objective for the system being controlled.
- A means of measuring results along the dimensions defined by the objective.
- Knowledge of the effects of possible actions.
- A choice of relevant alternative actions available to the controller.

These requirements can be illustrated by reference to the NHS, as follows.

Objective

A private sector organization may have defined a particular level of profit as its single objective. In the NHS, the objective may be to stay within its external financing limit (see Chapter 10). The problem, of course, is that the NHS as a whole has complex objectives – maintaining and improving the nation's health at minimum cost – which are hard to specify in detail. It is very difficult to say that something falls outside the objectives. However, some specific parts of the NHS may have very clear objectives, while other parts may have conflicting objectives.

Measurement

Costs (economy) can be easily measured, as can process activity (efficiency), in terms of, say, bed occupancy, number of surgical procedures, number of prescriptions etc. However, outputs/outcomes (effectiveness) are much more problematic.

Knowledge of effects

In a system involving people and being influenced by external forces, prediction is about probabilities, not certainties. Within the NHS it is difficult to predict the consequences of the various actions available, not least because of the sheer size of the organization and the time needed for change to take effect.

Choice of actions

In a not-for-profit organization there are usually far more outside influences on the control of the organization than would be the case in the private sector. Decision-making tends to be complex with little managerial freedom. Many options may be ruled out on political grounds, and real choice of action can only really take place in the medium to long term.

Budgeting for local units in the public and private sectors

Large organizations, whether in the private or public sector, provide their services on a national basis through a large number of local supply centres, known as multiple units. Public sector examples include schools, hospitals, libraries and a wide range of local authority services. Private sector examples include banks, hotel groups, supermarkets and other shops in common ownership.

The public sector has traditionally taken a bureaucratic approach to the management of these geographically-separate units, but recently a number of changes have been made in the UK in an attempt to reduce central bureaucratic control of local units by devolving more power to them. The manager of a local unit has a similar job, whether in the public or private sector, and there is an obvious superficial similarity between providing specialized services through geographically-dispersed units in both sectors. However, there are also differences to consider:

- The problem of determining provision: the public sector has to provide services, whether economic and efficient or not. Hospitals and schools within a reasonable range of the communities they serve are essential. The private sector on the other hand can choose to withdraw from attempting to provide a universal service, which simplifies the provision problem.
- Public sector units have to provide some sort of service to all sorts of 'customers' (hospitals, for instance, cannot easily turn away emergencies; the police cannot 'pick and choose' who they are prepared to help).

In the private sector, however, organizations can market the goods and services they wish, fully aware that this may exclude some customers.

• Public sector decisions on local provision are basically centralized, determined by experts and formulae, but often politically-modified (e.g. hospitals in London). Local decision-making can lead to different levels of service being offered in different parts of the country. In the private sector there is usually a clear line of command from the centre and much less local discretion.

• Public sector units are placed in a position where they are mainly competing against each other for limited funds (a zero sum game). Private sector units on the other hand, such as chain stores and hotels, are typically competing against units belonging to another company.

There is, however, a case for devolving authority and budgeting to local management in the public sector. Recent developments have involved the need to raise the awareness of professionals (e.g. NHS consultants) as to the importance of costs and cost management. This has been problematical in that most managers were appointed before business skills became important and many are much better at professional leadership than budgeting, let alone competing for customers. This development has followed the increased 'marketization' of public service activity, designed to increase efficiency through competition and to depoliticize decision making by allowing 'the market' to determine resource allocation rather than politicians (the NHS is again a good example: see Chapter 10, and Common et al. 1992; Edwards et al. 1995).

Budgeting, outsourcing and compulsory competitive tendering

One of the recent features of much public sector activity has been the extent to which a large range of services has been 'outsourced', i.e. delivered by external organizations (see Chapter 2). This has mirrored similar tendencies in the private sector, where a number of large organizations have outsourced services and disposed of peripheral businesses to concentrate on what are perceived to be core activities.

One advantage of this is that it simplifies operational management and saves management time and effort, regardless of the economics of comparing internal and external costs. Instead of managing staff and purchasing separately all supplies, there is just one contract to place and monitor. Similarly, the budgeting process appears easier because it is all settled by the contract and there is nothing left to discuss. However, there are significant other effects on the budgeting process. Control of the cost of outsourced services depends on three factors:

1 The contract duration: if it is a long-term contract, say anything from seven years upward, this is likely to constrain interim action. Most potential suppliers look for the security of a long contract to justify investment.
2 The difficulty in changing to an alternative supplier, regardless of contract length. This can be very significant with, for instance, outsourced information technology (IT) services if there are several hundred programmes running on a mainframe.
3 The extent to which the contract is for a fixed annual sum (e.g. for office space or equipment), or entirely volume-related, or a combination of the two. If volume is significant, the implications of outsourcing may be controllable but the effects of reduced spending on a lower volume of services may have more consequences, depending on the detail of the contract, than if an internal budget is cut. If volume has little effect, contract duration is the only issue.

Another complication arises from the fact that budgeting is often used by central and local management as a means of controlling or reducing costs, as well as to plan for the forthcoming year. This is valid if costs can be controlled within a one-year framework, but less so for costs to which an organization is committed for several years or where, in the first year, cancellation costs would exceed ongoing savings. The annual budget is unlikely to provide useful control over committed costs. Attempts to squeeze total budgeted costs can produce major problems if a significant part of the budget is taken up with long-term contracts for outsourced services. The pressure on the relatively few internal items that can be cancelled in the short term can become unreasonable. Policy will tend to be determined on the basis of which services can be cut, rather than those that ought to be cut.

Conclusion

The aims of budgeting and budgetary control appear similar on the surface in the market and non-market sectors, but there are significant differences. These are best explained by the certainty of negotiated income from taxation in the non-market sector, and by the motivational role of budgets and budget-related reward schemes in the market sector in order to achieve maximum income from the market. However, there are considerable similarities in the processes of budgeting and budgetary control, viz. the mechanical processes of reporting actual results and comparing them with the budget. Both sectors emphasize formal process and formal approval of budgets, but for different reasons. In the market sector, emphasis is placed on motivation to maximum achievement, where budgets help managers to succeed in the market. In the non-market sector, the process is essentially the political problem of negotiating for funds from taxation. The budget is a formalization of a set of quite separate discussions.

References

Argyris, C. (1953) *The Impact of Budgets on People*. New York: The Controllership Foundation.

Bellamy, S. and Kluvers, R. (1995) Program budgeting in Australian local government: a study of implementation and outcomes. *Financial Accountability & Management*, 11 (1): 39–56.

Briers, M. and Hirst, M. (1990) The role of budgetary information in performance evaluation. *Accounting, Organizations and Society*, 15 (4): 373–98.

Brownell, P. (1982) Participation in the budgeting process: when it works, and when it doesn't. *Journal of Accounting Literature*, 1: 124–53.

Brunsson, K. (1995) Puzzle pictures: Swedish budgetary processes in principle and practice. *Financial Accountability & Management*, 11 (2): 111–26.

Chartered Institute of Management Accountants (CIMA) (1996) *Management Accounting: Official Terminology*. London: CIMA.

Common, R., Flynn, N. and Mellon, E. (1992) *Managing Public Services: Competition and Decentralisation*. London: Butterworth Heinemann.

Coombs, H. M. and Jenkins, D. E. (1994) *Public Sector Financial Management* (2nd edn). London: Chapman & Hall.

Edwards, P., Ezzamel, M., Robson, K. and Taylor, M. (1995) The development of local management of schools: budgets, accountability and educational impact. *Financial Accountability & Management*, 11 (4): 297–315.

Emmanuel, C., Otley, D. and Merchant, K. (1990) *Accounting for Management Control* (2nd edn). London: Chapman & Hall.

Hofstede, G. (1968) *The Game of Budget Control*. London: Tavistock Institute.

Jonsson, S. (1984) Budget making in central and local government, in A. Hopwood and C. Tomkins (eds) (1984) *Issues in Public Sector Accounting*, pp. 128–46. London: Philip Allan.

Midwinter, A. and Monaghan, C. (1995) The new centralism: local government finance in the 1990s. *Financial Accountability & Management*, 11 (2): 141–51.

Pettersen, I. J. (1995) Budgetary control of hospitals – ritual rhetorics and rationalised myths? *Financial Accountability & Management*, 11 (3): 207–21.

Preston, A. M., Cooper, D. J. and Coombs, R. W. (1992) Fabricating budgets: a study of the production of management budgeting in the National Health Service. *Accounting, Organizations and Society*, 17 (6): 561–93.

Samuelson, L. A. (1986) Discrepancies between the roles of budgeting. *Accounting, Organizations and Society*, 11 (1): 35–45.

Wildavsky, A. (1975) *Budgeting: Comparative Theory of Budgetary Processes*. Boston: Little, Brown.

Further reading

You are advised to keep up to date by referring to the academic journals, notably *Financial Accountability & Management* and *Accounting, Organizations and Society*. In addition, refer to the publications of the professional bodies, including CIMA and CIPFA.

four

Costing and pricing in the public sector

Christopher J. Pyke

Key learning objectives

After reading this chapter you should be able to:

1 Classify costs for decision making.
2 Understand the techniques available for costing products and services.
3 Explain the factors relevant to pricing products and services.
4 Appreciate the complexities of costing and pricing in the public sector.
5 Understand the techniques for pricing services in an internal market.

Introduction

Since the mid-1970s the public sector has been under pressure to reduce its overall expenditure and at the same time to increase both the quantity and the quality of the services it provides. The introduction of compulsory competitive tendering (CCT) for local government, the internal market for the National Health Service (NHS), and market testing for the civil service during the 1980s added further pressures to improve efficiency (see Chapter 2). A major consequence of these initiatives has been the need to improve the quality of costing information and to develop adequate pricing systems. In this chapter some of the different techniques used for costing and pricing products and services in the public sector are reviewed.

Costing products and services

Purpose of costing

Managers in both the public and private sectors are responsible for planning, controlling and making decisions about the future of the resources entrusted to their care. They will use a wide range of information to help them, including costing information. The purpose of costing is to calculate as accurately as possible how much a product, process or service has cost, is costing, or will cost. On the basis of such information, important management decisions can be taken, for example how much to charge for a particular product or service, or to assess whether a change in the method of service delivery is required, or identify where savings can be achieved.

Classifying costs

When using costs for decision making it is useful to classify them. The method of classification will depend on the nature of the decision being taken and the costing technique used. One of the main classification methods used by accountants, particularly for forecasting costs, is cost behaviour. There are four basic cost behaviour types:

1 Fixed costs, which do not change (in the short term at least) with the level of activity, e.g. rent and rates.
2 Stepped fixed costs, which are fixed between certain ranges of activity. At a critical level of activity the costs step up to a new plateau, e.g. supervision costs in a children's day centre might be fixed for supervising between one and five children, but a sixth child may require an additional child-carer to be employed.
3 Variable costs, which vary in direct proportion to the volume of activity, e.g. in the health service the total cost of vaccines will vary in direct proportion to the number of patients vaccinated.
4 Semi-variable costs, which include both an element of fixed and variable costs, e.g. a telephone bill is made up of a fixed line rental charge plus a variable usage charge for the calls made.

Figure 4.1 shows graphical representations of these behaviour patterns.

Another method of classifying costs is by their relationship with the final product or service, i.e. whether they are *direct* or *indirect* costs. Direct costs are those which can be traced in full to the product, service or department that is being costed. Indirect (or overhead) costs are those which are incurred while producing a product (or service), but which cannot be directly traced to that product or service.

Other cost classifications include:

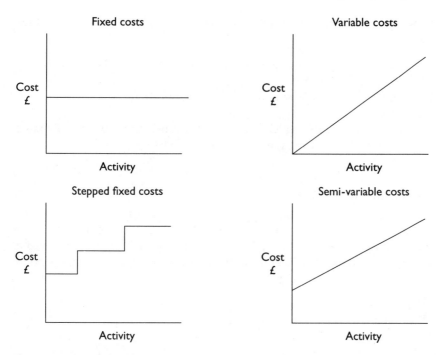

Figure 4.1 Cost behaviour patterns

- Relevant costs: those which will change as a result of the decision under consideration. Costs which will remain unaffected by the decision are referred to as *non-relevant.*
- Sunk costs: those already incurred and which will be unaffected by the decision to be taken.
- Opportunity costs: costs which represent the sacrifice made when a choice of one course of action precludes the pursuit of an alternative course of action.
- Marginal or incremental costs: the additional costs which arise from the delivery of additional units of service (or product).
- Controllable costs: those which can be controlled by the budget holder's decisions and actions. Costs which cannot be influenced by the budget holder are *non-controllable.*

Responsibility accounting

For costs to be managed economically, efficiently and effectively it is necessary to have a costing system which identifies where the costs arise and who was responsible for incurring them. This system is known as responsibility accounting and is based on the recognition of individual areas of responsibility, called responsibility centres. Drury (1996: 47) identifies three main types:

1 A *cost centre* where managers are accountable only for the expenses that are under their control.
2 A *profit centre* where managers are accountable for sales revenue and expenses.
3 An *investment centre* which is similar to a profit centre but the manager is also responsible for capital investment decisions.

Approaches to costing

The process of costing is not an exact science. It requires both judgement and estimates to be made, hence there is scope for different techniques and assumptions to produce significantly different outcomes. In this section three approaches to costing are considered:

1 Full costing (or absorption costing).
2 Marginal costing (or variable costing).
3 Activity-based costing.

Full costing

Full costing exercises in the public sector can be quite complex, though the principles are relatively straightforward. Costs are initially collected and categorized as either direct or indirect (overhead) costs. In local government, for example, indirect costs arise at two tiers in the organization: at service department level and at the corporate level.

When ascertaining the full cost of a front-line service, a proportion of the indirect costs must be allocated to that service through a process of cost allocation and apportionment. For example, consider the process for costing a mobile library service provided by a local authority. The direct costs would include the driver's wages, petrol, the depreciation costs and maintenance of the vehicle, the book stock and any other materials. The indirect costs would include an element of the library service's departmental costs, e.g. mobile library supervisory costs. In addition, an element of the local authority's overhead costs would also have to be allocated, e.g. an element of the payroll administration costs. There is clearly a cascading allocation of overhead costs through the organization, and these need to be taken into account to ascertain the full cost of the mobile library service – see Figure 4.2.

The main advantages of full cost apportionment when applied in the public sector are that it:

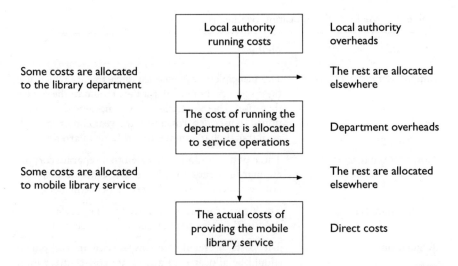

Figure 4.2 Allocation and apportionment of costs to a front-line service
Source: Based on Jones (1995: 86).

- shows the full cost of the service being provided;
- ensures maximum revenue is received, e.g. where a service is grant funded;
- demonstrates compliance with legislation, e.g. where there is a need to demonstrate that a particular rate of return has been achieved;
- enables cost comparisons between internal and external service suppliers;
- enables inter-authority cost comparisons, perhaps to ascertain whether value for money is being achieved (see Chapter 8).

The way in which overhead costs are allocated at the different levels in the organization will depend on the particular approach adopted by a local authority. The view of the Chartered Institute of Public Finance and Accountancy (CIPFA) on accounting for overheads by local authorities was issued as guidance in 1991 (see CIPFA 1991). CIPFA classifies overheads into four main categories:

1 Support services, e.g. payroll, personnel, finance.
2 Corporate management.
3 Service management.
4 Regulation.

The method for allocating these costs is outlined in Table 4.1.

Marginal costing

The marginal costing approach requires a distinction to be made between fixed and variable costs. The marginal cost of a product is the sum of its variable costs, which are normally taken to be direct labour, direct materials,

Table 4.1 Methods for allocating overheads

Overhead	Method
Support services	The principle is that service departments which use these services should pay for the amount of the service they use. Therefore, these costs need to be apportioned to user departments at the year end or through an internal charge made monthly or quarterly.
Corporate management	These costs should be allocated to a separate corporate management expenditure cost centre and should not be allocated to other service departments.
Service management	These costs should be allocated to the services managed in the same way as support service costs.
Regulation	The costs of regulating any service to the public should be allocated to a separate cost centre within the accounts of the service and should not be apportioned to divisions or units of service.

Box 4.1 Marginal cost equation

Let S = Sales revenue
   V = Variable cost
   C = Contribution
   F = Fixed costs
   P = Profit

Therefore: S − V = C
           C − F = P
or   C = F + P
Therefore: S − V = F + P (the marginal cost equation)

---

expenses and any variable part of overheads, i.e. direct overheads. The Chartered Institute of Management Accountants (CIMA 1994: 38) defines marginal costing as: 'the accounting system in which variable costs are charged to cost units and the fixed cost of the period are written-off in full against the aggregate contribution'. Contribution is defined as the difference between sales revenue and variable cost.

The main use of marginal costing is as a basis for providing information to management for planning and decision making. It is particularly appropriate in the private sector for short run decisions involving changes in volume or activity. The marginal cost equation, given in Box 4.1, enables

---

Box 4.2 An example of how marginal costing can be used to calculate the effect on profit at different levels of activity

Units of activity	100	200	300	400	500
	£	£	£	£	£
Sales	1,000	2,000	3,000	4,000	5,000
Less variable costs	500	1,000	1,500	2,000	2,500
Contribution	500	1,000	1,500	2,000	2,500
Less fixed costs	1,000	1,000	1,000	1,000	1,000
Profit/(loss)	(500)	–	500	1,000	1,500

Break-even is achieved at 200 units of activity. Above this level of activity a profit is made.

---

management to cost quickly the implications of any decision. This is possible because it can normally be assumed that fixed costs remain constant and are therefore not affected by a particular decision, and contribution can be calculated at any level of sales activity as variable costs are assumed to vary in direct proportion to the sales revenue. Fixed costs can then be deducted.

An example of the application of marginal costing and how it can be used to calculate the profit or loss at different levels of activity is given in Box 4.2. Under marginal costing, once all fixed costs have been covered by total contribution, each extra unit sold results in an additional amount of profit (or surplus). The point at which total contribution equals fixed costs is referred to as the break-even point.

Some of the weaknesses of marginal costing are that:

- costs cannot always be easily divided into fixed and variable categories;
- variable costs do not necessarily vary in direct proportion to activity at all levels of activity;
- fixed costs may change to some extent with increases or decreases in activity.

The application of marginal costing techniques is particularly relevant in the public sector when considering pricing decisions. This is discussed later in the chapter under 'Marginal pricing' (see page 88).

Activity-based costing

One of the main developments in cost accounting in recent years has been activity-based costing (ABC) (Cooper and Kaplan 1988). Initially developed in a manufacturing context, this approach has been considered in the public sector, in particular for costing health care (HFMA 1992; Chan 1993; CIMA 1993; King *et al.* 1994).

ABC originally developed from the failure of conventional costing systems in manufacturing to deal adequately with the overhead element of cost. As the consumption of overhead costs by individual units of output cannot be directly observed and measured, a surrogate measure has to be found for tracing the various patterns of resource usage to products and services. This has traditionally been done by using a time-based measure of production volume, e.g. direct labour hours or machine hours. This approach assumes that overheads are related closely to production time and output volume. However, this assumption may mask the true cost consumption patterns in the organization and consequently generate misleading information for management.

ABC attempts to allocate non-volume driven overheads in a way that more accurately reflects the bases upon which they are consumed by product or service outputs. This is achieved by assuming that activities consume resources and that products (or services) consume activities. Under ABC, activity cost pools are created based on an analysis of the major activities or transactions being undertaken in the organization. Transactions which are identical (or very similar) provide the basis for each activity cost pool.

The allocation of costs to products or services involves a two-stage approach: first, the attribution of costs to individual activity cost pools; second, the attachment of each activity cost pool to the organization's final outputs. In the first stage, some costs can be allocated directly to products or services, which is relatively straightforward. However, it is more difficult where costs are shared between two or more activities. ABC apportions these costs using factors that influence the cost of a particular activity. The term 'cost driver' is used to describe the events that determine the costs of an activity, e.g. in a production environment, scheduling costs will be affected by the number of production runs, therefore the number of production set-ups would be the cost driver for production scheduling. A cost driver rate can be computed by dividing activity costs by the number of cost drivers. This rate can then be applied to each product or service based on the number of transactions (i.e. the cost driver volume) pertaining to it. Figure 4.3 shows the key stages in developing an ABC system.

Application of ABC to the public sector

The application of ABC to public-sector organizations could in theory follow the procedures described previously for manufacturing operations. The end service provided could be regarded as consuming a portion of each activity which contributes to it. To establish an appropriate ABC system, an organization would need to identify its major activities. The relationship between activities could then be traced to provide a framework for tracking

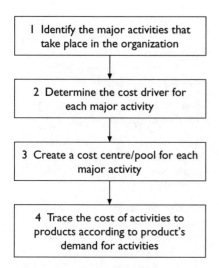

Figure 4.3 Outline of an ABC system
Source: Based on Drury (1996).

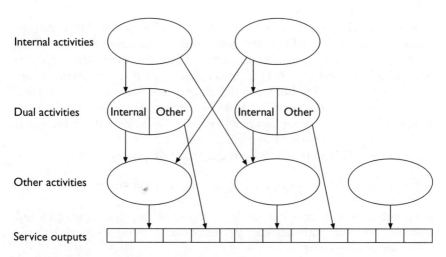

Figure 4.4 ABC structure in a service context
Source: Lapsley *et al.* (1994: 97).

cost flows through the organization to its final output (see Figure 4.4). This can be done by using measures of activity output as the cost driver and therefore the basis of each activity cost rate. Service flows can then be costed using these rates with all costs being apportioned to front-line services (Lapsley *et al.* 1994).

Lapsley *et al.* (1994: 97) argue that mapping the organization's internal relationships for an ABC system has other benefits. For example it: 'highlights

Table 4.2 Radiography: ABC analysis

Activities	Cost drivers
Patient movement	Number of in-patients
Booking appointments	Number of patients
Patient reception	Number of patients
X-ray equipment preparation	Work time
X-ray patient preparation	Work time
Radiological examination	Work time
Patient aftercare	Work time
Film processing	Number of images
Film reporting	Number of images

Source: Kirton and Hazelhurst (1991).

all supplier/customer links and by encouraging contact between these parties it can facilitate analysis of how structures can be enhanced and how services can be improved'.

Studies by HFMA (1992), CIMA (1993), and King *et al.* (1994) demonstrate the potential of ABC in the health service and stress the possibilities of ABC for producing significant cost revisions. For example, a study by Kirton and Hazelhurst (1991) identified four activity cost pools and four cost driver rates for a radiography department (see Table 4.2). The application of ABC produced costs for X-ray services which ranged from £10 to £90, clearly demonstrating that previously-used average costs had seriously under-costed or over-costed particular types of X-ray.

Kirton and Hazelhurst (1991) argued that this exercise also:

- promoted a better understanding among accountants of how services worked;
- provided visibility on where and why the significant costs were incurred;
- highlighted the potential cost of rework and thereby supported total quality management initiatives.

Pricing products and services

An organization may be concerned with two types of pricing decisions: those for selling goods or services externally to customers or clients, and those related to prices used for internal transfers between parts of the same organization, known as transfer pricing. The problems of pricing products and services for external consumption are considered first.

In a free or competitive market, prices have an important function: they signal what consumers are prepared to pay to receive a product and provide information to producers about how much to produce of a given good or service. Consumers are regarded as price takers, as they have no power over the price of goods or services, since the price is determined by the market.

When pricing its products or services, there are many factors an organization needs to consider, including:

- The objective of the organization. This may differ according to whether it is located in the public or private sector. Is it concerned with maximizing profit or revenue, or is it concerned with providing a service which meets a social need?
- The market in which it operates. What is the extent and nature of competition, if any? Is the organization sufficiently powerful to be a price-maker or does it have to take the market price?
- The demand for the organization's products or services. Is the expected level of demand at various price levels known? How sensitive is demand to price changes, i.e. what is the elasticity of demand? Are there readily-available substitutes for the product or is the product clearly differentiated?
- The cost of the product. What are the expected future marginal and fixed costs?
- Current and expected levels of activity. Is the organization working at full capacity or below it?
- Government restrictions or legislation. Are there any regulations or laws governing prices?

Not all these factors will be relevant to every pricing decision and on occasion some of the information will be difficult to obtain, in particular demand information. Many organizations attempt to identify likely demand for their product through customer surveys, market testing and market research. In practice there are three main methods of pricing:

1 Cost plus.
2 Marginal.
3 Market rate.

These are now discussed.

Cost-plus pricing

Most private and public sector organizations use cost-plus pricing methods to establish a selling price. There are two elements to this methodology: first, what is the relevant cost to include in the price; second, what is the profit margin which must be added to the costs to arrive at a selling price?

There are two main-cost plus systems:

1 Full cost pricing.
2 Rate of return pricing.

Full cost pricing is where a percentage mark-up is added to the cost of a product to establish its selling price. The main difficulty with this method is deciding the level of mark-up. For example, the mark-up may be related to risk and rates of stock turnover, or it may be influenced by market conditions. In addition, this approach may result in an organization which is operating below full capacity turning away work which is available at less than normal price, even though this work may be priced above marginal cost and would therefore make a contribution to fixed costs.

Rate of return pricing is adopted by those organizations (e.g. direct labour organizations) where performance measurement is based on the concept of a rate of return on capital employed (ROCE). Management will therefore need to know what selling price would be necessary to achieve a given rate of return on capital employed. This approach involves establishing a target rate of return on capital employed and then estimating the total costs for a normal year and the amount of capital employed. The percentage mark-up can be calculated using the following formula:

$$\frac{\text{Capital employed}}{\text{Total annual costs}} \times \text{Planned rate of return of capital employed}$$

For example, if the required rate of return on capital is 10 per cent, the amount of capital employed is £2m and the estimated annual total costs are £8m, the required mark up on costs would be 2.5 per cent:

$$\text{Mark-up} = \frac{2.0}{8.0} \times 10\%$$

$$= 2.5\%$$

Both full cost and rate of return pricing methods are essentially long-term pricing strategies which, if applied rigidly, lack the flexibility to deal with short-term pricing decisions. In addition, these approaches do not take account of demand as they assume prices are only cost-related.

Marginal pricing

Marginal pricing is sometimes referred to as variable cost or contribution pricing. This method aims to establish prices which cover variable costs and maximizes a contribution towards fixed costs and profits. It is therefore more flexible than cost-plus pricing in that there is no automatic percentage mark-up on cost to arrive at a selling price.

Box 4.3 An example of marginal pricing

The variable costs per unit of product Z are as follows:

	£
Direct materials	50
Direct labour	75
Variable overheads	25
Total variable costs	150

The selling price of product Z must be at least £150 to recover the variable (or marginal) costs of producing the product. A higher selling price would result in a contribution towards paying for the fixed costs of the organization. Once all the fixed costs have been paid for then any contribution would become profit.

In the private sector, marginal pricing can only be used in the short term as in the long-term prices must cover all costs plus a reasonable margin of profit (or surplus). Marginal pricing enables an organization to develop and penetrate new markets. For example, a business might tender for a contract with a local authority using a marginal cost pricing approach, while recovering its fixed costs on other core work. Public sector organizations might use marginal pricing to establish social charges for certain services – charging the client for just the marginal costs, with a subsidy being provided to cover the fixed costs – see Box 4.3.

Market-rate pricing

Organizations who choose to maximize their profit will price their products and services at the going market rate. Therefore, the main decision for a profit-maximizer is how much of the product or service to provide to the market. The graph in Figure 4.5 illustrates the choices facing an organization using this approach to pricing. If an organization decides to produce at output Q1 then the going market rate or price is P1. Alternatively, it could produce an output of Q2 and sell it at price P2. In practice the volume of output will be determined by the organization's costs.

Pricing products and services within an internal market

The introduction of devolved budgeting, internal markets and competitive tendering have compelled public sector organizations to develop internal transfer pricing systems. In the private sector the primary function of transfer pricing systems is to determine the profitability of internal resource

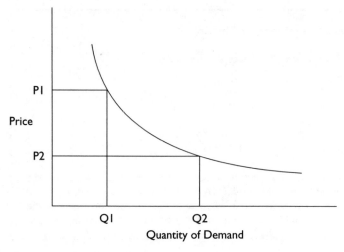

Figure 4.5 The demand curve in a competitive market

centres (profit centres). In general terms, transfer pricing should not affect the profitability of the whole organization.

Successful transfer pricing systems must fulfil three key objectives:

1 Goal congruence between resource centre managers and the organization as a whole.
2 Performance appraisal: prices should enable reliable assessments to be made of a resource centre's performance.
3 Resource centre autonomy: prices should enable maintenance of maximum autonomy so that the benefits of decentralization (motivation, better decision making, *etc.*) are maintained.

In practice, achieving these objectives is not easy. Setting prices centrally at levels where organizational objectives are met may conflict with maintaining the autonomy of the resource centres. Likewise, if resource centres are able freely to set transfer prices, they will seek to maximize revenues in what may be an uncompetitive market.

There are three main methods for establishing transfer prices:

1 Market-based transfer pricing, where the price which prevails in the external market is used, rather than cost-based prices, as market prices provide a better indication of the value added to products and services.
2 Cost-based transfer pricing, most appropriate where no external market for the product exists. The main weakness with this approach is that it may hide inefficiencies, though this may be avoided by transferring products at a standard cost rather than actual cost. A standard cost is a predetermined cost based on the efficient use of resources; i.e. it will take account of any normal waste or machine down-time.

3 Full cost-transfer pricing plus a profit. This approach differs fundamentally from the market-based pricing approach as there is no limit on
prices charged and the costs incurred are recovered with a profit. Consequently, this approach does not encourage internal suppliers to use
resources efficiently.

Transfer pricing in the public sector

The introduction of transfer pricing (or charging) for services in the public
sector was intended to introduce the efficiency of the market into the
allocation of public resources. The prices charged by service providers in
the internal market are not a function of demand but of cost, and therefore
the efficiency of providers. The task of producing prices for services is
crucial. In local government, for example, a surplus made by an internal
service provider represents lost resources to a front-line service. In the
health service, where there may be particularly severe budget constraints,
an inaccurate price may lead to non-treatment, which could be the difference between life and death. Therefore, if internal markets are to encourage the efficient allocation of resources and fulfil their objectives, the
methodologies for pricing services and contracts needs to be appropriate.

The NHS

In the NHS (see also Chapter 10), the approach to pricing contracts for the
internal market was set out in *Costing and Pricing Contracts: Cost Allocation Principles*, produced by the NHS Management Executive (NHSME)
in October 1990. It stipulated that:

- contracts should generally be priced at full cost;
- all costs, including depreciation at current cost, and 6 per cent interest
  on capital assets should be included;
- there should be no planned cross-subsidization.

The Department of Health explained its chosen price mechanism as
seeking to imitate the 'ideal hospital market' (Department of Health 1989).
Prices were to be based on long-run average cost, with providers being
given a large degree of discretion in producing their prices. However, the
NHSME (1990) stressed the need to document the pricing process for
audit purposes. It was envisaged that purchasers would be guided to the
most efficient providers by comparative prices based on resource usage.
However, in practice, the ability of prices to reflect resource usage was
greatly undermined by inadequate costing systems. In an early survey by
Ellwood (1992) of the prices and methods used by acute hospitals in the
West Midlands in 1991–2 considerable differences were identified in prices

Table 4.3 Specialty prices 1991–2: West Midlands region

Specialty	Price per consultant episode (£)		
	Average	High	Low
General medicine	1,160	1,472	923
Paediatrics	767	1,139	371
Dermatology	1,830	3,417	469
General surgery	1,148	1,477	713
Urology	985	1,714	595
Orthopaedics	1,493	2,311	854
Ear, nose and throat	754	1,203	457
Ophthalmology	934	1,483	518
Gynaecology	635	915	443
Obstetrics	761	1,353	350

Source: Ellwood (1992).

per consultant episode (see Table 4.3). For example in obstetrics, depending on the hospital selected, a consultant episode could cost from £350 up to £1353. In theory, if the internal market was operating satisfactorily then the price differentials should have been indicative of efficiency or quality. In fact, Ellwood found that price differences in the West Midlands were due to inadequate costing and pricing methods.

On this basis, in 1991–2 cost-based pricing was having fundamental problems in fulfilling its role in the NHS internal market. In response to these problems, in April 1993 the NHSME issued *Costing for Contracting* (NHSME 1993a) which provided guidance on how providers were to approach cost allocation and apportionment. The guidance emphasized the need:

- To treat as many costs as possible as direct costs.
- For overheads to be fed through patient treatment services.

The guidance also detailed a 'minimum level sophistication for the treatment of costs as variable, semi-fixed and fixed' so as to encourage a marginal costing approach. The guidelines, though not obligatory, were to be regarded as 'strong guidance' (NHSME 1993b). The 1993 costing for contract guidelines also identified the need to develop more meaningful contract categories: 'each specialty should be divided into a manageable number of conditions to represent treatment grouping' (NHSME 1993c, Annex B: 8).

The treatment groupings chosen were 'healthcare resource groups' (HRGs). In 1995–6, to inform the contracting process, the NHS executive asked providers to cost HRGs in at least one of three specialties (orthopaedics, gynaecology or ophthalmology). This was increased to six specialties

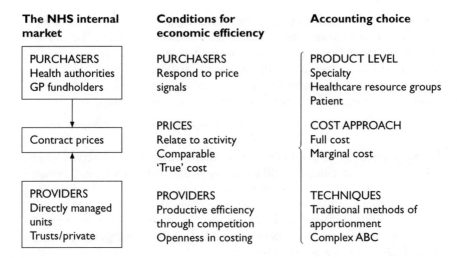

Figure 4.6 The NHS internal framework for efficient pricing
Source: Ellwood (1996).

in 1996–7. In a more recent survey by Ellwood (1996), again in the West Midlands, it was found that little use had been made of HRG cost information in negotiating 1995–6 contracts. However, there was general support for the development of HRG costs as a means of facilitating price comparisons.

The current NHS internal framework for ensuring efficient pricing is summarized in Figure 4.6. The key assumptions are:

● cost based prices which are reasonable measures of resource consumption can be determined for health care services
● prices can be meaningfully compared between alternative providers
● price is a function of quantity i.e. the volume of activity determines contract value.

(Ellwood 1996: 285)

Ellwood (1996: 285) goes on to argue that in order for prices in the health service to operate as effective signals:

● providers must be encouraged to achieve productive efficiency through competition and or openness in costing and pricing (i.e. yardstick competition); and
● purchasers must respond appropriately to price signals.

Local government

Transfer pricing in local government (see also Chapter 9) is less sophisticated than in the health service. Trading relationships exist mainly between front-line services and support services, e.g. legal, information technology, personnel, and finance. The fundamental difference between the internal markets in the NHS and local government is that purchasers (front-line services) in local government do not usually have a choice of support service provider, and consequently there is no competition. There are four main reasons for charging for support services in an internal market:

1 To ascertain the true costs of the front-line services provided by the authority.
2 To ensure there is a proper and justifiable charge to all service users. Overstating the charge could cause particular difficulties for those services which have to achieve a statutory rate of return. Understating charges to some user departments may mean that grant income is lost.
3 To provide purchasers with information relating to the costs of using internal support services, thereby enabling them to judge whether they are receiving value for money.
4 To comply with CIPFA requirements on the treatment of support service costs. CIPFA's current requirements are set out in an institute statement issued in March 1991 (CIPFA 1991). It requires that all support service users should pay for the actual amount of services they use. A revised institute statement was issued in 1995 (CIPFA 1995), though no fundamental changes in the treatment of accounting for support service costs were proposed and the general rule of full allocation of support service costs remains.

The purpose of the internal market in local government is to provide some transparency in support service costs and consequently to create internal pressure, either at officer or member level, to question internal costs. However, local authorities have a large degree of freedom in determining the basis for making the charge. The charging basis chosen has an important role in influencing the behaviour of support service managers in the way they manage costs. For example, if a support service manager is simply able to recharge all costs incurred there is no incentive to control costs.

There are three main bases for producing transfer prices or charges:

1 Input based.
2 Partly input-based.
3 Output based.

These different bases were evaluated by the District Auditors Society (1992) using six key characteristics: accuracy; accountability; certainty; cost; comparability; flexibility. See Box 4.4.

The main conclusion from this evaluation is that output-based methods of charging provide a better basis for producing charges, mainly because outcomes and charges are predetermined. If a provider overspends in delivering

Box 4.4 An evaluation of charging options

Type of charge	Description	Accuracy/ efficiency	Accountability/ efficiency	Certainty/ consistency	Cost/simplicity	Comparability	Flexibility/ user choice
Input	Based on resources used. Charge rate and final charge not known before use, e.g. time sheets.	Variable: relies on accurate recording.	Poor: no incentive for efficiency and no accountability.	Poor: user billed for cost after use. Likely to be inconsistent and no certainty.	Good: base is simple. Administratively cheap.	Poor: service specification vague and not questioned.	Poor: provider led. Little incentive to discuss service requirements.
Part input	Based on assessment of average resources needed. No specification. Charge rate but eventual charge not known, e.g. £X per hour.	Fair: standard fees provide some consistency but no guarantee that similar jobs charged at same rate.	Fair: some incentive to keep costs within hourly rate.	Fair: rate is published before use.	Variable: simple to understand but monitoring costs are high.	Good: can compare to other published rates.	Fair: user able to choose if rate unacceptable to them.
Output	Based on resources used to produce output. Output specified with charge rate and eventual charge known before use, e.g. £X per invoice.	Good: rate for a specific job.	Good: provider has to keep within rates stated.	Good: user knows charge rate and can estimate charge for period.	Variable: simple to understand but records must be available and monitoring cost could be high.	Good: comparisons of charges easier.	Good: user can choose level of service depending on output and promotes discussion.

Source: District Auditors Society (1992).

Table 4.4 Some examples of methods of charging for
finance services

Activity	Output base
Budget preparation	Fixed charge plus hourly rate
Budgetary control	Fixed charge plus hourly rate
Final accounts	Fixed charge plus hourly rate % of turnover
Debtors	Per debtor account Per value of accounts
Creditors	Per number of payment Per urgent payment Per non urgent payment
Payroll	No. of employees Per wage/salary payment Per cheque/cash/BACS payment
Internal audit	Per time plan

Source: CIPFA (1991).

a service then the cost has to be absorbed by the provider, not the purchaser.
Some examples of output bases for various finance activities are shown in
Table 4.4.

One of the recognized problems when charging for support services is
that each of the support services will inevitably receive services provided
by the other support services. Therefore, problems arise when determining
the actual cost which needs to be charged to end-user departments. For
example, the full cost of an activity recharged within the finance department will not be known until all of the other recharges from other support
services are determined. The recharge to the finance section from other
support services will not be known until the finance charges have been
actioned. Consequently, a reciprocal charging loop is formed. This problem is usually overcome by making fixed charges between support services.

Conclusion

Throughout the last decade the public sector has been under increasing
pressure to adopt much more commercial practices. In this chapter some
of the main costing and pricing techniques available to public service
managers have been discussed. However, following the election of the
Labour government, it seems likely that the belief in the supremacy of
the market mechanism, as held by successive Conservative governments, as

the best means of allocating resources within the public sector, will be challenged. Indeed, the government, in the Queen's Speech (May 1997) announced its intention to dismantle the health service internal market. However, public services managers will still need to demonstrate that they are operating economically, efficiently and effectively. Consequently, the importance of adequate costing systems should not be underestimated.

References

Chan, Y. C. L. (1993) Improving hospital cost accounting with activity based costing. *Health Care Management Review*, 18 (1): 71–7.

Chartered Institute of Management Accountants (CIMA) (1993) *Activity Based Costing and its application in the NHS*. London: CIMA.

Chartered Institute of Management Accountants (CIMA) (1994) *Management Accounting Official Terminology*. London: CIMA.

Chartered Institute of Public Finance and Accountancy (CIPFA) (1991) *The Management of Overheads in Local Authorities*. London: CIPFA.

Chartered Institute of Public Finance and Accountancy (CIPFA) (1995) *Accounting for Central Services in Great Britain*. London: CIPFA.

Cooper, R. and Kaplan, R. S. (1988) Measure cost right: make the right decisions. *Harvard Business Review*, September/October: 96–103.

Department of Health (1989) EL(89) MB/171 *Contracts for Hospital Services, Pricing and Openness – Discussion Document*. London: HMSO.

District Auditors Society (1992) *Charging for Central Services*. London: HMSO.

Drury, C. (1996) *Management and Cost Accounting* (4th edn). London: International Thomson Business Press.

Ellwood, S. (1992) *Cost Methods for NHS Health Care Contracts*. London: CIMA.

Ellwood, S. (1996) Pricing services in the UK National Health Service. *Financial Accountability and Management*, November: 281–301.

HFMA (1992) *Health Care Financial Management Association, Costing: Activity Based Costing*. London: CIPFA.

Jones, B. M. (1995) *Local Government Financial Management*. London: ICSA Publishing Ltd.

King, M. T., Lapsley, I., Moyes, J. and Mitchell, F. (1994) *Activity Based Costing in Hospitals: A Case study Investigation*. London: CIMA.

Kirton, R. and Hazelhurst, M. (1991) *Activity Based Costing in the Luton and Dunstable Hospital*. London: CIMA.

Lapsley, I., Llewellyn, S. and Mitchell, F. (1994) *Cost Management in the Public Sector*. London: Longman.

NHS Management Executive (NHSME) (1990) *Costing and Pricing Contracts: Cost Allocation Principles*. London: HMSO.

NHS Management Executive (NHSME) (1993a) EL(93) *Costing for Contracting*. London: HMSO.

NHS Management Executive (NHSME) (1993b) EL(93) *Costing for Contracting*. London: HMSO.

NHS Management Executive (NHSME) (1993c) EL(93) *Costing for Contracting*. London: HMSO.

Further reading

There are many good management accounting books covering costing and pricing techniques. Perhaps the most comprehensive and authoritative is by Drury, C. (1996) *Management and Cost Accounting* (4th edn) (London: International Thomson Business Press). Should you be interested in further information concerning pricing and charging for services in the public sector, you are recommended to refer to: Walsh, K. (1995) *Public Services and Market Mechanisms, Competition, Contracting and the New Public Management* (London: Macmillan Press); and Rose, R. (1989) 'Charges as contestable signals' which appears in the *Journal of Public Policy*, 9 (3): 261–86.

five

Capital investment appraisal

John Williams and Anita Carroll

Key learning objectives

After reading this chapter you should be able to:

1 Understand the methods of investment appraisal used in the private sector.
2 Understand the basis of these methods of investment appraisal and their limitations.
3 Appreciate how public sector investment decisions and supporting processes differ from those in the private sector.
4 Appreciate the background and broad logic of developments current in the Private Finance Initiative (PFI), a new approach to making the use of capital assets available to the public sector without the need for public capital funds.

Introduction

For much of the period since 1979, under successive Conservative governments, the emphasis was placed on selling public sector assets, i.e. transferring them to the private sector (privatization – see Chapter 2), rather than investing in them. This policy, involving the sale of capital assets to finance current expenditure, was accompanied by placing considerable resource constraints on those organizations that remained in the public sector. Whenever actual or planned expenditure reductions have to be found, often it is the capital budget which is the first victim. The result has been a declining public sector asset base, in terms of volume and quality, and, it may be argued, underinvestment in key areas, including education, infrastructure and, most notably, housing. As Jackson (1997: 18) states: 'The dramatic decline in public sector housing expenditure reflects the [previous] Government's attempts to contain public spending by cutting back on capital spending'. To illustrate the point, as a percentage of gross domestic product (GDP), housing expenditure fell from 3.13 per cent in 1979 to 0.65 per cent in 1995 (see Jackson 1997: 18, Table 4).

Table 1.2 in Chapter 1 (see page 10) showed general government expenditure (GGE) 1997–8 as £315.3bn. Total public sector capital expenditure is forecast to be £7.6bn for 1997–8 (excluding debt interest which counts as current expenditure and net of £9.4bn depreciation) (see HM Treasury 1997: 117). Given the limited resources available for capital expenditure, it is even more critical that objective technical analysis informs, as far as practicable, political decision-making given the importance, for individuals, organizations and society, of investing in the future.

Investment decisions, whether taken in the public or private sector, are important, and problematic, involving as they do the commitment of significant resources over long periods, perhaps for up to 60 years. The length of time involved also means that investment decisions are risky in that it is not possible accurately to predict what will happen during, or at the end of, the time of the investment.

Public sector investment decisions raise two main areas of concern:

1 Scale: huge investments are required in certain services such as transport (e.g. the motorway network) and, in reality, can only be undertaken by governments.
2 Policy and revenue consequences: decisions taken will have knock-on effects on future policy and revenue expenditure, effectively determining policy in a number of key areas for many years ahead.

In considering capital investment in the public sector, it is necessary also to consider private sector methods of appraisal as the theoretical rationale of the latter, in many respects, underpins the former. This chapter will consider the nature of investment decisions and the methods used by both private and public sectors.

The nature of investment decisions

Investment decisions are made by individuals and organizations alike, e.g. an individual buying a house, a local authority building a new school, or a manufacturing company buying a new machine. An investment decision may, and usually does, involve a large tangible asset and a large sum of money. The decision requires much consideration and, after it has been taken and acted upon, there is a valuable asset owned and to be protected.

However, investment decisions are more varied than this and may include an agreement to:

- purchase a licence to use a particular computer programme (no tangible asset involved);
- purchase the registration of a professional footballer, by paying a transfer fee;
- lease a car for three years;
- lease a property for 99 years, on payment of a premium, and agreement to pay a ground rent thereafter;
- rent a shop for a period of years.

A theme which unites all the above decisions is that they involve future benefit. The initial approach may be to think of cost now and benefit later (though cost could also be deferred) provided there is a firm long-term commitment.

Confusion may arise as a result of a failure to differentiate between the long-term nature of a decision and the nature of the asset, if any, acquired (the latter may determine the way the transaction is accounted for, or financed). For the purposes of this discussion, a broad definition of decisions involving forecast benefits is adopted. In theoretical terms, these are long-run decisions involving costs or revenues in more than one time period.

Public sector definitions

Within the public sector certain expenditure is defined as 'capital' and separately controlled. Any definition of public sector capital expenditure would include:

- The acquisition, reclamation, or enhancement (meaning either lengthening the life of the asset, or increasing its market value, or improving the extent to which it can be used) of land, roads or buildings.
- The acquisition, installation or replacement of plant, machinery or vehicles.
- The acquisition of capital in any other body.

A similar set of definitions is used for taxation purposes, splitting the repair and maintenance of plant and buildings (allowable as a charge against taxable income) from any element of improvement of plant or buildings, deemed to be capital and hence not allowable as a direct charge against taxable income. Depreciation of the enhanced value of the asset will however be allowed over a number of years.

Most public bodies have taken the view that, where possible, expenditure on major items for future benefit should not be met from current revenue but, ideally, by borrowing the necessary funds and repaying the funds (i.e. the principal) and the interest cost incurred over the years that benefit from the investment. This would avoid 'unfair' charges in the current year and provide 'fair' charges to successive generations of users. However, this approach has not been used where future benefits are uncertain, or when future revenues from all sources are uncertain. The main difficulty with this approach is the assumption that all costs over the life cycle of the asset, including maintenance, repairs and modernization, can be estimated and hence the total related cost can be fairly spread. Spreading just the capital element can be misleading if costs in later years are likely to be a substantial part of total costs.

Another problem with the above approach is that it moves the control of the expenditure to a different 'pool' with different rules. For historical reasons, different ways of controlling current (i.e. revenue) and capital expenditure have evolved in most public bodies. In the public sector as a whole, current expenditure is tightly controlled for the obvious reason that it has to be raised from taxation. Capital expenditure can only be financed from:

- Current revenue.
- Capital grants.
- Proceeds from the sale of capital assets.
- Approval of requests to be permitted to borrow.

The last is usually the most important, and this too is tightly controlled because most capital expenditure commits future costs, such as interest payments, as well as promising future benefits.

These definitions are unhelpful for the current purpose of indicating the range of transactions discussed in this chapter. It is possible to devise transactions which in form do not comply with these rules and are hence deemed not to be capital transactions. But, in substance, these can represent significant assets and decisions with long-term consequences, and can be regarded as effectively the same decisions in a different legal form. The discussion of the private finance initiative (PFI) (see page 119) illustrates this problem. Leasing agreements, which differ from PFI contracts, also demonstrate the problem.

Techniques of investment appraisal

Decision makers have to choose between competing, often mutually exclusive, projects with finite resources. They want to be able to compare projects and assess whether they are worthwhile. In this section, the three main approaches are discussed and their limitations indicated. They are divided into non-discounting methods, comprising payback and accounting rate of return (also described as return on investment, ROI, or return on capital employed, ROCE), and the discounting method, known as net present value (NPV). An alternative presentation of discounting, known as internal rate of return (IRR) is also discussed, but in less detail.

Payback

This is the simplest method of evaluating investments and is widely used in small businesses and as one of a range of methods in larger organizations which increasingly use multiple methods of evaluation. Net benefits are accumulated year by year until they match the original investment – the payback period. This is a calculation using cash flows, i.e. the investment is shown when it occurs, and there is no attempt to spread this by a depreciation calculation. Thus if a project costs £100,000 and shows favourable cash flows of £50,000 per annum, it recoups the investment, i.e. reaches payback, in two years. This method has significant advantages:

- Simplicity: the possibility of erroneous calculations or of managers misunderstanding the calculations is very limited.
- Concentration on the relatively foreseeable, rather than the distant future: the calculation emphasizes the short term and depends little on the more difficult, distant, future. Often, in the private sector, it is combined with a general policy of only looking at the next two to three years. The method also matches short-term perspectives in the City.
- It is a very useful first approximation to use when evaluating an investment. If there is no payback, there is no proposition to evaluate further. If there is only a distant payback, the rate of interest will be critical and the investment will be difficult to justify.

There are, however, also significant weaknesses:

- It does not allow for variations in timing within the payback period.
- It does not take account of the time value of money, i.e. that a pound now is worth more than a pound will be worth in three years time.

To take a simple two-project example:

Project	A £000	B £000
Investment [year 0]	<u>100</u>	<u>100</u>
Cash inflows:		
Year 1	80	10
Year 2	10	10
Year 3	<u>10</u>	<u>80</u>
Total inflow	<u>100</u>	<u>100</u>

Project A receives the same total return as project B, but recoups the majority of funds earlier, which is clearly advantageous. The projects are ranked the same, paying back in three years.

The next example shows how the method does not consider total project inflows after the payback period.

Project	C £000	D £000
Investment [year 0]	100	100
Cash inflows:		
Year 1	50	50
Year 2	50	50
Year 3	50	NIL
Total inflow	150	100

Both projects pay back in two years, and would appear equal, but the additional return in the third year in project C has been ignored. This would make project C preferable.

The last example shows how the method ignores initial losses which may be unacceptable to a private sector company trying to meet profit targets or to a public sector body facing revenue constraints.

Project	E £000	F £000
Investment [year 0]	100	100
Cash inflows:		
Year 1	[50]	50
Year 2	150	50
Total inflow	100	100

Both projects pay back in two years. The initial loss in project E, which would concern most managers, is not highlighted.

To summarize, though the method is imperfect and approximate it is very widely used and effective for projects with a limited life.

Accounting rate of return

This method links with the normal methods of evaluating an ongoing investment by looking at return on capital over the period of the investment. It does not work from cash flows but from 'accounting' numbers. The accounting profit after depreciation is compared with the value of the assets shown on the balance sheet.

The general definition is:

Net returns less depreciation
Average investment over period

The definition and the depreciation policy will vary between organizations and hence strict comparability is not always possible. Notably, many American firms make calculations on the initial rather than the average investment, and some British firms adjust for the working capital investment to be more comparable with ongoing investments.

First, to simplify, the cash flows and paybacks are shown for two projects:

Project	G £000	H £000
Investment [year 0]	100	100
Cash inflows:		
Year 1	[50]	50
Year 2	50	50
Year 3	100	30
Year 4	50	20
Total inflow	150	150

Project H pays back in two years; project G in three.

To put this evaluation of two projects into accounting rate of return form using the same figures:

Project	G £000	H £000
Average investment (100–0)/2	50	50
Depreciation: 100/4 = 25 per annum		
Profit = cash flow – depreciation		
Year 1	[75]	25
Year 2	25	25
Year 3	75	5
Year 4	25	[5]
Total profit [4 years]	50	50
Average per annum	12.5	12.5
	25%	25%

This method has significant weaknesses and few advantages. The weaknesses are:

- It ignores timing within the period, possible earlier or later returns.
- It ignores losses during the period.

- The calculations can be distorted by the inclusion of accounting numbers, such as depreciation, which do not represent cash flows.
- There are countless minor variations in the accounting definitions of profit and capital employed.
- It can be difficult to compare project evaluations across organizations.

The advantages are:

- It provides an easy comparison with existing investments.
- Managers in the private sector are accustomed to using return on investment as a performance measure.
- Investment appraisal is based on the same measure that is used each year for performance appraisal.

NPV

This is the method recommended in virtually all textbooks and in such official guides as the HM Treasury (1991) guide to investment appraisal in the public sector. It is a method which takes account of the time value of money (that money now is worth more than money in the future). This is universally recognized in interest payments; interest has to be paid on money borrowed and is paid on money offered for deposits.

A very simple explanation will be provided with arithmetical examples, avoiding algebraic formulae. The explanation will be simplified by assuming annual inflows and outflows of cash and using simple discount factor calculations with only two significant figures to derive a simple table of factors, rather than using a more elegant algebraic explanation. In practice, a spreadsheet programme would be used.

Assuming a 10 per cent interest rate for both borrowing and lending, £100 now will be worth:

In 1 year: 100 + (10/100 × 100) = 110
In 2 years 110 + (10/100 × 110) = 121

Conversely, future money is worth less than today's value; £100 in the future is today worth the sum that would need to be invested to achieve the £100 in the future. £100 now is worth £110 in one year (as above), so, using these proportions:

100 × 100/110 is worth £100 in one year
100 × 0.91 = £91
£100 now is worth £121 in 2 years (as above)
100 × 100/121 is worth 100 in two years
100 × 0.83 = £83

Thus a list can be derived of present values of £1 receivable at particular times:

£1 now in 0 years	1.00
£1 in 1 year	.91
£1 in 2 years	.83
£1 in 3 years	.75
£1 in 4 years	.68

This can now be applied to the first example illustrated in the explanation of the payback technique:

Project	A £000	B £000
Investment (year 0)	100	100
Cash inflows:		
Year 1	80	10
Year 2	10	10
Year 3	10	80
Total inflow	100	100

Both pay back in three years.

	Discount factor	Project A		Project B	
		Cash £000	Discounted cash £000	Cash £000	Discounted cash £000
Initial investment		100	100	100	100
Cash inflows:					
Year 1	.91	80	72.8	10	9.1
Year 2	.83	10	8.3	10	8.3
Year 3	.75	10	7.5	80	60.0
		100	88.6	100	77.4
			(11.4)		(22.6)

The example demonstrates the advantage of receiving the returns earlier, which escaped the payback and accounting rate of return methods of evaluation. However, in the example, while A produces a higher return than B (£88,600 as against £77,400), in neither case does the discounted inflow reach the level of the investment. Were the inflows to exceed the investment, the decision rule, comparing investments, would be to select the investment showing the highest net present value (inflows minus investment).

Using the same logic of discounting, a different form of arithmetic, search (trial and error), can be used to find the rate of interest at which discounted inflows exactly equal the investment, effectively measuring the percentage return on the investment – the Internal Rate of Return (IRR). Many investors find it easier to understand and use this form of discounted measure. The calculations are easy with a spreadsheet, but some care is needed not to produce misleading answers in circumstances such as a project with two or more investment phases where in some years there are outflows with inflows in preceding and following years.

The use of discounted cash-flow techniques (NPV and IRR) appears to eliminate all the obvious problems of the earlier techniques discussed (payback and accounting rate of return). They are widely used in large companies, though the extent to which these use multiple methods of assessment make it extremely difficult to ascertain which measure is most influential in persuading decision makers, or indeed whether any specific measures are more influential than strategic plans. Discounted cash-flow techniques are widely used in the public sector where they are officially recommended in HM Treasury publications. Virtually all textbooks follow the route taken thus far, pointing out the deficiencies of alternative measures and recommending the use of discounted cash-flow approaches.

However it is possible to take a more critical view of the claim that discounted cash-flow measures can solve all problems. It is important to try to explain the reluctance of most decision makers to trust any one method of investment appraisal and emphasize instead the need for judgement.

The limitations of investment appraisal techniques

Assumptions of the discounted cash-flow model

The discounted cash-flow technique is based on the normal decision-making model of economics and follows logically from this model. The basic model in economics is a single-period model dealing with costs and revenues in that period, under conditions of perfect information. This model does not deal with:

- Past costs, i.e. sunk costs, which are deemed to be irrelevant.
- Future costs and benefits beyond the period.
- Risk and uncertainty because it assumes perfect knowledge.

It also assumes that:

- All relevant factors can be quantified, which, in the case of quality, is particularly problematic.
- Decisions in one period have no consequences for decisions in future periods.

In addition, the discounted cash-flow model attempts to link successive single periods by the use of an interest rate and, further, it assumes a perfect capital market in which a firm can borrow as long as it has projects which show a return in excess of that obtainable in the market. This assumes a perfect capital market with no transaction costs and the same rate for borrowing and lending. If the market rate is 10 per cent, the firm would lend to the market rather than back a project at 9 per cent and would borrow if it had a project whose return was 11 per cent.

However, despite what appear to be very restrictive and unrealistic assumptions, the model has significant advantages, including clear logic and a clear link to a short-term performance measure. None the less, there are potential problems with the model in the real world:

- Capital markets are not perfect and firms have limited access to capital. Under capital rationing, the firm is likely to use an artificially high discount rate, which biases against long term projects. This could be even more of a problem in the public sector than the private sector, given the long-term nature of much decision making.
- The firm is never likely to be able to consider all projects at one time. It never has perfect knowledge of all present and future opportunities. Hence it is always comparing returns on present projects with hypothetical returns on future projects, within an indeterminate timescale before it may be able to acquire more capital.
- There is a problem of relative risk. Real projects are risky; perfect information in the model includes perfect project forecasting and this does not exist in the real world.

With regard to risk, a number of different approaches could be adopted, including:

- Sensitivity analysis: looking at the effects of possible changes in forecast costs and revenues.
- Scenario planning: looking at a range of possible future conditions and project scenarios.
- The use of differential interest rates, reflecting market judgement of risk and required return. This is a practical solution, but not necessarily logical for single project investment, as opposed to portfolio investment (see below).

Special considerations regarding irreversible investments

There is considerable present debate on the validity of the net present value rule for irreversible investments; most investments, especially public sector infrastructure investments, are irreversible. There is no alternative use for a channel tunnel, for instance, nor is there any way in which such an asset can be disposed of for a particular fee. This is quite different from buying a delivery van, knowing that it can be sold again if the anticipated workload for which it was bought fails to materialize.

The difficulties arising from irreversible investments are explained in a variety of critical approaches to investment decisions. The simplest to understand is the concept of robustness (Rosenhead 1980), which involves maintaining flexibility and keeping options open in the face of uncertainty. The search is not for the optimal plan but for the plan that fits a range of alternative futures. Such a plan might involve:

● Investing in stages to allow for alteration at later stages.
● Investing in facilities with scope for flexible operation.
● Building facilities that can easily be expanded.
● Investing in facilities with alternative use possibilities that can be disposed of if desirable.

More complex is modern 'real option' theory (Dixit and Pindyck 1994), the implications of which are still being explored. The concept of options, to buy or sell in the future at determinate prices, is well known from financial markets and literature on the best ways of valuing these options has existed for some time. Options are widely used by public and private sector organizations to hedge interest rate and foreign currency exposure. The concept of real options is to take the same general methodology of pricing financial options and apply it to options to change investment strategy. Examples of this approach include:

● The costs of temporary mine closure, with maintenance to permit reopening.
● Offshore oil leases, which can be exploited if the price of oil is attractive.
● New products developed by research, that can be launched at a future date if the market appears suitable.

An important conclusion from early studies is that there is considerable latitude for delaying the exercise of real options. It may in a range of circumstances be advantageous to delay exercising an option, even if profitable, because it may be even more profitable to exercise it later.

Investments are often implicitly presented as 'now or never' choices. This is unrealistic; there are hidden choices. Waiting may mean a lost opportunity, or learning more and finding a better way to invest to achieve the same objectives.

It could be argued that the traditional net present value model has another hidden assumption that does not fit with the real world: that there are perfect markets in capital goods, which can be bought and sold at will, in the same way as it assumes perfect financial markets and perfect information. The perfect capital markets assumption would fit with shares, which can always be sold, but at a price; it does not fit with many tangible assets.

In particular it does not fit well with many very specific public sector investments. Alternative uses for prisons or hospitals may be hard to find.

Coordination of budgets, strategic plans and investment decisions

This section discusses the interrelationship between strategic planning and investment decision-making and the budgeting process. It does not attempt to discuss strategic planning or budgeting.

It is fairly straightforward to see the appropriate processes for a modest investment, say the replacement of a machine by an improved model which reduces costs:

- A review of the activity as contained within the strategic plan.
- The management action formulated from the strategic plan; the stage referred to by some American texts as 'programming'.
- The budget for the year will include provision for the investment, either specifically, or within an agreed provision for minor plant improvements.
- The investment is duly approved, orders placed, the machine installed and paid for.
- The machine comes into use and the expected savings are realized.

For these processes to work successfully, a very wide range of formal planning and control processes have to work individually and fit together. The problem that needs to be addressed is that they are unlikely to work effectively if there are significant delays in the system. There is also the possibility, even probability, that, being prepared at different times, the policies and decisions incorporated in the key documents will not be completely consistent.

When major investments are considered it is fairly easy to see how the coordination of systems comes under strain, even if all the separate parts are functioning satisfactorily. This occurs for a variety of reasons, but mainly because investment approval procedures were established by most organizations before strategic planning systems became the norm; there is a pattern in many companies of giving general approval to strategies and policies in the strategic plan, but then needing to review each separate investment proposal for approval at the appropriate level, which will usually be the main board for significant investments. The board approval is the key to action and is normally a genuine review in the sense of not being an automatic approval because the investment is in the strategic plan. This stage is described with different emphases by Scapens *et al.* (1982) and by Pike and Wolfe (1988).

The general results from a range of surveys suggest varying practice, informal discussion and strategy evaluation. These usually lead to the withdrawal of proposals unlikely to be accepted as the risk of a formal rejection is too great. The submission by a senior executive of a major proposal is similar to seeking a vote of confidence.

A notable feature of many organizations is that the systems for taking major investment decisions are very prone to delays. Delay has complex effects on budgets. Delay on a major project normally has more effect on any future budget being prepared than on the current budget. It is not unusual to start budget preparation on the assumption that a major investment will be approved by the start of the budget year and be in place during the year, only to need to revise completely before the start of the budget year when the situation changes.

There are two sets of controls on capital investment:

1 Project authorization, linked to investment justification, linked to formal approval.
2 Expenditure authorization, linked to cash planning and the availability of funds. Cash constraints can be solved by reconsidering 'lease or buy' decisions, or by extracting credit from machinery suppliers. Cash constraints may lead to project delays, because this is one of the few items of expenditure that can be delayed. There may be little feasible alternative action in particular circumstances.

The difficult part for the designers and managers of control systems is seeing that this range of controls (from strategic planning to short term cash management) can interlink, and ensuring effective consistency in their separate interpretations of the situations and problems.

Investment appraisal in the public and private sectors

This section discusses the ways in which the public sector differs from the private sector and how these differences affect approaches to investment appraisal. This involves a significant level of generalization, which cannot always apply. There are some examples of public sector investment which are almost indistinguishable from those in the private sector, such as replacing the office photocopier.

The budgeting cycle

The example of the replacement of the office photocopier, which at first sight appears an identical decision in both sectors with similar costs and justification criteria, also illustrates a basic difference – the rigidity of most public sector budgets. Once the budget has been agreed for the year, it becomes an instruction to spend money in a particular way, with limited scope for varying the way it is spent and virtually no scope for changing the amount of money available. The limited scope for virement and systems of contingency reserves may well cover genuine emergencies. A manager who produces a case for change, however excellent, which is non-urgent, is likely to be told to budget for such expenditure in the *next* financial year. A local authority, for instance, cannot easily obtain more money until then and there is marked reluctance to reallocate resources or release contingency funds until it is clear what is unspent towards the end of the financial year.

In the private sector, there are inevitable beaucratic rigidities in the systems of large groups which will appear similar to the public sector systems, but, if they were so minded, the board of a company could decide to approve additional expenditure at any time. If they are satisfied that the investment is worthwhile and that the required funds are available from borrowing capacity and current trading, they are at liberty to change the budget and decide to invest in the new photocopier. The funding decision depends on the current financial situation, which depends on current trading. It does *not* depend on irrevocable annual decisions on overall funding linked to proposed taxation.

The board of a large private sector company would not consider something as small, and in their scale of operations as insignificant, as a photocopier. Systems of delegation are needed to ensure that the board would only consider the most significant investment decisions, involving sums in the tens or probably hundreds of millions of pounds. These systems of delegation will permit managers at varying levels to approve capital investment up to certain costs per item, subject to approval of a total budget and the approval of systems of control. This is similar to the public sector system; but the board can always overrule the system if it wishes. A public sector authority, other than the government itself, cannot do so; taxation decisions have been taken and can only be changed during a year in quite exceptional circumstances, such as a financial crisis, a new government or a military crisis.

Conversely, changes of this sort are not unusual in the private sector. Major investments, such as acquisitions of other companies, whether for cash or shares, are normally not budgeted, but approved by the board on the basis of the project justification and the funding available.

The cost of money

The cost of capital for discounting purposes in the private sector is a weighted average of debt and equity finance, the cost of equity being the expected return on equity investment (in dividends and capital growth) over the period. The calculation may be untidy, but the underlying logic is clear. The rates are market rates, in money terms.

In the public sector, the discount rate, which serves as a cost of capital, is simple in that it is laid down by the Treasury and no calculations are involved. The difficulty is understanding which of the various possible arguments for such a rate applies. Is it:

- The opportunity cost argument, whereby resources could be used for other purposes? At the margin, the use of funds in the public sector should be no less efficient than in the private sector.
- The classic time preference argument? The incentive to invest, not consume.
- The need to compare in-house and contracted-out supply, where a rate equivalent to private sector low risk projects would be appropriate?
- The need to be comparable with financial targets for commercial government bodies?

A real (i.e. excluding inflation) rate of 6 per cent is used for most purposes, to be comparable with a low-risk cost of private capital, a mixture of debt and equity. The approximate arithmetic is to look at a real cost of long-term risk-free debt of around 4 per cent in real terms, and a real return on equity of around 6 per cent, but to expect both to rise. The rate is varied for some purposes. For outputs sold in commercial markets and for industrial assistance or transport a rate of 8 per cent tends to be used. There is a reluctance to use nominal rates, or actual borrowing costs, as these will change frequently, and it is desirable to look at an appropriate rate over the life of a project.

The timescale

While similar investments in both public and private sectors tend to be considered over similar timescales, certainly at the lower end, for such investments as cars and computers there tend to be significantly more very long-term investments in the public sector and investments considered over a longer term.

The public sector has traditionally considered and financed such investments as council housing and hospitals over a 60-year period. This has been justified by seeing these investments as very long-term and wishing to achieve equity between the various generations of users, rather than weighting the cost on the generation funding the project and the early users.

The private sector has very rarely looked beyond 25 years for any project in terms of investment justification or funding, though it may have taken a longer term for depreciating fixed assets such as prime city-centre retail or office property. Sixty years may once have looked sensible for assets which would last forever and always be needed and appear sensible for such investments as the conventional semi-detached house, but the same principle applied to tower blocks of flats which tenants have shunned and councils have been unable to maintain has caused major financial problems.

In the same way, investments in sanatoria for tuberculosis patients, isolation hospitals for infectious diseases and large mental hospitals, have become redundant as a result of changing patterns of health and medical technology. The difference in timescale has become a major problem with the PFI (see page 119).

Given the rate of change in almost all things in society, the private sector attitude, which displays a reluctance to forecast into too indefinite a future, appears realistic. The problem is that a 30-year loan requires twice the annual capital redemption than is required for a 60-year loan, effectively a better rate of return.

There is another problem with very long-life projects to which there is no possible answer. Projects are justified by comparing forecast costs in the near future with forecast returns over a range of future times. These are prepared by fallible managers, who will be concerned that the events in the near future are forecast accurately, because they will still be managers and responsible for achieving the costs and benefits forecast but will be nowhere near as concerned with long-term forecasts over 30 or 60 years, by which time the responsibility for accuracy will no longer be theirs.

Costs and benefits compared with cash inflows and outflows

There is a clear distinction between the public and private sector in their consideration of relevant beneficiaries. Within the private sector the objective is maximizing shareholder wealth, defined as the net present value of future forecast cash flows into the enterprise. This has considerable advantages in focusing and simplifying requirements. Only future cash flows from and to the enterprise need be considered; costs and benefits to third parties are irrelevant unless they have legal consequences. Pollution does not matter unless it leads to penalties or a public relations problem that affects sales and profits.

Some future benefits to the private sector organization are difficult to estimate because models of cause and effect are not perfect. Taking as an example an investment in computer-controlled machine tools, it may be easy to calculate the direct effects of saving labour and scrap but difficult to estimate the effects of flexibility in providing faster customer service and of more precise control in providing better quality, both of which will eventually produce more sales. The usual problem in the private sector is in making an adequate estimate of these secondary benefits because invalid comparison with the assumption of no change in competitive pressures leads to significant understatement.

The public sector has broader, less easily defined aims, which can enable projects to be justified on some form of community benefit. A set of techniques has been developed for such approaches, known as cost benefit analysis.

Cost benefit analysis

This developed as a means of establishing criteria for public sector investment in terms of net social benefit by, as far as possible, placing monetary values on all social benefits. A simple example is that of the construction of a motorway. There are first some tangible costs and benefits, mostly costs:

● Initial investment in construction.
● Compensation to landowners badly affected.
● Motorway maintenance.

The tangible benefits of such a project are:

● Tolls if a toll road.
● Increases in property prices to reflect greater convenience.
● Value of local employment during construction and multiplier effect of this investment injection into the local economy.

The intangible costs will be the disturbance or destruction of quiet countryside. The intangible benefits will be:

● Time-saving by users. This assumes that it is possible to value the average users' time. If this is taken into account, the tolls should be ignored as part, but not all, of this benefit.
● The 'option value' to potential users that the motorway is there and could be used if wished. This could be reflected in changing property prices.
● Less accidents per mile travelled; less emergency service costs.
● Greater personal mobility; faster travelling making shopping and working at greater distances feasible.

There are a range of potential problems with this approach:

● Pricing problems for both costs and benefits in the absence of a market test.
● Difficulties in estimating the number of potential users/beneficiaries of a free service.
● Forecasting motorway usage has frequently been grossly inaccurate; too low for the M25, far too high for the Humber bridge. The planning for the National Health Service (NHS) after the war assumed that with a healthier population the demand for medical services would decline even if those services were free.

Despite the problems associated with cost benefit analysis, it at least gives some structure to the decision-making process. It enables decision makers to recognize the scale of assumptions they would be making by authorizing a project. It is also the only possible route forward when market prices either do not exist or would be unacceptable. Thus, where medical resources are finite and have to be rationed, the approach is more acceptable than that which may result from market forces or bureaucracy.

Cost effectiveness analysis

An alternative approach in theory is that of cost effectiveness analysis. If the objectives can be clearly defined, it should be feasible to find alternative ways of achieving identical objectives. These can then be compared, and the most effective, a mixture of quality and cost, can be chosen. This is the argument for outsourcing (see Chapter 2 and the discussion on compulsory competitive tendering within the section 'Conservative policy and NPM', page 38), typically something like information technology. Instead of investing in, or leasing, new computer equipment and continuing to employ staff to provide a service, outsource to a specialist supplier who will invest, employ staff and provide the service required. The approach of cost effectiveness analysis works well where precise objectives can be defined and quality measurement is straightforward and reasonably inexpensive. An example of difficult quality measurement is outsourcing the provision of residential care for the old.

The diffculties with cost effectiveness analysis include:

- Providing a clear definition of the aims and objectives.
- Finding an alternative solution which satisfies the same interests in the same proportions.
- The problem of unplanned beneficiaries from the alternatives.

These difficulties can be illustrated by the hypothetical comparison between meeting inter-city transport needs by motorway investment or railway investment. Some requirements are clearly better met by one or other solution. Rail has advantages for bulk transport and for inter-city passengers travelling between city centres. Road has advantages in terms of flexibility. Road and rail have varying environmental impacts, partially obscured by spare capacity on the rail network. Social costs of such a project are significant; while the programme aim may be transport between X and Y, the alternatives will have differing impacts on other possible journey planning. Different people will use road or rail for different journeys; there will be disparate beneficiaries.

Costs and benefits that are not cash flows to the entity

This section assumes the general validity of a public sector organization justifying a project on the basis of cost: benefit analysis, as discussed above, where benefits flow to 'stakeholders', not to the entity, the organization, itself. There are two resulting problems that this creates for the public sector that do not exist in the private sector: acceptable distribution of benefits; and funding.

With regard to the first, within the private sector all inflows are to the entity and shareholders are entitled to dividends. The division of gains is clear. Within the public sector, benefits flow to various parts of the population. For instance, investment in schools is no direct benefit to pensioners; investment in day care centres for the elderly is only of direct benefit to the elderly.

The assumption is made that the political process or the consultative process will produce a broad balance between beneficiaries – that a spread of projects will provide some sort of benefits for all, or at least most, groups. This is not always the case; examples can easily be found where the distribution of benefits is most uneven, possibly even deliberately biased. Reference in the USA to 'pork barrel' politics is about the division of the spoils of political victory.

The problem is relating costs incurred by a particular group – those paying taxation to support the public sector body – to the benefits gained by that group. Overall benefits may exceed overall costs but be received by different people. This is not primarily an accounting problem, but a political problem; the justification of a particular allocation of taxation. Some cross-subsidy is normal and accepted in most societies; the richer pay more tax to provide social security benefits for the disadvantaged; those of working age support the elderly and the young. All accounting can do is clarify the issues involved. It cannot provide a solution. An excess of benefits over costs can be seen to be a necessary, but not a sufficient, justification of investment. The benefit allocation has to be politically acceptable.

With regard to funding, there is also a financial management problem when benefits are received by 'stakeholders' rather than by the organization. This is the problem of solvency, or the need to continue to provide funding. This can be illustrated by the provision of a local authority sports or leisure facility such as a swimming pool. The initial investment is predictable and may be relatively easy to finance in terms of grants available or special loan facilities. Thereafter, there are substantial benefits to users and an 'option benefit' to those who feel they can use the facility if they wish, but do not do so. But the charges that can be levied on users without deterring use are limited. High charges would mean that the pool was little used and little benefit/received by stakeholders. Probable charges will lead to a continuing cash outflow, a loss, comparing receipts with running costs and interest charges. The authority will have to find more resources every year to gain the promised benefits for the stakeholders. This may be difficult if there are severe pressures on current resources and may be deemed impossible if priorities change; if the authority decides, for example, that transport should be given priority over leisure.

An investment such as a swimming pool has two particular problems:

1 Commitment: committing, or attempting to commit, future managers or decision makers to continue to support a facility once provided. The cost to 'free' or available resources may be much greater than that involved

in the orginal decision; revenue resouces may be tightly stretched, but borrowing permission for capital projects relatively easy to obtain.

2 Irreversibility: it is more difficult to close or discontinue a service than to decide to provide a new service; there are clear losers who will complain, and the general benefit – of saving money – is thinly spread. Even if the service is discontinued, there is rarely an obvious alternative use for the physical investment, especially public sector investments such as schools and swimming pools.

The PFI

The general background to the initiative is the long-term problem of funding adequate investment in public infrastructure, given perceived constraints on additional public finance to be raised from further borrowing or further taxation. There is a second background problem of a perception of the public sector as having managed long-term assets badly, with too great an emphasis on initial cost and too little on long-term flexibility.

The general aim and emphasis is not pure funding of capital projects but involvement in the design, building and operation of a capital asset by a service provider.

There is inevitably a degree of scepticism regarding any government or political aim. In the case of the PFI, there was the criticism that it would entail the substitution of private finance for public finance as a way around finance limits. However, the fundamental requirement for a PFI contract is that risks should be allocated to whoever is best able to manage them. These risks are seen to be those associated with:

- Design and construction (cost and time).
- Operation (operating costs and performance).
- Residual value and obsolescence.
- Demand (volume/usage).
- Project financing.
- Regulation.

Some of these are unexceptionable. For example, the concept of relating the costs of initial construction to the operating costs and to the residual values is well established, involving looking at asset costs over the whole lifecycle, rather than purely looking at the initial cost. However, transfer of the financing risk is a problem. This is lower for the public sector than for even the strongest potential private provider. Transferring this risk implies extra cost to be recouped by savings elswhere. There are persistent problems with new quasi-independent public sector bodies, such as NHS trusts, as well as with older independent bodies such as universities, in clarifying the degree of government guarantee for meeting future contract obligations. There are regular announcements that the problem has been solved, but firm contracts with these bodies are still slow to materialize. One part of the financing risk problem has been clearly resolved: the private sector is not going to finance anything over the 60-year timescale that the public sector used to adopt. Thirty years appears to be the limit.

The transfer of demand risk is clearly problematic. If the public sector is the sole paymaster and sole customer it is meaningless. In other fields it is valid for suppliers to face the risk of losing custom if the service provided is poor. Some contracts, where payment is designated to be volume-related could produce undesirable consequences. It is argued that, for a contract to design, build and operate a new road under the PFI, remuneration on the basis of vehicle usage could be an incentive to encourage increased traffic rather than to ease congestion.

The ideas behind the PFI and its broad aims can be seen as remarkably similar to those concerning the private sector in looking at irreversibility and project robustness and options. Specific investments for long periods are not desirable in a rapidly-changing world and value for money must include a significant degree of flexibility as well as cost minimization. Options for future change or development are very valuable and much of the negotiation of PFI contracts is in fact negotiating the value of such options.

The Labour goverment has declared its intention to continue with the PFI as there is little scope within the limits of the public finances for all desirable projects. The number of projects under consideration has been scaled down considerably, which is clearly sensible until the ground rules for these projects are completely clear.

Summary and conclusions

This chapter has highlighted that all transactions which produce costs and benefits in more than one period involve the cost of money and uncertainty. The techniques of the main methods of investment appraisal were discussed, stressing the logical basis for net present value, which is the preferred method for many private and public sector organizations. The limitations of this approach were discussed at length. The dangers of a precise, apparently scientific, quantification of 'best guesses' were also stressed. Other limitations on the process of investment appraisal were discussed, including the linkages between a variety of decision-making systems. Much of the chapter applied equally to public and private sectors: the same calculation methods; the same net present value technique; the same difficulties with overlapping information and decision-making systems. Both sectors also experience the problem of irreversible investments, but this is more acute in the public sector.

The main differences between the public and private sectors were explained, with particular emphasis on the problem of benefits being received by stakeholders, not the organization, with major implications for funding and the extent to which future decision-making is committed.

Cost benefit analysis was discussed, and could have been discussed at much greater length. Further reading in this area is recommended below, but it should be recognized that cost benefit analysis is still only a process of making guesses about the future, and does not provide any better insights into what that future might be.

It is still too early to see in any detail what the Labour government will do with the PFI. It is also difficult to be convinced that any scheme which meets all the requirements proposed for the PFI would be remotely attractive to any private sector supplier.

References

Dixit, A. K. and Pindyck, R. S. (1994) *Investment Under Uncertainty*. Princeton: Princeton University Press.

HM Treasury (1991) *Economic Appraisal in Central Government: A Technical Guide for Government Departments*. London: HMSO.

HM Treasury (1997) *Financial Statement and Budget Report*. London: HMSO.

Jackson, P. (1997) Economic performance, in P. Jackson and M. Lavender (eds) *Public Services Yearbook 1997–98*, pp. 13-28. London: Pitman.

Pike, R. H. and Wolfe, M. B. (1988) *Capital Budgeting for the 1990s*. London: CIMA.

Rosenhead, J. (1980) Planning under uncertainty: a methodology for robustness. *Journal of the Operational Research Society*, 31 April: 31 (4): 331–41.

Scapens, R. W., Sale, J. T. and Tikkas, P. A. (1982) *Financial Control of Divisional Capital Investment*. London: CIMA.

Further reading

You are recommended to refer to the finance and general textbooks on the public sector, including: Coombs, H. M. and Jenkins, D. E. (1994) *Public Sector Financial Management* (2nd edn) (London: Chapman & Hall); and Jones, R. and Pendlebury, M. (1996) *Public Sector Accounting* (4th edn) (London: Pitman). In addition, please refer to: Samuels, J. M., Wilkes, F. M. and Brayshaw, R. E. (1995). *Management of Company Finance* (6th edn) (London: Chapman & Hall); Smith, P. (ed.) (1996) *Measuring Outcome in the Public Sector* (London: Taylor & Francis); and to the Treasury publications (as given under HM Treasury above) for the official guidance. The ongoing development of the private finance initiative is producing many interesting insights into the different problems of the public sector, as well as purely financing problems, and useful analyses of these problems often appear in the quality press, especially the *Financial Times* (which published a PFI supplement on 17 July 1997). See also *Public Money & Management*, 17 (3), July to September 1997, which contains four articles on PFI.

part three

Applied accountability

six

Audit quality

Bob Hopkins

Key learning objectives

After reading this chapter you should be able to:

1 Understand the statutory background to audit within the United Kingdom.
2 Understand the way in which the meaning, nature and perceptions of audit have evolved.
3 Discuss the key elements underlying the term 'audit quality'.
4 Understand the significance, in a competitive environment, of perceptions of audit quality.

Introduction

Part two considered some of the key techniques involved in financial management. However, following on from Part one, it will be appreciated that financial management is not undertaken in 'laboratory conditions' – political and economic considerations are of fundamental importance to the public service financial manager. Here, however, by focusing on another feature of financial management – audit – a further dimension is added, i.e. the behavioural dimension. This chapter considers the importance of perceptions of the quality of internal audit within the public sector at a time when the traditional providers of internal audit services are facing their greatest challenge from an increasingly competitive environment.

The concept of internal audit has moved from that of a single product provided to a single client to a wide range of internal audit services to a number of clients. Although perceptions of the integrity and independence of the auditor have changed very little over time there have been some significant changes to the perception of exactly who is the customer of internal audit. In fact it will be argued that it is essential for the success of internal audit to decide exactly what services are to be offered and who their key customers are. This is not as simple as it may seem. The answers will depend upon the perceptions of both the providers and purchasers of internal audit services in what is becoming an increasingly competitive environment. It is suggested that it is the extent to which both auditors and their prospective customers are hanging onto historical perceptions of the audit product that may compromise the ability of internal audit to offer the most effective and appropriate range of internal audit services for the future.

This chapter will demonstrate the evolutionary process underlying many of the current perceptions of internal audit quality, and show the importance of differing perceptions of the internal audit product within the competitive marketplace.

Audit: statutory background

Company law in the United Kingdom (UK), contrary to the majority of other countries, requires all limited companies to have their accounts 'externally' audited. The auditors' duties essentially relate to the production of an audit report which gives their opinion as to whether the financial statements show a 'true and fair' view. The various companies acts deal with the auditors' appointment, remuneration and duties. The auditors are normally members of major firms of accountants often referred to colloquially as the 'big six', recognizing that the majority of the market is handled by a small number of large firms.

Within the public sector the external audit of accounts is technically similar to the audit of accounts in the private sector. However, public sector external auditors have a wider remit as they are required to deal with issues as diverse as fraud investigations and value for money. The external auditors within the public sector are:

- The National Audit Office (established by the National Audit Act 1983), for central government.
- The Audit Commission (established by the Local Government Act 1982) for local authorities and the National Health Service (NHS) within England and Wales. The Audit Commission awards some of its work to approved private firms (typically 'big six' firms).

Unlike the external auditor whose principal responsibilities are to the shareholders or 'taxpayers', internal audit is a support service for corporate management. It is essentially concerned with the appraisal of activities and is intended to be positive in its contribution and aims at all times in order to provide an independent and objective service to management. Government departments, local government and all NHS bodies are required by law to have an internal audit function. There is no such statutory requirement for private sector bodies.

It would be incorrect to concentrate on the differences between external and internal audit as both sets of auditors are essentially concerned with the set of systems and controls that underlie the financial statements. As senior management has a duty to ensure that the financial statements do show a true and fair view, they need an internal assurance agency to inform them about the state of the internal systems and related controls. As external audit reports are, normally, produced annually, there is a demonstrable need for an ongoing appraisal function acting on behalf of management working across the organization as a whole. Internal audit, it is argued, is the most appropriate review agency for management.

Definition

'Internal audit is an independent appraisal function within an organization for the review of activities as a service to all levels of management. It is a control which measures, evaluates and reports upon the effectiveness of internal controls, financial and other, as a contribution to the efficient use of resources within an organization' (Chartered Institute of Public Finance and Accountancy (CIPFA) 1979).

This definition of internal audit contains the essence of what is perceived as the current role for internal audit, i.e. 'service to all levels of management': evaluating internal controls and examining both financial and non-financial controls including elements of value for money. The above definition would not have fitted the typical auditor of the early post-war years and may not be suitable for the auditor today. Research, to be described in this chapter, has shown that the definition may not fit with the current perceptions of auditees and auditors.

The evolution of internal audit

In order to understand the evolutionary process currently being undertaken by the best internal audit providers it will be necessary to understand the historical perspective from three different periods and perceptions. Please note that the periods are not fixed; rather, it is better to view internal audit as a gradually developing set of concepts established over time. However in a general sense the evolution of internal audit can be established post-war as having the following characteristics.

Traditional auditing (1946–'late' 1970s)

Internal audit was typically an unsophisticated activity within the financial department trying to establish the accuracy of the accounting records within the organization. A great deal of emphasis would have been placed on the accuracy, completeness and validity of records and transactions creating a view of internal audit synonymous with preventing and detecting frauds or finding errors. It is doubtful if the internal auditors had any perception of 'a range of business orientated products' or the concept of the 'customer' (terms used by CIPFA 1992 to suggest a 'modern' role for internal audit). Key words associated with internal audit from this period would be 'check', 'verify', 'find', and 'detect'.

Modern internal auditing (1980–'late' 1980s)

The advent of modern internal auditing, with its emphasis on the systems-based approach, measuring, evaluating and reporting upon the effectiveness of internal controls, helped to widen the range of internal audit services. Once the concept of auditing systems and their related controls was accepted, internal audit was able to expand its activities into the audit of non-financial systems and consultancy. Internal audit was indeed able to be a service to management by addressing issues of value for money, the audit of operations and other areas outside of their previous scope.

Internal audits' perception of the customer now changed from the 'organization' to senior managers and/or the audit committee, and it was necessary for auditors to establish close links with their 'customers'. It will be shown that it is in the area of close working relationships that the perceptions of auditors and their customers concerning the quality of the audit product differ significantly. Modern internal auditing is often associated with key words analogous to 'assess', 'review', and 'appraise'.

Post-modern auditing (1990s–)

Modern organizations are increasingly embracing the concept of empowerment. Empowerment essentially allows the organization to devolve the responsibility for controls down to the lowest level consistent with the effective management of associated risks. The key idea is to allow groups of individuals (often across a range of disciplines) to decide the most appropriate level of controls to handle perceived risks within their combined areas of control. The creation throughout the organization of a number of teams or 'workgroups' establishes a subtle and complex set of relationships handling corporate activities at levels that previously might have been unimagined. The resulting set of communication issues raises a number of challenges for internal audit. The range of audit customers will now have expanded to all managers, not just senior managers. The controls and risks being discussed at 'workgroup' level are likely to be non-financial in nature rather than the more traditional financial risks and controls previously associated with internal audit. All of the workgroups may have new, valid, and challenging perceptions of what they require from the audit product. It is unlikely that internal audit will be able to ignore the requests for a wider and more challenging role for internal audit services from a set of customers who will represent the organization as a whole.

Internal audit's role may well be to provide assurance to the organization as a whole, through its board or audit committee, but it will first have to meet the considerable challenge of auditing within a new environment. If internal audit is to meet this challenge then its perceptions of the quality of its services will have to incorporate those of its key customers. The rest of this chapter will demonstrate that there are currently a number of significant differences in the perceptions of what a quality internal audit service is, and that this may compromise the ability of internal audit to offer the product that is required in the post-modern 1990s. Associated key words might be 'integrate', 'facilitate', and 'core activity'.

The current environment

Within an increasingly competitive environment in the public sector, created by a number of changes of which compulsory competitive tendering and 'market testing' have been the main drivers, one of the greatest challenges to traditional in-house providers of internal audit services is survival. Perhaps the best means of ensuring survival is for internal audit to demonstrate its value to the organizations it audits. 'Value' is a qualitative term and may be subject to differing interpretations from the perspectives of the clients and the would-be providers of audit services. If differing perceptions of internal audit quality do exist then there may be inherent risks for any internal audit service trying to demonstrate a quality audit product to an organization who may 'see' internal audit in a fundamentally different way.

If internal audit is to survive beyond the 1990s, a number of writers have suggested that it will need to change its focus. The main thrust of this will be a closer link with the organizational objectives and culture. Sawyer (1992) warns internal auditors that competence, integrity and loyalty will not be enough to succeed and that they must understand the politics and culture of an organization and appreciate where the real power is, in order to succeed. Hagasset-Bellamy (1994) claims that internal audit must market itself to top management and promote a separate identity. In promoting itself, it must demonstrate unequivocally that it offers a quality product. The problem, as will be demonstrated, is that there are differing perceptions of the meaning of audit quality between internal auditors and their prospective clients, and that these differences, if not addressed, might limit the chances of internal audits' survival in a competitive environment.

Modelling for quality

A number of new models have been proposed for internal audit (see McCrindell 1993) which suggest a closer relationship with management and the overall strategic objectives of the organization. The NHS, for example, has adopted the controlled self-assessment model (originating in Canada) which requires that:

- Management embrace fully their responsibilities for internal control.
- Auditors are used as facilitators or monitors of key groups dealing with significant organizational risk.
- Control theory is based around trust through empowerment and addresses key organizational issues.
- Internal auditing involves the auditee through teamwork.

These modern ideas have their roots in the 'total quality management' paradigms of the 1980s, though some writers have suggested that many of the principles on which internal audit is founded are incompatible with the new internal audit paradigm suggested for the 1990s (Hawkes and Adams 1995).

If internal audit embraces the necessity for change then it will be of the utmost importance to understand not how it is currently perceived within the organization, but how it sees itself. Any differences found may be major stumbling blocks for the internal audit provider trying to demonstrate a quality product.

In 1992 CIPFA published *Promoting Internal Audit* (CIPFA 1992). This advised auditors about the problems inherent in promoting a quality audit service, indicating that 'the audit section must therefore ensure that it is aware of the needs of its customers', that 'at the end of the day, the section's performance will be judged by the extent to which it has communicated its role and objectives to the organisation as a whole' and that 'the head of audit and his staff need to convince the potential client that audit understands the business, fully appreciates the organisational structure and the objectives and ambitions of the potential clients' (CIPFA 1992: 53–5).

The provision of quality audit services to clients therefore requires a more 'participative approach' but that in itself depends on an understanding of customers' perceptions and the culture within which these perceptions flourish. Balkaran (1995) claims that the importance of culture to business success is often overlooked by internal auditors in their preoccupation with audit plans and their desire to demonstrate their value to management. Balkaran claims that corporate culture can be likened to the personality of an organization. The culture will explain what things are considered important and how things are done. The corporate culture will therefore shape the perceptions of organizational members. Balkaran states that 'culture' may embrace such elements as corporate identity, decision-making methodologies and approaches to personnel management. Auditors can overlook the importance of culture and this may compromise the ability of the audit report to address real quality issues that would be valued by management. Such a development may contribute to the existence of a quality expectations gap, an important concept in understanding the differing perceptions of audit quality between providers of the audit services and their potential purchasers. Hopkins (1995) showed that there are significant differences between the perceptions of auditors and auditees and that these were likely to affect the chances of internal audit services' success in a competitive environment.

In building on this work, Hopkins (1997) focused on the following key questions:

1 Given that an expectation gap exists, what are the key variables affecting the quality of audit as perceived by audit providers and their customers?
2 Given that audit quality exists, what are the key objectives, attributes and skills that, taken together, mean 'quality audit'?
3 Once the key objectives, attributes and skills are derived, where does the expectation gap lie and what are the consequences for auditors, their customers and their organization?

In attempting to answer the above questions, a definition of quality was derived to try to establish the parameters of the search criteria for the key variables (see Question 1). Audit quality needed to fall within the following parameters for any survey to be successful:

- Quality attributes are those that touched upon the excellence of the audit product, either in a positive (good quality) or negative (poor quality) manner.
- Quality attributes are those that gave a general excellence to audit work taken as a whole (leading to a high-quality service).
- Quality attributes are distinctive, associated with auditors and auditing (characteristic traits).

The attributes used were ranked in order to demonstrate their relative weighting in the overall assessment of audit quality. The distinctiveness of particular key attributes and variables was also demonstrated so that, where significant expectation or perception gaps existed between auditors and auditees, a clear exposition of these differences was given. This had a particular contribution to make towards a general understanding but also towards such key areas as the training and development of auditors and auditees within an appropriate organizational culture.

Within the above parameters, a comprehensive literature search was undertaken to establish the key words or phrases used when auditing is being discussed. The main literature examined was textbooks, academic journals, professional journals, articles and newspapers. It became apparent that auditing standards, as issued by the accountancy profession, were (quite naturally) a rich source of key words and, as a result, auditing standards were given a high profile in the survey to reflect their obvious importance.

The literature search picked up over 2000 words which were aggregated into key concepts forming 39 key words and phrases which accounted for over 60 per cent of the word list used in the survey of public sector auditors and auditees. The words appeared to fall into three categories: objectives; activities; qualities and skills.

All variables were ranked in terms of the highest ranking variable associated with quality auditing, ranked 1. The rankings for both auditors and auditees are shown in the Appendix, with the ranking differences between auditors and auditees given in the final column. Larger 'ranking differences' show variables where there is evidence of an expectation gap between auditors and their clients. For example the largest ranking difference is with the variable 'prevent and detect fraud' which auditors rank as 26th whereas the auditees ranked it 7th, a difference of 19 places. Possible reasons for the findings are discussed below.

The highest quality rated variable for both auditors and auditees is 'have integrity'. This finding does not mean that both groups attach equal weight to the concept. To demonstrate what weight is attached to a variable the normalized mean has been calculated and is shown in the Appendix for each variable. For example, although both the auditor and auditee rate 'have integrity' as their number-one ranked quality attribute, the auditee normalized mean of 1.61 is higher than the auditors' 1.08, which indicates that the auditee attaches even more importance to the concept of integrity relative to the other variables than does the auditor. Taking the use of the normalized mean further using 'prevent and detect fraud' as an example, it is shown that the auditor normalized mean is −0.27 (attaching less quality value than the average auditor variable) while the auditee normalized mean is 0.87 (attaching a significant amount of quality to this variable).

Although the approach used in Table 6.1 can identify the quality expectation gaps between auditors and auditees and weight the value attached to the variables used in the survey, further analysis was required to test whether the quality variables are seen in isolation or whether they cluster together to form larger concepts. It is in fact unlikely that all the variables are 'seen' in isolation in the minds of those who come into contact with 'quality audit services'. It is likely that a number of the variables are associated with each other in some way, i.e. 'possess qualifications' may be associated with 'possess experience'. This association may either be positive (both variables move in the same direction) or negative (the variables move in different directions). The set of perceptions taken together will form a paradigm or model of internal audit that exists within organizations and also in the minds of their internal auditors.

The association between variables can be statistically generated using correlation techniques. The number of replies to the survey (1400) make this a robust method to use. However, because the 39 terms used in the survey were already associated with the concept of audit it would not have been surprising had many of the terms correlated with one another. This in fact turned out to be the case. The maximum number of statistically sound correlations between one variable and the others was 23 with a minimum figure of 1. This is in itself an interesting result; the 23 correlations stem from 'offer business skills' (auditees) while the correlation of 1 relates to 'the chief financial officer should be able to influence the recommendations of the audit report', auditors being unable to link this with any other concept (perhaps not surprisingly).

By considering how each variable linked with other variables it was possible to infer how auditors and auditees understand each variable. By examining the differences between the links established between the variables it was possible to 'see' the perceptual differences that exist between auditors' and auditees' understanding of the term 'audit quality'. For a complete analysis of all of the key variables see Hopkins (1997). The analysis and discussion below centres on a number of the key findings.

For example, 'have integrity' for an auditor has an excellent association with 'be objective' and a strong relationship with 'make recommendations'. There is also a good relationship with 'have good communication skills'. Auditees on the other hand relate 'have integrity' directly to 'be independent', and 'have good communication skills' directly to 'provide a service to management'.

The use of the word 'independence' is noteworthy. The Research Committee of the Institute of Chartered Accountants of Scotland (1993) claimed that one of the criticisms made of internal auditors is that they are not independent of the executives. However, no *definition* of independence is given. Perhaps it is assumed? CIPFA (1990) defined independence in terms of organizational status and personal objectivity which permits the proper

Table 6.1 Attributes of auditors and auditing

Variable	Auditor		Auditee		Ranking
	Normalized mean	Rank (1 = high)	Normalized mean	Rank (1 = high)	Difference
Have integrity	1.08	1	1.61	1	0
Have good communication skills	1.05	2	0.84	8	−6
Be independent	1.03	3	1.27	2	1
Be objective	1.03	4	1.22	3	1
Provide a service to management	0.98	5	0.92	6	−1
The audit report should prompt management action to implement change	0.95	6	0.62	13	−7
Internal audit should make a positive contribution to the overall management of the organization	0.95	7	0.68	12	−5
Internal auditors and management should meet to discuss audit findings prior to the audit report	0.88	8	1.01	5	3
Internal auditors should foster constructive relationships	0.80	9	0.78	9	0
Internal auditors should be appraisers of internal control systems	0.80	10	0.16	23	−13
Internal audit plans should be flexible and respond to change	0.78	11	0.77	10	1
Make recommendations	0.75	12	0.69	11	1
The audit report should provide a formal record of points arising from the audit and of agreements reached with management	0.73	13	0.49	15	−2
Appraise	0.68	14	0.14	24	−10
Evaluate	0.58	15	0.42	18	−3
The internal auditor should be consulted about significant proposed changes to systems	0.55	16	−0.36	27	−11
Advise	0.53	17	0.45	16	1
Draw conclusions	0.53	18	0.33	21	−3
Internal auditors should consult with management on audit priorities	0.48	19	1.05	4	15

Statement					
Be analytical	0.28	20	0.50	14	6
Pursue value for money	0.06	21	0.41	19	2
Be innovative	0.03	22	-0.56	29	-7
Possess experience	0.03	23	0.34	20	3
Internal auditors should occasionally make unannounced visits	0.03	24	-0.34	26	-2
An audit should be planned in consultation with management	0.03	25	0.42	17	8
Prevent and detect fraud	-0.27	26	0.87	7	19
Possess qualifications	-0.34	27	-0.78	30	-3
Offer business skills	-0.44	28	-1.26	33	-5
An internal auditor should exercise personal judgment when determining what evidence is necessary for consideration	-0.59	29	-0.86	31	-2
Internal auditors should offer a wider range of business-orientated services	-0.60	30	-1.39	35	-5
The internal auditor should set objectives independently of management	-0.97	31	-1.55	36	-5
Find errors	-1.32	32	-0.04	25	7
Internal auditors should keep suspicions of fraud or irregularity to themselves until they have conclusive proof	-1.32	33	-1.29	34	-1
Internal auditors should periodically be attached to other departments	-1.37	34	-0.36	28	6
Internal auditors need have no technical knowledge of the organization	-1.82	35	-2.05	38	-3
Internal auditors should verify that the statements show a true and fair view	-1.84	36	0.29	22	14
An internal auditor can give total assurance that control weaknesses and irregularities do not exist	-2.26	37	-0.99	32	5
The chief financial officer should be able to influence the recommendations of the audit report	-2.36	38	-1.97	37	1
Internal audit is a test of the personal performance of individuals	-2.54	39	-2.47	39	0

performance of auditors' duties. It is interesting that CIPFA suggest two elements to independence, with effect to the organization itself and to the individual concerned. The research shows that the auditor links independence with a service to management (the organizational context) while the auditee links independence with integrity (the personal context). There is good evidence therefore that a fundamentally different perception of the key concept 'independence' exists between the auditor and the auditee and that any discussion of this key term should carefully define the context of its use.

All other variables can be similarly defined in terms of their key relationships with other variables. Three specific examples will illustrate the potential of this analysis, and attempt to explain three interesting differences between auditors and auditees.

Example 1: 'prevent and detect fraud'

Preventing and detecting fraud are historically associated with the internal audit function. Although any modern internal audit section will be spending a reduced amount of its time on probity-type audits in order to concentrate more on value-added audits and new initiatives, the survey detected that, as far as the clients are concerned, 'prevent and detect fraud' is a high-quality audit activity ranked 7th by auditees but 26th by their auditors. Perhaps it is not surprising that fraud maintains a strong link with audit – research in the USA highlights the importance for every organization of remaining vigilant to improve the ability to combat fraud and provides evidence of strong links between fraud, internal controls and internal audit. In 1995 the *Journal of Accountancy* (p. 20) stated that 'there is no such thing as an unimportant fraud'. Other research (Lower and Pany 1993) showed that potential jurors in auditor malpractice claims trials agreed that the auditor is a public watchdog and a ferreter of fraud.

Auditors relate 'prevent and detect fraud' to 'find errors' and 'exercise judgement when determining what evidence is necessary for consideration'. Both connections seem natural from the auditor's perspective. The auditee also relates 'prevent and detect fraud' to 'find errors' but also connects 'prevent and detect fraud' to 'possess qualifications' and 'verify that the statements show a true and fair view' therefore widening the applicability of the concept to personal skills and the wider role of auditors generally. The risk for an auditor when selling the audit staff as well 'qualified' becomes clearer. Auditees might well associate this announcement with an audit service directed at fraud and error finding – not the natural connection that an auditor might assume would be applied.

Example 2: 'find errors'

Ranked 32nd by the auditors and 25th by the auditee.

Auditors only correlate 'find errors' with 'prevent and detect fraud'. This closed set of probity-related concepts is consistent with the auditing guideline in this area (see CIPFA 1990). Auditees do make this natural link but also correlate 'find errors' with 'be analytical', 'evaluate' and 'possessing qualifications' – central audit terms used quite differently by auditors. For example 'possess qualifications', for an auditor is linked to 'appraisers of internal control systems'; a de-personalized systems-based view and one which is central to an auditors' perception of quality-audit. It can be inferred at this stage that the auditees' perception of 'quality audit' gives a higher prominence to 'fraud' concepts than that of the auditor. Further evidence is provided by the normalized means. The auditor mean of –1.32 shows a low quality perception. The auditee figure is –0.04: significantly higher.

Example 3: 'provide a service to management'

Auditors and auditees both rank this variable very highly (5th and 6th respectively). 'Service to management' therefore has a very high association with a quality audit service.

For auditors, this means linking 'provide a service to management' with:

● The audit report as a formal record of points raised during the audit.
● Advising.
● Consulting internal audit with regard to changes in the system.

However, auditors did not link 'provide a service to management' with 'verify that the statements show a true and fair view' (a 'good' negative correlation exists between these two variables).

Auditees recognize none of the above links in terms of their own key relationships, linking 'provide a service to management' with:

● The auditors having 'good communication skills'.
● The auditors 'pursuing value for money'.
● The auditors 'fostering constructive relationships'.

It can be concluded that there is good evidence of a highly different interpretation of the same quality audit concept.

Interpreting the quality audit concept

Many of the variables exhibited the same issues: namely, differing associations between the key concepts even when the concepts exhibited similar

rankings. It was therefore concluded that there exists a different consensus between auditors and auditees as to what the phrase 'quality audit
services' actually means. This conclusion raises considerable problems
for any audit service which is attempting to market itself using either a
traditional or 'post-modern' set of audit terms which may be both valued
and interpreted differently by their customers, the auditees. This conclusion may imply that there are significant risks in a competitive situation where differing would-be suppliers of an organization's internal audit
services may compete in terms of cost and the quality of delivery but
might be differentiated in their ability to communicate 'quality' to the
customer.

It is possible to analyse the major links by concentrating on the strongest
correlations that do exist between the highest-rated quality audit variables.
This can be carried out for auditors and auditees with the purpose of
establishing where the most significant differences exist. For any variable
that appears to exert a fundamental influence it might prove interesting to
explore its full set of relationships.

The process began by using 'have integrity' as the first point because it
had already been proved that this was the most important concept in terms
of its absolute, relative, and Quality Expectations Gap (QEG) figure. All of
the top-ten quality concepts were considered, together with their most
strongly associated quality variables. For a complete discussion of the
findings, see Hopkins (1997).

The key findings, however, clearly show a number of interesting differences between the auditors and auditees. It is proposed that the differences
discovered show that there is a perceptual difference between the meaning
of key audit concepts as understood by the provider, and their meaning as
understood by the purchaser of those services, and that these differences
may have consequences for the future of internal audit in a competitive
market.

For the auditor the key concepts tend to centre on technical and personal skills and attributes which eventually focus on the audit report, i.e.
appraising, analysing and evaluating, leading to drawing conclusions, giving advice and 'innovation' as a service to management.

The key term appears to be 'appraise', which links a number of key
concepts. It was an earlier conjecture that auditees personalize the audit
process (and that this may indicate a 'traditional' view of internal audit)
and that this individualization means that all 'assessing' concepts are associated with a 'personal integrity rating' that attaches to individual auditees
and not to the systems they work within. 'Appraise' for the auditor has a
short route to 'service to management' through 'advise' whereas the auditee
map has no such direct route. The auditee linking 'service to management'
with the far more personal 'good communication skills' and the 'softer'
'value for money'.

The auditees link 'advise' to changes which are in turn strongly associated with reporting and internal control. It was a previous conjecture that auditees resist 'change' at the best of times, but in periods of major public-sector upheaval in local government and the health services further perceived 'change' may carry strong negative connotations. It is perhaps to mitigate this negative perceived aspect of auditing that the auditees construct a set of concepts all linked to establishing closer relationships. Here the key words and high quality ratings for 'consult', 'foster constructive relationships' and 'flexibility' are interestingly grouped. If the concept of 'empowerment' is actively embraced by organizations then the internal auditor will have to recognize that key relationships and communications are essential elements in establishing a quality set of perceptions regarding the internal audit product. Failure to address this issue would be a fundamental risk for internal audit.

Note that the auditors link 'foster constructive relationships' directly to 'appraisers of internal control systems', the behavioural aspects being secondary to the task of gaining information. It should also be noted that auditors link 'flexible plans' to 'consult with management' but do not link these two concepts with any other group. The auditee however links 'flexible plans' to 'foster constructive relationships' and 'consult with management', emphasizing the importance of working more closely with the auditor.

To echo a theme already discussed it is worth repeating that the auditors link qualifications and experience directly to internal control appraisal and reporting while the auditees link qualifications and experience to fraud, error etc.

As the meaning of the concepts can be inferred from the variable attached to them, there is further evidence of a number of key perceptual differences between auditors and auditees in their understanding of the fundamental nature of the overall concept of 'quality audit services'.

Before moving on it will be instructive to examine one of the key audit concepts in some depth. The term is 'internal audit should make a positive contribution to the overall management of the organization' and will be examined from the point of view of the auditee only. There are several reasons for this analysis:

- 'Internal audit should make a positive contribution to the overall management of the organization' is a highly rated quality concept for the auditee. An overall auditee mean value of 3.4 gives a value label between 'strongly agree' and 'agree'.
- The phrase has the largest number of significant correlations with all of the other variables (26 out of 39) showing this variable to be a 'key player' in understanding the auditees true perception of the quality value of internal audit.

● Finally, if internal audit is to survive as a quality service and a core activity central to every organization's well-being then it will be essential for every auditor to understand how their customers see the main quality audit contribution.

The key terms that correlate significantly to 'internal audit should make a positive contribution to the overall management of the organization' are given below. All concepts are ranked in order of the strongest link first. For the auditee, making a positive contribution to the overall management of an organization is therefore strongly associated with:

1 Audit report should prompt management action to implement change.
2 Appraising internal control systems.
3 Consulting the internal auditor with regard to proposed changes.
4 Auditors fostering constructive relationships.
5 Evaluating.
6 Audit report is a formal record of points arising.
7 Advising.
8 Providing a service to management.
9 Making recommendations.
10 Appraising.
11 Flexible plans that respond to change.
12 Discuss audit findings prior to the report.
(All correlations are given at the 0.01 level of confidence)

It can be seen, therefore, that the auditee requires an internal audit service that can help the organization deal with 'change' and that can best be handled through a systems-based approach where the auditor involves management throughout the process. By establishing closer relationships with the auditee, the auditor can better sell modern ideas of audit quality and secure a better understanding of the value that internal audit adds to any organization. The greatest risk is that some auditees strongly associate internal audit with probity-related issues and until this historical association is removed it may be difficult for a modern internal audit service actively to promote itself as being 'modern' and having 'added value'.

Conclusion

It might be erroneously concluded that all auditors have to do to sell a high-quality image to management would be to use the terms above to describe what audit is offering. The problem is that auditors do not necessarily 'see' the above terms in the same 'quality' manner as do the auditees. The quality associations dealt with in this chapter show that there is a demonstrable need for auditors to understand the perceptions of their customers. Jacka (1994) claims that internal auditors should deal with their audits in a way that satisfies their customers and that the audit functions should be assessed in relation to their customers. Jacka notes that this implies a shift away from traditional approaches and that internal auditors might have to reflect on how these changes will affect their perceptions of risk. He goes on to state that definitions of audit risk will have to emphasize their customers' practices. It will be important for auditors to consider relaxing overburdening controls where they may hinder the success of the organization. Jacka finishes by noting that it will therefore be important for auditors to determine whether or not their customers are satisfied.

It will be necessary for auditors to study the quality language of audit with a new perception. Key terms routinely used by auditors may carry completely different weights and meanings when considered by the auditee. Effective communication between the provider and purchaser of quality audit services can only take place when there is an effective consensus on the meaning of the terms being used to describe the audit process. In the absence of consensus, a 'gap' will continue to exist.

By understanding the nature of the expectations or perceptual quality gap, audit managers can:

- Enhance their own understanding of 'quality audit'.
- Increase their behavioural skills.
- Carry out effective training of their audit staff.

Just as importantly, they can also decide whether it might be necessary to try to establish how much 'education' their *clients* may need to understand fully the modern concept of internal auditing. The perceptual quality gaps discussed here have shown that education is needed for clients as well as their auditors. Auditors will face the considerable challenge of having, in some cases, to change the culture of the organizations that they audit before any post-modern auditing could be accepted or would be likely to flourish within those organizations.

All of the above challenges and changes may carry a cost. However, the cost of doing nothing may be at the expense of the future of internal audit services in a competitive environment. Research has shown that customers are prepared to pay more for a quality audit product. Internal audit cannot afford to gamble with the expectation gap.

References

Balkaran, L. (1995) Internal auditing – corporate culture. *Internal Auditor*, August: 56.

Chartered Institute of Public Finance and Accountancy (CIPFA) (1979) *Statements on Internal Audit Practice in the Public Sector*. London: CIPFA.

Chartered Institute of Public Finance and Accountancy (CIPFA) (1990) *Auditing Guidelines*. London: CIPFA.

Chartered Institute of Public Finance and Accountancy (CIPFA) (1992) *Promoting Internal Audit*. London: CIPFA.

Hagasset-Bellamy, A. M. (1994) Do we need a change of direction? *Internal Auditing* (UK), September: 18.

Hawkes, L. C. and Adams, M. B. (1995) Total quality management and the internal audit: empirical evidence. *Managerial Auditing Journal* (UK), 10: 31.

Hopkins, R. N. (1995) Internal audit – perceptions of quality and the expectations gap: a question for management? *The Journal of Applied Accounting Research*, 3: 105–30.

Hopkins, R. N. (1997) The nature of audit quality – a conflict of paradigms? *International Journal of Auditing*, 1 (2): 117–33.

Jacka, J. M. (1994) The upside-down pyramid. *Internal Auditor*, June, 51: 62.

Journal of Accountancy (1995) Combating fraud: know the facts. September: 20.

Lower, D. J. and Pany, K. (1993) Expectations of the audit function. *CPA Journal* (USA), August: 63-8.

McCrindell, J. Q. (1993) The new management paradigm. *Management Accounting*, February: 31.

Research Committee of the Chartered Accountants of Scotland (1993) *Auditing into the Twenty-First Century*, a discussion document.

Sawyer, L. B. (1992) The Political Side of Internal Auditing. *Internal Auditor* (USA), February: 26.

Further reading

You are advised to refer to academic and professional journals, including: *International Journal of Auditing*; *Accounting, Organisations and Society*; *Auditing: a Journal of Practice and Theory*; *Journal of Applied Accounting Research*; *Internal Auditor*; and *Management Accounting*. In addition, more information on the research reported in this chapter can be obtained by referring to: CIPFA (1997) *Perceptions of Audit Quality* (London: CIPFA).

seven

The mismanagement of financial resources

Alan Doig

Key learning objectives

After reading this chapter you should be able to:

1 Evaluate critically the impact of change on public sector standards.
2 Appreciate the potentially adverse consequences of empowerment and managerial enterprise without appropriate controls and supervision.
3 Understand issues relating to the stewardship and accountability of public funds within the context of continuing, complex organizational change.
4 Appreciate the role of senior management in ensuring that propriety and probity are integral issues on any management agenda.
5 Appreciate the range of procedures and controls that are available to prevent mismanagement or misconduct and to appreciate the importance of focusing on people as the most effective means of ensuring that the procedures and controls work.

Introduction

This chapter focuses on the mismanagement of financial resources as a means of highlighting both the issues and the reforms that should be addressed by organizations in the public sector as they learn to operate with substantial degrees of independence and initiative. The chapter uses the National Health Service (NHS) to illustrate these issues because it has undergone managerial and structural changes since the early 1980s similar to those elsewhere in the public sector. The NHS also provides three case studies to illustrate what can go wrong when resources, staffing and management approaches are mismatched within changed cultures and devolved financial and management responsibilities without appropriate controls and procedures. The NHS provides a range of institutional responses across a number of areas which, again, have been the subject of debate and discussion elsewhere in the public sector since the end of 1993 and the start of 1994 with the publication of two official reports.

In December 1993 the Audit Commission published a report on probity in local government which reported that 'fraud and corruption and the stewardship of private and public sector accounts have never had a higher profile' (p. 1) at a time when ensuring public probity had been

> rendered more demanding and complex by numerous recent changes to the nature and operation of local government services. Many of the changes, such as the delegation of financial and management responsibilities, while contributing to improved quality of service, have increased the risks of fraud and corruption occurring.
>
> (Audit Commission 1993: 2)

In January 1994, the Committee of Public Accounts (CPA) reported that there had been 'a number of serious failures in administrative and financial systems and controls within departments and other public bodies, which have led to money being wasted or otherwise improperly spent. These failings represent a departure from the standards of conduct which have mainly been established during the past 140 years' (Committee of Public Accounts 1993–94: v–vi). At a time of change, it argued 'it is important to ensure that proper standards are maintained in the conduct of public business . . . at such a time it is even more essential to maintain honesty in the spending of public money and to ensure that traditional public sector values are not neglected in the effort to maximise economy and efficiency'. Later the same year, the Audit Commission's report on the NHS stated that 'some of the current arrangements to prevent fraud and corruption are weak and leave at risk large amounts of the taxpayer's money . . . it is important that, despite the pressures and demands they face, probity is not taken for granted and allowed to slip down the management agenda' (Audit Commission 1994: 4). It was thus clear that those charged with responsibility for overseeing the stewardship of public funds and the propriety of public expenditure were concerned that the existing procedures and controls, as well as the traditional public service culture, were being shown to be inadequate or ineffectual. They appeared particularly concerned about some of the consequences of the comprehensive changes to the structure and delivery of public services, as well as the growth of what is termed new public management (NPM – see Chapter 2) as the management style and attitude embodying changes to the personal and organizational cultures in the public sector.

The agenda for change

The short reference in the 1979 Conservative manifesto – that the reduction of waste, bureaucracy and overgovernment would yield substantial savings – has been elevated to a blueprint for reform, but was originally a general phrase to deal with the cost and size of government. Unlike the 1968 Fulton Report, set up by the then Labour government to recommend ways to modernize the skills, staffing and management of the civil service, which proposed management reform within a given public service framework, the process of change initiated by the Conservative government had no clear blueprint, no milestones and no goal other than a continuous reduction of the size and cost of the public sector with an underlying belief that the private sector approach provided the model for the delivery of public services. While the government privatized its commercial or trading assets or activities, its initial approach within the public sector was to reduce expenditure, cut back on the growth of non-departmental public bodies (NDPB) and, in relation to the civil service, conduct a series of reviews of administrative costs and activities. From the Rayner scrutinies and the financial management initiative (FMI) in the early 1980s up to the Efficiency Unit's 1988 'next steps' report, the underlying themes were:

- The introduction of financial and management information systems.
- Good management practice through cost awareness and responsible and devolved management.
- Measures of performance and targets for individual managers who would be held accountable for achieving an agreed level of performance (*Government Observations* 1982).

The 'next steps' report, however, went a stage further. It focused on structural reform that differentiated functional responsibility and encouraged organizational independence in the delivery of those functions in terms of staffing, form of delivery and an emphasis on cost and customer focus as the vehicle to overcome the lack of urgency and alter 'cultural attitudes and behaviour of government so that continuous improvement becomes a widespread and inbuilt feature of it' (Efficiency Unit 1988: 1). This approach was echoed across the public sector to create the context for similar change (Wilson and Doig 1996).

The NHS structure had undergone a number of changes since its inception (see Chapter 10): it experienced a process of organizational reform to improve decision making, resource allocation and service delivery during the 1970s with the creation of regional health authorities (RHAs) as the executive agencies between the Department of Health and Social Security and the tiers which dealt with health care provision. Nevertheless, Conservative governments from 1979 viewed with concern the inadequacies that the changes had institutionalized or would be unlikely to resolve, including the limitations of negotiated or consensual strategic planning which were embodied in the earlier reforms, the rapid escalation of costs (particularly salaries and wages), and (to the Conservatives) the conservatism of the various vested interests. The concern provoked further reviews and initiatives in the early 1980s which were designed primarily to push down expenditure, introduce means to optimize the delivery of scarce resources and promote efficiency and productivity. In 1982 a single delivery tier – district health authorities (DHAs) – were set up. Both their and RHA memberships were redrawn to reflect business and management competencies. DHAs were to be responsible for the purchase and delivery of health services, leaving the RHAs responsible for policy, resource allocation, capital expenditure and provision of common services (Ham 1985; Klein 1989; Gabe *et al.* 1991; Spurgeon 1991).

Within this framework, Conservative governments then sought to introduce various efficiency and productivity measures, focusing on weighted allocation formulae and effective management to implement the resource management initiative (RMI): 'the linking of clinical activity data, for both volume and quality (at individual patient and case-mix level), to resource utilisation such that costs can be identified on a projective basis' (Spurgeon 1991: 80). The cornerstones of managerial change were the 1982 Korner Reports on information systems and the 1983 Griffiths Report on management in health authorities. Together they pointed towards a devolved managerial responsibility with access to managed, accurate and up-to-date information, working to balance costs and clinical needs with population needs and available resources. The reforms, however, were still constrained by the existing structure and traditions which were dominated by the hierarchy of the medical profession which left consultants with the power effectively to commit large proportions 'of hospitals' resources in ways which did not necessarily accord with the longer-term plans being developed by the administrative hierarchies' (Pollitt 1993: 190). The structural context for NPM and a more cost-focused approach to the use of resources emerged with the introduction of the internal market with a range of suppliers and providers across general practice (through the establishment of fundholding practices), district and regional boundaries, in a series of contractual relationships (see Chapter 10).

The reforms had two effects on the management of the NHS up to the mid-1990s, after which time further changes were made at regional level. First, the devolution of multiple functions to single agencies, with RHAs becoming significant financial players within a context of cultural change, was not matched by the revision or adaptation of those procedures and controls (such as separation of duties, audit trails, levels of financial responsibility) that would have been considered as important balances to the potential impact of disaggregation, devolution and delayering. Second, little attention was given to wider societal and cultural changes, including the uncritical enthusiasm for private sector values and approaches to the delivery of public services (Doig 1995; 1997a) that meant that NPM could be both enterprising and innovative but also an area of risk, misunderstanding and conflict of purpose.

NPM and the NHS

Both NPM and structural change in the public sector combined to require of those working in the sector to assume new duties and responsibilities, adopt private sector approaches to the management and delivery of public services, and look to new technologies and management practices within a context in which the traditional means of ensuring public service standards and means of accountability were changing. The changes had several major effects. First, they meant that management took on a number of new functions such as 'the devolution of estate and personnel services, for example, and new functions of contracting and marketing, and, in some, posts such as risk management or public relations' (Ferlie *et al.* 1996: 50). Such changes were in part compounded by increasingly close relations with private sector organizations, particularly where public sector organizations attempted to buy-in expertise and technology to improve or accelerate services and delivery as part of their performance and productivity profile.

Second, such managerial primacy and empowerment, together with the rapid drive for devolved and redesigned frameworks for delivery of functions or services, left within the responsibility and remit of those working in the sector the authority to make a range of decisions relating to themselves, their organization, their suppliers and their users, often without guidance and appropriate supervisory and scrutiny arrangements. In such circumstances:

> to treat the establishment of the conditions for effective achievement of public purposes and the resolution of conflicts between efficiency and effectiveness in the public sector as questions of 'managerial discretion' is either simple-minded or question-begging on a huge scale. The enormous complexity of defining public purposes and translating these into objectives and targets; of establishing machinery to integrate and co-ordinate different bodies; of monitoring the outcomes of action and inaction and the environment in which public policy operates, all require learning processes.
>
> (Birkenshaw *et al.* 1990: 165)

Third, there have been assumptions about the role of new technology to assist the process of change, as well as to offer means for savings, that have been problematical in practice in terms of development, staffing and use:

[the] recruitment and retention of information and information technology staff has been difficult and the technological infrastructure has been
bedevilled by a lack of standardisation. The immediate consequences
of the reforms have been an increased demand for more sophisticated
systems, the rapid extension of the resource management initiative
to facilitate detailed costing of activities, a strong commitment to net-
worked systems linking GPs, social services, hospital and community
services, and an emphasis on information interpretation skills.

(Moon and Kendall 1993: 186)

Furthermore, while the NHS, the Department of Health, together with
the NHS Management Board (and its successors, the NHS Management
Executive and the NHS Executive) pushed for RHA-led information technology (IT) provision as a core requirement for change, it has been 'hard to
overestimate the sheer complexity of the data collection systems that would
ideally be required to generate reliable and timely data about the efficiency,
effectiveness, responsiveness and equity of health care services' (Harrison
et al. 1990: 143). Assumptions about the costs and capabilities of information technology, particularly in untested circumstances, as well as reliance on
the advice of consultants and on the employment of private sector companies to offset staff skills shortage, have been made without realizing that:

IT as an instrument of policy is not an uncontentious or problematic
issue. It cannot be used as a straightforward cost-cutting tool in isolation from the rest of the administration. If it is viewed as such by
'new' public managers, then the public sector will become increasingly
vulnerable to risk.

(Margetts and Willcocks 1993: 56)

Fourth, the fragmentation of organizations and the primacy of the contract culture affected how officials perceived their roles and their functions.
While still in theory working within a public service ethos, officials have
been more likely to see themselves as employees of a specific organization
and subject to its particular terms and conditions of service, as well as its
culture, leadership and style of management. The 'next steps' report denied
the concept of a unified public service and blamed uniformity of pay and
grading as a deterrent to effective management, and the head of the civil
service argued in 1988 that the unifying framework of the changing public
sector would develop from 'requirements of equity, accountability, impartiality and a wide view of the public interest' (Drewry and Butcher 1991:
237). However, little thought was given to how this would be achieved
against the countervailing influences of organizations developing their own
approaches to the delivery of public services in the NPM context. Once
agencies were encouraged to develop their own recruitment, pay, grading
and career development criteria for staff, the issues of personal ambitions,
expectations and job satisfaction also arose:

the rewards and incentives required to encourage managers to take risks are not a regular part of the civil service environment. Accommodating these requirements will mean greater organisational diversity and new personnel management problems, which would set up some strains in the system as career opportunities and rewards could be expected to diverge.

(Metcalfe and Richards 1990: 165)

High salaries to recruit and retain staff, particularly those whose careers have been in the private sector, as well as the use of performance-related rewards, have not been unknown in the civil service, but there was a more general expansion of the range of perks, benefits and pay-related payments, with the focus on personal reward for individual initiative and responsibility, without a concomitant adaptation of the means to inculcate and monitor the public interest perspective.

Fifth, and one of the recurring themes of the process of reform, was the adaptation of means of accountability to offset the development of devolved organizations. When the Fulton Committee assessed what type of civil service was needed to support the changing roles and responsibilities of government in the 1960s, its recommendations foreshadowed the structural and managerial reforms that were to take place during the 1980s, operating according to predetermined and assessable performance criteria; 'accountable management' outside 'the day-to-day control of Ministers and the scrutiny of Parliament' (Fulton Committee 1968: 61). The Committee accepted, however, the creation of 'hived-off' bodies and that 'the drawing of the line between them and central government would raise parliamentary and constitutional issues' (p. 61), but at the same time it expected greater mobility of personnel to and from the private sector. Nevertheless it believed that such developments would take place within a civil service where 'there is a strong sense of public service' and 'integrity and impartiality are unquestioned' (Fulton Committee 1968: 13), working within an appropriate accountability framework determined by government and Parliament.

Accountability

The issue with accountability is that it has a number of interpretations, not least the differences between political accountability – 'those with delegated authority being answerable for their actions to the people' – and managerial accountability – 'those with delegated authority accountable for carrying out agreed tasks according to agreed criteria of performance' (Ferlie *et al.* 1996: 198). There is also the wider concern 'that the traditional mechanisms used to ensure the accountability of public services – along with their supporting organisational culture – have been eroded as a result of recent organisational restructurings, with consequent loss of traditional standards of probity' (p. 197). Although governments have placed substantial emphasis on management measurement, both through the Citizens Charters, 'next steps' reports and the Audit Commission's extensive publications on performance indicators (see Chapter 8), and while there has been substantial debate on whether 'traditional methods of parliamentary accountability have been jettisoned and . . . accountability by contract is the mechanism which has replaced those methods' (O'Toole 1995: 69), the issue of standards and probity have received less attention.

While the Efficiency Unit's 1988 report was dismissive of monitoring any adverse effects of change, saying that 'pressure from Parliament, the Public Accounts Committee and the media tends to concentrate on alleged impropriety or incompetence, and making political points, rather than on demanding evidence of steadily improving efficiency and effectiveness' (p. 4), it did argue that the role of the 'centre of government' included a requirement 'to set and police essential rules on propriety for the public service in carrying out its essential functions' (p. 12). In a context in which the Treasury and Civil Service Committee was praising departments for their 'hands-off approach' to agencies and inviting them to pursue 'cultural change' and 'a large scale re-writing of the rule-book' (Treasury and Civil Service Committee 1989–90: xviii) ministers and senior civil servants endorsed organizational independence (or *de facto* organizational autonomy), claiming the continuation of uniform standards and arguing that change had not only not affected those standards but had led to greater transparency and accountability (*Government Reply* 1991; Treasury and Civil Service Committee 1992–93; Cabinet Office 1994).

Yet in only one area – NDPBs – did governments act to lay down guidance on how to ensure standards and accountability in changed circumstances. Thus in 1985 the Cabinet Office and the Treasury published a set of guidelines on a number of issues (Cabinet Office (MPO) and HM Treasury 1985). Thus NDBPs were expected to have 'good standards of management' (p. 34) including standards of conduct and internal management budget and information systems. Sponsoring departments were expected to review management and control systems and practices, communicate information on ministerial priorities and policies, receive costed proposals for future work and the allocation of resources 'for the sponsor department (and the Treasury) to appraise its viability and efficiency' (p. 37), and 'appraise any spending proposals which are not within the body's delegated authority' (p. 37). The 'prime responsibility for maintaining high standards of management' (p. 43) in carrying out its functions rested with the NDPBs; the ultimate responsibility, particularly if things went wrong politically, lay with the minister.

There was, however, less attention given subsequently to the implementation of the guidelines by sponsoring bodies while many NDPBs did not have (or sometimes did not wish to have) a clear understanding of the parameters of their independence, autonomy and powers, particularly in relation to their sponsoring department (Doig 1988). Nevertheless, at least guidance existed for parts of the public sector, but others were specifically excluded from their remit, including health authorities on the grounds that 'there are statutory and other arrangements for regular scrutiny and monitoring overseen by the health departments' (Cabinet Office (MPO) and HM Treasury 1985: 57). In practice, however, the fragmentation of the NHS, and the predilection for arm's length relationships, fractured lines of accountability with Parliament, the Department of Health and the NHS Executive (and its predecessors). The responsibility for scrutiny and monitoring lay primarily with audit. Even here there were concerns about internal audit's effectiveness. In his 1987 report the Comptroller and Auditor General noted that his predecessor had been concerned in 1981 that 'generally there was a lack of audit planning and reporting; the coverage of computer systems, capital expenditure and family practitioner services was deficient; and in England staff numbers were below those recommended by regional treasurers to achieve satisfactory financial audit standards' (National Audit Office 1987: 1). He himself noted in his 1987 report that 'most had not achieved the defined minimum acceptable level of audit coverage' (p. 3). More success, however, was secured through the creation of the Audit Commission and the strengthened powers and confidence of District Audit in promoting economy, efficiency and effectiveness. They have carried out studies into areas of general concern, including the examination of existing procedures and tests to identify specific patterns of fraud and/or to inform management of the inadequacies of and need for effective protective procedures, regulations and decision-making systems. Within this framework, two of District Audit's inquiries were to raise significant issues about the impact of change on public sector organizations' capabilities to manage significant financial resources within changed cultures and structures.

The Shock: two case studies in new public mismanagement

Case study 1: the Wessex Regional Health Authority

In 1984, believing that effective management had to be underpinned by a sophisticated IT strategy, Wessex Regional Health Authority (WRHA) proposed a five-year plan, involving £25.8m capital costs and £17.5m recurrent costs, to computerize offices, hospitals and wards for hospitals, manpower, estates, community care and financial information. In April 1990 the plan – Wessex's Regional Information Systems Plan (RISP) – was abandoned at a cost of at least £20m with few of the systems in place either in whole or in part. The WRHA had defined its requirements between 1982 and 1984, underlining the need for the WRHA to manage the project, for the DHAs to be closely involved to ensure the project's success, and for clear lines of responsibility between them and the project managers. The project was to be funded by 'top-slicing' the RHA's annual capital allocation.

Originally the tendering process was intended to produce a number of contractors to supply a mix of software and hardware requirements for three core systems. In the end a single contractor was engaged for the whole project. During the tendering process, lasting some 12 months, District Audit alleged that the successful bidder, already a WRHA consultant, took part in the tender evaluation and debriefing meetings, used privileged information in their submissions and lobbied at a senior level for the bid. District Audit also alleged that WRHA officials amended the criteria to assess tenders, amended the tender specifications without re-tendering, made decisions at inquorate meetings, did not pass up decisions to the RHA board, ignored other consultants' advice, removed safeguards and performance requirements from the contract with the successful tenderer and allowed decisions to be taken without delegated authority.

The project was abandoned after a number of concerns over what RISP would do, and how it would be implemented, with the DHAs refusing to use new software because of licensing costs, rejecting new software in favour of retaining their existing systems, or buying in a variety of interim systems to suit local needs. This in turn reflected WRHA's inability to define and restrict the systems it would finance and its faith that other systems could later be integrated in RISP. In looking at RISP, District Audit found that the RHA's budgetary control was so weak that 'it took until half way through the following financial year before the total commitment for the earlier year could be estimated with any accuracy' (Committee of Public Accounts 1992–93a: 33). Poorly-defined consultancies were handed out on the basis of verbal agreements reached at informal meetings, contract procedures were ignored, no internal audit work was carried out between 1985–9 (when £38m was spent) and no attempt was made to ensure value for money.

Following a report from another consultancy firm over RISP's progress, WRHA accepted a proposal from the consultancy (whose lead consultant was a former WRHA senior manager) that WRHA enter into a partnership with it to undertake IT work for the WRHA. WRHA IT staff were privatized by being transferred into Wessex Integrated Systems (WIS), a company set up by WRHA and the firm but whose set-up costs were paid for by the WRHA and whose contract with the WRHA was drafted by WIS's solicitors. Not only did the contract specification differ substantially from the original tender documents but it contained 'no effective performance requirements or any details of work to be undertaken' (Committee of Public Accounts 1992–93a, Minutes of Evidence: 57). Attempts by some WRHA officials to instil progress-reporting against specific targets, quality assurance and budgetary compliance, were rejected as a 'set of overbureaucratic procedures' by WIS (Minutes of Evidence: 58). This view was accepted by WRHA and, 'in the absence of independent advice, realistic development plans, adequate financial and budgetary control, the WRHA was totally dependent on its contractor which was able to exert abnormal influence over the decisions to be taken by the WRHA' (Minutes of Evidence: 61).

This influence led to: WRHA paying for drawing up WIS's business plan; paying for the recruitment and training of WIS staff; accepting WIS's overestimation of the work WRHA would require of it and WRHA's consequential commitment for potential payments that 'could not be afforded' (Minutes of Evidence: 78); allowing WIS to prepare the WRHA's IT budgets (including WIS's own likely costs); taking advice from WIS to purchase an IBM computer it did not need and which incurred a loss in value of over £3m; underwriting inflated staff costs at WIS by failing to identify the WRHA staff who actually transferred; accepting agreements on underwritten redundancy costs; and the disengagement of WIS's services and performance measures that substantially favoured WIS at the WRHA's expense.

The weakness of the arrangements, according to the district auditor, meant that the WRHA never knew what work was done, and whether what was done was done by appropriately-skilled staff to agreed standards. Nor did they know whether the costs and quality of work done were acceptable, whether they were being overcharged or double-charged, who owned the equipment WIS bought but charged to WRHA and how WIS was able to order supplies directly on WRHA's account, 'signing delivery notes and representing to potential suppliers that they had the power to commit WRHA financially . . .' (Committee of Public Accounts 1992–3, Minutes of Evidence: 99). District Audit alleged WIS was at fault in failing to give the WRHA 'independent and unbiased advice' (Minutes of Evidence: 78), and that the consultancy firm had 'exploited weaknesses in the management structure to its advantage when it was being paid to advise the RHA and to protect its interests' (p. 78). At best the firm's advice was negligent; at worst 'it was knowingly or recklessly intended to promote its own interests and those of its subsidiary, WIS, at the expense of the RHA and public funds' (Minutes of Evidence: 78).

The causes of WRHA's difficulties were several. First, the pressure for (and faith in) sophisticated IT systems was not supported by a clear WRHA board policy, detailed planning or continuity of leadership. For example, the post of regional information systems manager (RISM) changed four times in five years. The use of outside consultants deprived the RHA of experienced in-house staff and created the potential for conflicts of interest (two of the four RISMs between 1985 and 1990 were seconded from firms bidding for WRHA work), while the volume of work involved in monitoring the activities of consultants invariably outstripped WRHA's capacity and capabilities for effective monitoring to the point where misconduct and mismanagement occurred. Examples of such behaviour included the raising of orders and authorizing expenditure by the same officer; ignoring tender and contract procedures; consultants drawing up plans the implementation of which was to be their responsibility; officials setting budgets for contracts for which they would later tender; officials awarding contracts to firms by whom they were either employed or were later employed; and the employment of senior employees of contractors as WRHA advisors. Information on the progress of the project and the activities of officials and consultants was not forwarded to or raised with the WRHA board by senior management. No attempt was made to require regular performance, implementation and budgetary reports from the contractors.

Subsequently WRHA, as a result of the disasters it had visited upon itself, recommended the steps that should have been taken in the first place: the review of IT contracts; an IT directorate with effective contract management; a strengthened finance department with improved budgetary and financial control; overhauled financial systems; use of legal redress against overpayments; competitive tendering; monitoring procedures for contracts; and 'improvements in the standard and style of reporting of all major issues to all members of the WRHA' (Committee of Public Accounts 1992–3, Minutes of Evidence: 22). In 1992, after the damning District Audit reports, the then NHS Management Executive's chief executive wrote to all RHA regional general managers reminding them of the importance of: rigorous systems for tendering for, managing, and monitoring contracts with outside consultants; strict propriety in standards of business conduct; ensuring senior management's accountability for economy, efficiency and effectiveness in the use of public funds; and having proper personnel practices.

Case study 2: the West Midlands Regional Health Authority

During the changes to the NHS during the early 1980s the West Midlands Regional Health Authority (WMRHA) undertook a wide-ranging review of core (statutory and strategic management functions) and non-core services. The latter were those services managed by the RHA but delivered to DHAs as part of the former's secondary role as a 'common service agency'. In 1986 WMRHA set up the Regionally Managed Services Organization (RMS) to deal with central non-core functions such as supplies, management services (including computer services), blood transfusion and ambulance services. It appointed a director of regionally managed services (DRMS) who was described as bringing a new 'culture' to the RMS and, in particular, to its regional supplies division (RSD) which was responsible for negotiating contracts for the supply of goods and services to the DHAs.

The DRMS chose to define WMRHA policy – that non-core functions should adopt a more commercial approach to their provision – as a mandate both for rapid managerial reform and possible future privatization. His first major departure from RHA procedures and policy took place in

1989 when he hired a management consultancy firm to make the supplies division commercially viable by 1992 and, according to the consultancy firm, have it 'in good shape' if it were to be privatized (Committee of Public Accounts 1992–93b, Minutes of Evidence: 43). The tendering process was inadequate while the consultancy firm's 'contract' consisted of a single letter from the company to the director discussing what they would do and what they would charge – £48,885 a week for 34 weeks and expenses 'in accordance with our standard practice' (Minutes of Evidence: 57; see also p. 47). Although the letter was never seen by the WMRHA board, the supplies board which was supposed to oversee the activities of the RMS, or the regional solicitor's department, WMRHA paid over £2.5m to the consultancy firm, including, it was later alleged: paying for VAT twice; paying out on unsupported invoices; paying for rented houses for American executives and their wives; and paying for private aircraft charter. What the consultancy firm proposed led to conflict between the RHA and the DHAs and finally to internal and external inquiries. District Audit, noting that the total cost of the whole affair was nearer £4m, alleged that the conduct of the DRMS showed 'a cavalier disregard' (Minutes of Evidence: 41) for the standards of conduct expected from public officers, did not follow RHA procedures and ignored standing orders on contracts. The District Audit report also drew attention to the potential conflict of interest arising from the DRMS's relationship with other private sector organizations with whom he had worked and who were working for him, including 'off-payroll' consultants for senior management positions in the RSD.

At the same time RSD decided to develop end-to-end electronic trading, an innovative system whereby customers (such as hospital wards) and suppliers were linked via a database of supplier capabilities and a broking system (to deal with quotes, discounts and technical specification) to streamline ordering and delivery. The WMRHA and the East Anglian RHA (who later withdrew from the project) agreed to fund joint development work and provide the successful contractor with a business strategy, a list of requirements and an IT strategy. In April 1990 a meeting between a contractor – who had been selected rather than chosen by open tender – the DRMS and RSD's chief executive, led to the WMRHA being committed to £1.4m of development work without standing orders and tendering procedures being followed, and without explicit board authority. In less than two years the system contractor had billed WMRHA for £7.3m. This amount included work resulting from revisions to the contract without any competitive tender or any price being quoted.

The internal inquiry into the consultancy firm's contract in February 1991 had noted the need for a review of the electronic trading project but the funding continued until payment was suspended in January 1992 and the development ended. From the beginning the project was badly planned and executed within WMRHA. The high level of investment in the project was believed acceptable on the incorrect assumption that it would be offset by high royalties from sales to other RHAs among whom electronic trading was generally accepted as the key to the future for NHS supplies. The project cost over five years to the WMRHA was expected to be £5.3m and the expected royalties return was estimated at nearly £4m; in the event the WMRHA received £12,585 (Minutes of Evidence: 65). The contracting procedures and payments procedures were at variance with standing orders and orthodox accounting procedures and not properly costed and based on a business plan that was speculative. They lacked evidence of market research or of consultation with suppliers and hospitals and were in any case prepared by the contractor rather than WMRHA.

WMRHA had no clear strategy plan or monitoring process against which to supervise the developments. Senior management failed to monitor what was happening or to report to the board while still authorizing payments and contracts in contravention of agreed procedures. There was no effective, continual financial or management information system, no clear reporting mechanism, no clear rules on delegated responsibility, and no internal management control over the allocation and monitoring of resources.

Such weaknesses were evident elsewhere within WMRHA. Quality assured business services (QABS) was the vehicle for a £0.75m management buyout of the RHA's management services board (an entity known as MSD), which provided forecasting, budgeting and manpower control management services. WMRHA did not know MSD's financial position prior to the sale and therefore the management buyout team's business plan could not predict likely turnover. Other potential bidders for MSD had withdrawn because of this unpredictability and any likely financial liability that might arise from the sacking of any of the MSD staff who would have to be taken on under terms and conditions analogous to those of their WMRHA employment. QABS went into liquidation within 22 months, still owing the WMRHA 20 per cent of the purchase price and owing the DHAs nearly £1m in pre-payments for commissioned work. Again the WMRHA had not followed its own procedures: a committee empowered to review the sale and the acceptability of the buyout produced no minutes or working papers; did not value the business; failed to charge the new company 'all the costs associated with running a commercial company' (Committee of Public Accounts 1992–3, Minutes of Evidence: 78); committed itself to a turnover guarantee 'set at an unrealistically high level' (Minutes of Evidence: 79); ignored evidence of a projected 'continued and rapid decline' in the use of its facilities at the time of sale (Minutes of Evidence: 79); and failed to verify the buyout business plan's claims for a dramatic increase in non-RHA work.

When asked by CPA about the various issues – 'a dubious sell-off', £10m of lost resources, money diverted to 'pursue the personal aspirations' of a senior manager, 'fraudulent use of public money', undeclared outside activities, and confidential golden handshake packages – Sir Duncan Nichol, then chief executive of the National Health Management Executive, replied that 'I have already made it very clear just how seriously I regard these matters. The point that I have been trying to get across is that we are determined that the lessons should be fully understood' (Committee of Public Accounts 1992–93b, para. 602).

Getting the point across: the NHS Executive and the corporate governance task force

The cases described in the previous section were a salutary lesson for the NHS Executive which, either directly or through its corporate governance task force, and drawing on the 1992 Cadbury Report on Corporate Governance (intended to provide for organizational procedures and controls to prevent the recurrence of the financial scandals perpetrated by senior management in the City), produced a series of publications and instructions for the NHS. The documents covered:

- Standards of business conduct for NHS staff (NHS Management Executive 1993): this was reissued in 1993 for circulation to appropriate staff. It covered gifts, hospitality, conflict of interests, private dealings with suppliers, favouritism in the award of contracts, confidential information and outside employment, and included the Institute of Purchasing and Supply's ethical code.
- Internal controls (NHS Executive undated): this report outlined the control environment. It stated that it should include: an audit committee; documented internal control procedures; an independent internal audit function; published standing orders, standing financial instructions and a code of conduct; effective human resource development (HRD) and staff appraisal policies; and the imposition of sanctions for failure to observe the controls or to implement recommendations from internal or external audit. The environment would be devised after a risk assessment exercise, led by the board and involving all staff, that identified levels of risk for procedures and activities, and proposed appropriate controls (for example, from separation of duties to control on physical access). The new systems would be designed for and communicated to all staff; compliance and monitoring would be the responsibility of management, internal audit and external audit, but particular responsibility would also lie with the chief executives, the directors of finance, and non-executive directors on audit committees.
- The role of director of finance (NHS Management Executive 1994): this report described the responsibilities of directors of finance because of the pivotal role that the finance function had for 'sound financial management, probity and value for money' (NHS Management Executive

1994: 1). A director's responsibility included: corporate management; public accountability and stewardship; financial management; management of the finance directorate; an ability to ensure that the board and chief executive do not 'stray from the straight and narrow' (p. 9). He or she should be prepared to 'stand up and be counted' (p. 9) in such matters as complying with internal controls, ensuring adequate levels of internal financial control, collaborating with external audit, and ensuring proper relations with suppliers and rigorous monitoring of outposted or contracted-out services.

- Code of conduct and code of accountability (Department of Health 1994): the codes iterated that public service values – accountability, openness and probity – lay at the heart of the NHS. The code of conduct was made mandatory for all board members, and all staff were to 'subscribe' to its principles. It required that annual reports should be issued, and should be clear, comprehensive and balanced. Each board should have a public register of interests; each board member should have any potential conflict of interest recorded in board minutes before withdrawing from meetings. Hospitality, and particularly that involving suppliers, should be used circumspectly and, where appropriate, be formally recorded. There should be procedures for dealing with internal complaints or concerns. The code of accountability listed the various responsibilities for chairs, executive directors and non-executive directors. Collectively, boards were responsible for financial stewardship, high standards of corporate governance and the establishment of audit and remuneration committees. The codes were accompanied by guidance in April 1994 which detailed: the purpose, role and composition of audit committees; the committees' relations with internal audit and external audit; the remit and functions of remuneration committees (including best practice on 'properly defensible' remuneration packages); the differentiation between delegation of decision making and those decisions (such as standing orders, significant items of capital expenditure, appointment and remuneration of key staff, and audit arrangements) which were reserved for the board; financial reporting and annual reports; and declaration and registration of interests (including information on what should be considered a 'relevant' interest).

- NHS internal audit standards (NHS Executive 1995a): this handbook sets out nine standards for internal audit. They are: objectives; independence; staffing and training; relationships; due care; work planning; evaluation of the internal control system; evidence collection; and reporting and follow-up. It describes responsibilities in terms of malpractice, and the relations of internal audit with management, the audit committee and the external auditor.

- Audit committee handbook (NHS Executive 1995b): this handbook sought to expand on the role of audit committees in ensuring 'an environment of openness, honesty and integrity' (p. 2). It described the procedures that should be in existence, the system for internal control, reporting arrangements, the activities of internal and external audit, annual audit planning, and expected good practice.

Additionally, the NHS Executive has revised and issued an internal audit manual, issued model standing financial instructions, required each health authority and trust to designate the chief executive as the accountable officer (and sent a memorandum detailing proper stewardship of public funds and assets), and agreed with the Audit Commission that the latter place increased emphasis in probity in its audit work. The Audit Commission, whose manual on preventing and detecting fraud and corruption in the NHS was published in 1997 (Audit Commission 1997), had already conducted a general study on probity in the NHS in which it had indicated that it intended to encourage trusts to produce an anti-fraud and corruption strategy and response plan (Audit Commission 1994). These are now required from trusts, and usually explain what the trust's policy is on fraud and corruption and why it should be reported and investigated, before laying down procedures and personnel to be involved in the event of the receipt of complaints or allegations. Each trust's response plan should describe what types of action or behaviour are unacceptable or illegal, to whom suspicions should be reported, how internal inquiries will be managed, when external agencies may be involved, how preventative measures may be pursued and what sanctions are available to the trust.

Culture, change and consequences

In some trust strategies there is now an emphasis on culture and openness in the organization. Codes and standards, control environments and monitoring are only part of what the Audit Commission describes as an ethical environment (Audit Commission 1993) in which there are a number of components, including: an acknowledgement at senior level of the seriousness of the threat of misconduct; the need to act decisively against those who breach regulations or laws; corporate reviews and management self-assessment of prevention measures; public relations strategies to ensure cases are not presented negatively; careful staff recruitment; encouragement and protection of those who voice suspicions as well as a demonstrable linkage with consequential actions; awareness training; clear staff responsibilities and reporting arrangements; use of audit committees in risk assessment; effective internal procedures or staff for inquiries; standing links without outside agencies; full use of technology to analyse information, contracts and so on; developing best practice procedures; and sharing experience with similar organizations. Such components are themselves only part of the 'best practice' approaches to dealing with fraud and corruption

---

Box 7.1 Components of the ethical environment

Awareness of the law
On corruption
On computer misuse
On fraud or theft

Existence of internal rules
On register of interests
On conflict of interest
On disclosure
On standing orders and financial regulations
On codes of conduct
On disciplinary policy

Policies on staffing
Recruitment policy, including references
Regulations on canvassing
Open promotion and rewards procedures

Policies on decisions and procedures
Transparency and quoracy of decision making
Open access and communication
Formal recording
Instructions on expenditure and contracts

Prevention and detection plans
Guidelines on dealing with private-sector contractors
Effective and accessible management and financial information systems
Scrutiny or audit committees
Internal audit and external audit integration
Fraud response and contingency plan with designated and trained staff
Hotlines and/or ombudsman
Awareness training
Overt commitment of senior management

Source: Adapted from Audit Commission (1993); Audit Commission (1994) and Audit Commission (1997).

---

that seek to minimize opportunity and incentive while increasing the risk of detection and punishment. Box 7.1 provides a synthesis of the various aspects that any organization would need to address in order to minimize opportunity and concealment.

Such approaches acknowledge that procedures and controls are increasingly important as the traditional assumptions about public service values and standards appear to be somewhat compromised by the impact of some of the less welcome aspects of NPM, particularly in relation to management attitudes and organizational culture (Doig 1995). Within the NHS the corporate governance task force's own survey of 2600 board members reported that attitudes to probity were not uniform and that 'a substantial minority' of members would condone otherwise unacceptable behaviour in certain circumstances (including those relating to contract information and following standing orders) (West and Sheaff 1994: 29). In findings that the survey regarded as 'highly statistically significant' (p. 29), those with the most permissive attitudes were those who were executive directors, many of whom had 'gained the majority of their previous work experience within the NHS' (p. 29). This attitude appears to exist because:

> many managers in the NHS perceive a tension between following proper procedures and 'getting things done'. Indeed, the whole ethos of the NHS following the introduction of general management in the 1980s was one of many interpreted as 'business-oriented', 'risk-taking' and 'go-getting'. Such attitudes . . . were a deliberate move away from the image of the traditional, safe, risk-averse 'administrator' concerned with correct procedures and protocols.
>
> (Audit Commission 1994: 52)

Case study 3: the Yorkshire Regional Health Authority

Such attitudes were particularly noticeable in the 1996 report on the former Yorkshire RHA (National Audit Office 1996) which was later to be described by one member of CPA as 'a rogue management who were a law unto themselves' (Committee of Public Accounts 1996–97: p. 233), involved in what another member described as 'a catalogue of deception and greed and rule bending and rule breaking' (p. 264). Brought to the attention of the new RHA – Northern and Yorkshire RHA – by the district auditor, the allegations were the subject of an inquiry set up by the NHS Executive chief executive. The allegations concerned: 'irregular payments of relocation expenses amounting to £447,847' (p. 3) in advances on salaries or payments to cover losses on house sales; unauthorized appointment transfers intended to enhance redundancy settlements; unauthorized purchase or leasing of vehicles; payment of at least two chairmen through private companies; avoiding employer's national insurance contribution payments; the letting of a 'flawed' contract without tender to an American consultancy with a substantial prepayment, for which no value was received; an attempted land development with a private-sector company; a joint venture tender for waste incineration with a private-sector partner where there was no competitive tendering, no approval from the NHS Executive for the financial arrangements, an overlong contract and advice given to the RHA by a consultancy subsidiary of the partner; the disregard of financial regulations by a senior manager; the award of contracts by an executive director to their spouse, where there was a failure to declare an interest and the intention of the director to deliver one of the contracts on retirement; outsourcing of a number of services that bound the successor RHA to their continuation and which were likely to cost substantially more than if the work had been retained in-house; excessive hospitality; and reimbursement for untaken leave.

The later CPA report (Committee of Public Accounts 1996–97) fleshed out some of the details: the £695,000 spent on functions and dinners at Yorkshire hotels during two years (and its concealment in the accounts); the failure to ascertain, or follow, the rules on cars and payments; the details of the terms of reference of the American consultancy (including the time actually spent working in the RHA, as well as the provision of free accommodation and cars); the conflict of interests in relation to decisions on payments to senior managers by themselves or colleagues; and the failure to secure advantageous arrangements in joint ventures with the private sector. Of equal concern was the culture that senior management claimed lay behind their conduct. The National Audit Office report noted that two senior figures involved argued that, in one case, his judgement took precedence over the regulatory framework and that 'the new climate in the NHS at the time justified adopting an approach in which the highest priority was to ensure that problems were solved, even if the rules were bent or broken in the process' (National Audit Office 1996: 12.19), while, in the other case, she was acting 'within the entrepreneurial culture which appeared to be sanctioned by senior NHS management at the time' (p. 20).

Throughout the report senior management argued that it was the responsibility 'for the management on the spot' to make its own decisions rather than refer them to the NHS Executive (p. 21) and that it was known 'from personal experience' that many other authorities 'were already following novel or non-standard procedures' (p. 23). In the view of the NHS Executive inquiry, the RHA had 'an entrepreneurial culture where following the regulatory framework was seen as secondary to achieving results' (p. 57) and where local management claimed that the regulatory framework was being relaxed to, as one senior manager later told the Committee of Public Accounts, to give them 'space to achieve change quickly through the exercise of managerial discretion' (Committee of Public Accounts 1996–97: paragraph 94).

The Committee report was scathing about both the results and the discretion – 'failures of governance of the most serious kind which have resulted in the loss to public funds of millions of pounds which should have been spent on treating patients' (Committee of Public Accounts 1996–97: paragraph 112) – while condemning both management and the board:

> we are appalled too at the failure of the senior managers of the former Authority to provide professional, informed and independent advice

to the Board on a number of personnel and contractual matters. We also consider that the Chairman and the Board of the former Authority must share the responsibility. We are concerned that the Chairman and non-executive members of the Board failed to monitor adequately the actions of senior managers.

(Committee of Public Accounts 1996–97: paragraphs 114–115)

The National Audit Office was happy with the remedial actions of the new Northern and Yorkshire RHA. These actions included: a new executive and non-executive management team; adoption of the new standing orders and standing financial instructions; revisions to delegated powers; and new policies on car leasing, hospitality and relocation expenses. The National Audit Office also noted that the NHS Executive's own inquiry believed that the NHS Executive's Corporate Governance proposals 'provided considerable reassurance that the events they had investigated were unlikely to be repeated' (National Audit Office 1996: 60). Nevertheless the Committee of Public Accounts expressed concern that such changes lacked teeth and would continue to be less than effective if, as in the case of the Yorkshire RHA, 'staff can avoid repaying money that they have improperly received and can escape disciplinary action simply by moving to a different part of the National Health Service' (Committee of Public Accounts 1996–97: paragraph 116).

Conclusion: new cultures and more culture shocks?

The speed and direction of devolved managerial autonomy, together with the promotion of an entrepreneurial culture and of privatization as a goal for public-sector organizations, have raised questions about: the vulnerability of public-sector organizations; the weakening of the public sector ethos; the impact of private sector perspectives within a public sector context; the consequences of change as parts of an organization change in different ways at different times; the inevitable balance between public service and personal benefit; and the implications of change on existing but ill-defined relationships of accountability, monitoring and control. The three RHAs discussed in the case studies lacked clear strategy plans or monitoring processes for robust financial management through which to supervise major organizational and capital developments. Senior management failed to monitor what was happening or to report to the board while authorizing payments and contracts in contravention of agreed procedures. There were no effective, continual financial or management information systems, no clear reporting mechanisms, no clear rules on delegated responsibility and no internal management control over the allocation and monitoring of resources.

Box 7.2 Summary of the 1994 CPA report

Failures	Checklist for reform
Inadequate financial controls	Proper systems and procedures
Failure to comply with rules	Clear responsibility
Inadequate stewardship of public money and assets	Robust reporting arrangements
Failure to provide value for money	Trained staff
	Availability of information
	Regular expenditure programme appraisal
	Monitoring application of rules
	Accountability of decisions
	Open contract competition
	Clear disciplinary policy
	Effective risk assessment and project management
	Avoidance of conflict of interest

Source: Adapted from Committee of Public Accounts (1993–4).

Subsequently, as a result of the disasters they had visited upon themselves, the RHAs have taken steps to put in place review and monitoring procedures while the NHS Executive has continued to stress its commitment to the control environment. Inevitably other departments, NDPBs and other public sector organizations have stressed the action that they had taken or intended to take after evidence of mismanagement and poor stewardship of public funds has come to light (Doig 1995). In its 1994 report the CPA proposed a checklist of controls that were expected to be in place and operationally effective (see Box 7.2).

Nevertheless, procedures and controls are only a part of the means to deal with the circumstances which give rise to mismanagement and inefficiency and which may lead to fraud, corruption and conflict of interest. What matters at the end of the day is the integration of attitude and culture with the procedures and the controls. The latter are not effective without the appropriate organizational culture and individual commitment. This means addressing the circumstances of the changes which have introduced into NPM an implicit, and sometimes explicit, view among some public officials that, as T. Dan Smith once put it, public service should be combined with a 'piece of the action' (Doig 1984: 356). This view – that public managers should be able to decide for themselves their entitlement to the same types of benefits that are available to their private-sector counterparts – takes NPM towards a new public entrepreneurialism where issues of public service and personal gain become blurred, and public funds are used to pay for private-sector style perks and benefits of office (Doig 1997b).

The NHS Executive (1996) has now moved on to 'controls assurance' – the framework to identify and assess risks and then to confirm that they are being actively addressed – which has the double advantage that senior management understands the threats, as well as being aware of the responses, and can confirm their commitment to the implementation and effectiveness of the controls. The NHS Executive (1996) argues that controls assurance has developed for a number of reasons:

- The empowerment of NHS organizations 'within a national framework of accountability' (p. 1) where controls assurance ties this with the various corporate governance 'existing management control systems and procedures in the everyday world'.
- Following the Cadbury Report, company directors give reasonable assurance on the effectiveness of internal financial control which, in the NHS context, was seen 'as a useful way of encapsulating the whole purpose of management control and audit' (p. 2).
- The value of involving staff in the 'risk identification, management and control process' (p. 2).
- The need to provide the audit committee with the information to allow it to advise on controls and control systems that 'are in place to ensure that the direction set by the board is being followed by the organisation and are conducive to meeting the organisation's objectives' (p. 2).
- Expanding the role of internal audit into overall risk management, and harmonizing its work with that of external audit in seeking integrated control and review frameworks.

If successful, such a holistic approach will seek to mesh the personnel aspects with the procedural and control aspects – part of what is described as a 'decision tree' route (Manley 1992; Gorta and Forell 1995) to changing attitudes and to problem resolution, which also encompasses the whole organization and thus helps shape its culture (see Box 7.3).

While the current NHS view is that the concepts of control and risk are understood, and that an opinion should be given in the annual report on the effectiveness of internal control by the board, not all senior managers and board members have sufficient knowledge and training in terms of culture, procedures and control. They may not yet be able to give complete assurance as to whether their risks are properly managed. Furthermore, the culture shock of the three case studies is perceived as having now been addressed and resolved, while current risk is seen as externally-driven and largely non-financial, determined by such matters as litigation over clinical errors or the stability and fragility of the contract environment in which the NHS now finds itself. In its survey, the NHS Executive noted that, in terms of probity, 'overall issues of fraud, irregularity or error only account for a small fraction of the overall risks ... and that risks that are considered to be "probity" related are deemed to have the highest degree of

---

Box 7.3 The response route

Perceptions of conduct;
of the acceptability or justification;
of the status of those involved;
of the possibility of retaliation.

Focusing the response common understanding of conduct;
awareness of harmfulness;
avoid subjectivity or individual perceptions
of mitigating circumstances;
discourage collusion or ignorance;
promote common responsibility;
provide safe, effective and quick reporting
mechanisms;
ensure organizational change.

Building the decision tree the conduct in question is wrong;
the conduct should be reported;
the employee accepts that responsibility,
knowing:
– effective action will be taken;
– the action will be appropriate;
– the benefit of taking action outweighs the
cost of reporting;
– the organization is positive about both
reporting and taking action.

Source: Adapted from Manley (1992) and Gorta and Forell (1995).

---

control . . .' (NHS Executive 1996: 9). Whether controls assurance will provide the vehicle to match controls to culture is yet to be determined but, at present, the culture determines the controls, not vice versa, and, with the majority of those in the task force's own survey still in post, the NHS may find that controls assurance through controls alone may be insufficient to preclude future culture shock.

References

Audit Commission (1993) *Protecting the Public Purse, Probity in the Public Sector: Combating Fraud and Corruption in Local Government.* London: HMSO.
Audit Commission (1994) *Protecting the Public Purse 2: Ensuring Probity in the NHS.* London: HMSO.
Audit Commission (1997) *NHS Fraud and Corruption Audit Manual.* Abingdon: Audit Commission Publications.

Cabinet Office (MPO) and HM Treasury (1985) *Non-Departmental Public Bodies: A Guide for Departments*. London: HMSO.

Cabinet Office (1994) *The Civil Service: Continuity and Change*. Cm. 2627. London: HMSO.

Committee of Public Accounts (1992–93a) *63rd Report*, HCP 658. London: HMSO.

Committee of Public Accounts (1992–93b) *57th Report*, HCP 485. London: HMSO.

Committee of Public Accounts (1993–94) *Eighth Report*, HC 54. London: HMSO.

Committee of Public Accounts (1996–97) *Nineteenth Report*, HC 432. London: HMSO.

Department of Health (1994) *Corporate Governance in the NHS: Code of Conduct, Code of Accountability*. London: Department of Health.

Doig, A. (1984) *Corruption and Misconduct in Contemporary British Politics*. London: Penguin.

Doig, A. (1988) Advice, guidance and control: non-departmental public bodies and standards of conduct. *Teaching Public Administration*, 8 (2): 1–23.

Doig, A. (1995) Mixed signals? Public sector change and the proper conduct of public business. *Public Administration*, 73, Summer: 191–212.

Doig, A. (1997a) People or positions? Ensuring standards in the reformed public sector, in P. Barberis (ed.) *The Civil Service in an Era of Change*, pp. 95–113. Aldershot: Dartmouth.

Doig, A. (1997b) New public entrepreneurialism: changes to culture and conduct in the public sector. *Public Finance Foundation Review*, 14: 4–7.

Drewry, G. and Butcher, T. (1991) *The Civil Service Today*. Oxford: Blackwell.

Efficiency Unit (1988) *Improving Management in Government: The Next Steps*. London: HMSO.

Ferlie, E., Pettigrew, A., Ashburner, L. and Fitzgerald, L. (1996) *The New Public Management in Action*. Oxford: Oxford University Press.

Fulton Committee (1968) *Report*, vol. 1, Cmd. 3628. London: HMSO.

Gabe, J., Calnan, M. and Bury, M. (1991) *The Sociology of the Health Service*. London: Routledge.

Gorta, A. and Forell, S. (1995) Layers of decision: linking social definitions of corruption and willingness to take action! *Crime, Law and Social Change*, 23 (4): 315–43.

Government Observations on the Third Report from the Treasury and Civil Service Committee 1981–82 (1982). HC 236, Cmnd. 8616. London: HMSO.

Government Reply to the Seventh Report from the Treasury and Civil Service Committee 1990–91 (1991). London: HMSO.

Ham, C. (1985) *Health Planning in Britain*. London: Macmillan.

Harrison, S., Hunter, D. and Pollitt, C. (1990) *The Dynamics of British Health Policy*. London: Routledge.

Klein, R. (1989) *The Politics of the NHS*. London: Longman.

Manley, W. (1992) *The Handbook of Good Business Practice*. London: Routledge.

Margetts, H. and Willcocks, L. (1993) Information technology in public services: disaster faster? *Public Money & Management*, 13 (2): 49–56.

Metcalfe, L. and Richards, S. (1990) *Improving Public Management*. London: Sage.

Moon, G. and Kendall, I. (1993) The National Health Service, in D. Farnham and S. Horton (eds) *Managing the New Public Services*, pp. 172–87. London: Macmillan.

National Audit Office (1987) *Internal Audit in the Health Service*, HCP 314. London: HMSO.

National Audit Office (1996) *Inquiry Commissioned by the NHS Chief Executive into Matters Concerning the Former Yorkshire Regional Health Authority*, HCP 280. London: HMSO.

NHS Executive (undated) *A Guide To Improving Internal Control in the NHS*. Leeds: NHS Executive.

NHS Executive (1995a) *NHS Internal Audit Standards*. London: Department of Health.

NHS Executive (1995b) *Audit Committee Handbook*. London: Department of Health.

NHS Executive (1996) *Controls Assurance Project*. London: Department of Health.

NHS Management Executive (1993) *Standards of Business Conduct for NHS Staff*. Leeds: NHS Management Executive.

NHS Management Executive (1994) *The Role of the Director of Finance in the NHS*. Bristol: NHS Training Directorate.

O'Toole, B. J. (1995) Accountability, in J. Wilson (ed.) *Managing Public Services: Dealing With Dogma*, pp. 58–70. Eastham: Tudor.

Pollitt, C. (1993) Running hospitals, in R. Maidment and G. Thompson (eds) *Managing the United Kingdom*, pp. 188–212. London: Sage/OU.

Spurgeon, P. (ed.) (1991) *The Changing Face of the National Health Service in the 1990s*. London: Longman.

Treasury and Civil Service Committee (1989–90) *8th Report*, HC 481. London: HMSO.

Treasury and Civil Service Committee (1992–93) *6th Report*, HC 390. London: HMSO.

West, M. and Sheaff, R. (1994) Back to basics. *The Health Service Journal*, 24 February: 27–9.

Wilson, E. and Doig, A. (1996) The structure of ideology. *Public Money & Management*, 16 (2): 52–61.

Further reading

The literature on integrity and governance in the public sector is limited although there is an extensive literature on private sector ethics. The Audit Commission has produced reports on the role of audit committees and further reading may be found in: Manley, W. (1992) *The Handbook of Good Business Practice* (London: Routledge); Croall, H. (1992) *White Collar Crime* (Buckingham: Open University Press); Jones, P. (1993) *Combating Fraud and Corruption in the Public Sector* (London: Chapman & Hall); Albrecht, S., Wernz, G. and Williams, T. (1995) *Fraud* (Burr Ridge, IL: Irwin); and Hughes, O. E. (1994) *Public Management & Administration* (London: Macmillan).

eight

Performance measurement

David Gardner

Key learning objectives

After reading this chapter you should be able to:

1 Understand the essential features of performance measurement and its use for public services in the United Kingdom.
2 Appreciate the methodology and rationale of performance measurement.
3 Review critically its use and effectiveness in the provision of today's public services.
4 Develop your thinking on its potential use and evolution.

Introduction

From the 1970s onwards, there has been an emerging belief among those involved in the management and overseeing of public service provision in the United Kingdom (UK) that there is a need for objective measures of how organizations and their managers perform in delivering services to the public. Merely reporting on the extent to which budget allocations are spent in a particular financial year is now considered inadequate. The scrutiny under which public service managers find themselves, in a regime where government and its agencies require positive justification for services to remain in the public sector at all, has served to focus the minds of public service managers on ways in which they can best demonstrate the effectiveness of their efforts. The financial management initiative (FMI), launched in 1982, developed these ideas in government departments (see Chapter 2).

Government agencies, such as the National Audit Office and the Audit Commission, have been proactive in stimulating initiatives in the development of performance measures and in their use, both within the management processes of public service organizations (PSOs) and externally, as a means of furthering public accountability through the mechanisms of *The Citizen's Charter*. After initial scepticism towards early, input-driven initiatives, performance measures are now widely regarded as valuable management tools. The new Labour government has placed great stress on 'best value' and performance measurement in the provision of public services.

This chapter will explain the reasoning behind the use of performance measures in the context of PSOs, and consider how they might be employed within them or by external agencies in pursuit of accountability. It will evaluate critically alternative approaches to developing practical and useful performance measures and present a methodology for their deployment. Finally, it will discuss the operational difficulties that might be encountered in developing and using performance measures, and provide advice on how these difficulties might be avoided.

Performance measurement rationale

In explaining the need for performance measurement, it is first necessary to describe how it arises out of the notion of 'value for money' (VFM) in public spending, and then, how it has an important role in demonstrating accountability by public service organizations and their managers.

Performance measurement derives its underpinning primarily from the concept of VFM which became rooted in public service management thought in the mid-1970s. Rouse (1993: 61) defines VFM as '... the economic acquisition of resources and their efficient utilisation in the realisation of the purposes of the organisation'.

Modern writers interpret this concept as implying the achievement of the '3 Es', i.e. economy, efficiency and effectiveness. Economy is the measure of input and involves the acquisition of resources of a defined, appropriate specification at the least cost. Efficiency measures the relationship between input and output and involves maximizing useful outputs (services) from a defined and quantified level of resource input, or minimizing the quantity of resources consumed in producing a defined output. Effectiveness is the measure of output or impact. It involves measuring the extent to which output from a defined activity achieves the desired result or policy objective of the organization. Drucker (1974: 45) has stated that '[economy and] efficiency are concerned with doing things right. Effectiveness is doing the right thing'.

Effectiveness is the most difficult to measure and account for of the three. Measuring economy and efficiency tended to be tackled first in the

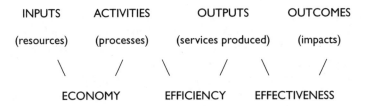

Figure 8.1 VFM concepts
Source: After Rouse (1993: 63).

development of performance measures because of the very real, practical difficulties of objectively defining and measuring effectiveness. The relationship between the '3 Es' is shown diagrammatically in Figure 8.1.

All three approaches to measuring performance are relevant and important individually and collectively. Some writers, notably Bovaird *et al.* (1988) add a fourth 'E', equity, which refers to the justice and fairness of processes and outcomes. However, in terms of the formal, practical application of performance measurement in public service organizations, the '3 Es' dominate.

Accountability is the need to demonstrate achievement to someone else, and to provide a reliable and meaningful account of how achievement came about. Accountability demands hard information about various aspects of performance, which is where measures of the '3 Es' are vital. In 1968, the Fulton Committee commented that accountable management meant 'holding individuals and units responsible for performance measured as objectively as possible' (p. 51). Three types of accountability are relevant here:

- Financial
- Managerial
- Political

Financial accountability demonstrates the lawfulness, probity, completeness and accuracy of an organization's actions. In private business, the need for this is fulfilled by the profit and loss account. According to the Audit Commission (1988), making a profit or avoiding a loss is a convenient performance indicator which, in a single expression, covers efficiency, economy and effectiveness.

This measure is not normally available or suitable for public service organizations. In most, there is no equivalent flow of revenue resulting from sales to match with costs of causal inputs. Nevertheless, other indicators, surrogates for profit, show that this form of accountability is generally achieved even in the public sector, though this information may be of limited use where the user of the service has no alternative supplier to which to turn if performance is less than satisfactory. Even in private businesses, the fact that profit is not reported until well after the event may well imply a need for further indicators of performance for internal use.

Managerial accountability is seen as the vital supplement to financial accountability in the public sector. This is the key form of accountability as it means that public service organizations are required to show that they have achieved their policy objectives while demonstrating attainment of the '3 Es'. According to Day and Klein (1987: 27), it means 'making those with delegated authority answerable for carrying out agreed tasks according to agreed criteria of performance'. The setting up of the Audit Commission in 1982 with its specific VFM responsibilities for local government was seen as a major step towards the delivery of managerial accountability.

Political accountability represents a more far-reaching form of accountability. It involves organizations being required to justify their decisions in terms of values currently supposed to characterize stewardship of citizens' interests (Pollitt and Harrison 1992). This is a very imprecise form of accountability as peoples' interests collectively are very difficult to define with precision.

Hinton and Wilson (1993) provide a comprehensive set of definitions of types of accountability, should the reader require further clarification, though they absorb financial into managerial accountability. For the purposes of this chapter, it is more appropriate that a distinction between the two is made.

Since the mid-1970s, there has been growing recognition in PSOs of the need to improve performance and to demonstrate improvement objectively to government and the public. Managerial accountability and VFM have been given considerable emphasis, and organizations have been encouraged to develop ways of communicating the achievement of VFM. Externally, statutory audit requirements applied to many PSOs now specifically include a need to report on the achievement of VFM. *The Citizen's Charter* publication and disclosure requirements now oblige PSOs in many parts of the public sector to generate and broadcast VFM and performance information. The accountability disciplines that all of this imposes on a PSO mean that its managers must be sensitive to measures of their performance. Measures are therefore widely used to appraise performance and to assist a PSO in achieving its external accountability targets as well as its policy objectives.

A source of potential confusion arises over the terminology used in the measurement of performance. The literature freely refers to both performance measures and performance indicators as though the terms are completely synonymous and interchangeable. While they are similar in meaning, performance measures imply greater precision than do indicators and are used where performance can be measured *exactly*. Burningham (1992) uses the analogy of employing performance measures as 'dials' or 'gauges'. An example here might be that a school has spent 80 per cent of its teachers' pay budget 75 per cent of the way through the financial year, suggesting that adjusting economies might be implemented. On the other hand, performance indicators should be used where there is a need for a warning signal, an alarm bell to alert management to the need for further consideration or analysis. An example might be an indicator that cost per pupil at one school is three times that at another. It doesn't necessarily indicate that the school is three times as wasteful, but flags the need for further investigation to provide an explanation. Despite these definitions, usage blurs the distinction.

Use of performance measures

It has been implied above that performance measures are of use within organizations and externally. In other words, they have uses at two levels, internal and external.

Internal usage involves accountable managers using performance measures and indicators to assist in:

- Policy planning.
- Control processes.
- Resource allocation decision making.
- Monitoring the achievement of objectives.

Jackson (1988: 12) argues for operational and strategic uses, stating that:

- they help to improve management practice;
- they increase the accountability of management;
- they provide a basis for policy planning and control;
- they provide essential management information by enabling activities to be monitored at several levels in the organization to confirm that the intended outcomes of various decisions are being achieved;
- they provide information for ex-post strategic post-mortems when policies and management practices and methods are reviewed;
- they can provide the basis of a staff appraisal system.

Burningham (1990) states that performance measures have a control and development role in that they identify opportunities for corrective action and are part of the learning cycle in a process of intervention and management change to improve performance. Jackson (1988: 9) observes that: 'High performance management requires a framework that enables a systematic approach to problem solving – one that will aid policy and priority formulation, implementation, monitoring and control'. He goes on to explain that:

Defining goals helps set priorities and helps senior managers to understand how the whole organisation fits together in delivering final output. Defining objectives, goals and targets assists in motivating individuals. Unless goals are clear, resource allocation tends to be arbitrary and the outcome of internal politics. If individuals know they have successfully achieved goals, morale is improved.

(Jackson 1988: 9)

Gould and Campbell (1987) specify the requirements for performance management:

- Managers at all levels should have clear objectives.
- Emphasis should be on outputs and outcomes with regard to specific objectives, not activities.
- Objectives should be set as targets or measurable indicators against which to review and assess performance.
- Each person should know what is expected of them, and that they are responsible for specific results.

All of this requires a culture in the organization consistent with performance-driven management, 'an attitude of mind, a commitment to good practice by managers, officials and politicians', according to Butt and Palmer (1985: 22).

Rouse (1993: 67) said an essential prerequisite for performance management is:

the establishment of the objectives of the activity, unit or organisation, preferably structuring performance measurement in terms of a hierarchy of organisational objectives [a cascade]. Performance indicators which are used 'simply' because information is currently available but are unrelated to objectives, are at best irrelevant and at worst positively dangerous.

There needs to be an integration of performance mechanisms into the working practices and structures of the organization. All involved should know and accept the purposes of performance measurement and not feel threatened by it. What is needed is a 'commitment culture', a 'non-threatening, participative environment' (Rouse 1993: 67) to empower managers and motivate them to accept the ethos and practices of performance management.

Further, managers need to be able to influence the performance indicators they are responsible for, and be assured that they are achievable by actions within their normal work remit. This means that contingencies will need to be built into targets to allow for changes outside the manager's control, though they should not be so flexible that they provide an excuse for poor performance. The individual's contribution to performance against target needs to be measured with precision. This demonstrates the need for information systems to be developed that are consistent with performance measures and to provide such information. Organizations need to be aware that this will mean incurring significant additional costs to be offset against the potential benefits of better performance.

Since the mid-1970s, there have been a number of experiments in changing the structure of incentives within organizations. Many have involved variations from the incremental budgeting arrangements that have been a traditional practice in most PSOs and which are predominantly input-based and lack a complete scrutiny of the budget content. Examples include programme or output budgeting (sometimes referred to as PPBS: planning, programming budgeting systems), identifying the cost of all the organization's financial objectives and phasing their achievement, and zero based budgeting (ZBB); regular scrutiny of the total budget in terms of the organization's aims. Other experiments have included:

- The devolution of decision making from the centre of organizations by establishing smaller more accountable units within them with delegated responsibility for finance and overall performance.
- The introduction of more supportable capital investment appraisal techniques (such as discounted cash flow, or cost benefit analysis which looks at the impacts of public choices on society as a whole – see Chapter 5).
- Systems of rewards for performance such as performance-related pay based on performance appraisal systems.
- The creation of internal markets in PSOs whereby they divide themselves into buyer and seller activities to stimulate competition within themselves (widely practised over the last 15 years).
- Systems of total quality management.

The need to improve management information systems and to develop schemes for measuring the performance of those who make decisions within such regimes is vital to every one of these initiatives.

External usage of performance measures derives from the increased emphasis ostensibly placed by government on public accountability and the need to empower the public. The aim appears to be to provide those outside the organization – the 'stakeholders' in the organization's work, including auditors, commentators, pressure groups and the press – with a basis for judging the performance of the organization and its managers for the benefit of the public/electorate (although it should be seen in the context of the move in the 1980s and 1990s, in reality, away from direct accountability with the delegation of decision making in many public services to government sponsored quangos). The most important development in this field has been the establishment of the National Audit Office in 1983, and in particular, the Audit Commission in 1982. Both are charged with the conduct of VFM audits, but the Audit Commission has been given a key role in the development of *The Citizen's Charter*, which necessitated the definition and publication of standards and measures of performance in many areas of the public sector.

While the aims of such a development are commendable, it is apparent that, if organizations are obliged to gear themselves towards the achievement of externally-defined targets, there may be incompatibility with internally-generated measures. The requirements for a commitment culture to ensure a sense of purpose and dedication towards the achievement of targets may be compromised. The privatization of state industries and the need to establish regulatory regimes to combat the monopoly power of such concerns has also created a need for the production of performance information for the consumption of external regulatory agencies such as OFGAS, OFFER and OFTEL (responsible for gas, electricity and telecommunications respectively), together with the public and the media. This too may create conflicts of priorities if the regulated industries have their own internal performance management and measurement arrangements.

In performing their internal and external roles, performance indicators support a kind of surrogate competition. League tables can be used to rank providers according to performance, across departments or organizations. Through the power of publicity, they can exert pressure for improvement. However, a single set of indicators may not serve both roles effectively, as user needs may differ significantly. The public sector lacks the measure of profit or loss, available to the private sector, which is often held, though wrongly, to be able to encapsulate in a single figure all aspects of measuring performance for all interested parties. For public services, Jackson (1988: 11) advocates the use of a 'complex mosaic of indicators' reflecting different aspects of a PSO's activities. This is more realistic as, in the public sector, there is no such thing as a perfect set of indicators serving both roles (though this may be said of the private sector also).

Developing performance measures: alternative approaches

In order to make performance measures useful, it is necessary for them to be produced in such a way that the performance they measure can be compared with a possible ideal, as portrayed in an achievement plan (Butt and Palmer 1985), with the result expressed as an amount of difference or variance. Comparisons can be made in a number of ways:

- Comparison between a PSO and other organizations.
- Comparison between a PSO's performance one year compared with previous years.
- Comparison of a PSO's actual performance with a predetermined standard or target.

A popular way is to compare performance in one PSO with other similar PSOs or with similar organizations in the private sector. Examples drawn from local government include comparative detection rates by police authorities and examination pass rates by schools and local education authorities. Comparisons can be made between providers or between one provider and a national average, or benchmarks such as those developed by the Audit Commission, government departments and CIPFA (Chartered Institute of Public Finance and Accountancy). They serve to flag areas of concern where further investigation or action is needed. Users are motivated either because they initiated the comparisons themselves (individual local authorities) or because they experience moral or political pressure when bodies like the Audit Commission publish comparisons referring to them directly. Those organizations performing below average should investigate why and take remedial action if necessary. There is a danger, however, that they will waste time and effort in explaining the shortfall rather than seeking improvement. Those performing above average may be less motivated to seek further improvement owing to complacency. There may be any number of reasons for deviations. In the case of school league tables, the classic explanation is the range of variation in the socio-economic background of children, resulting in a school located in a deprived area finding it much harder to attain a standard target than another from an affluent area. It is necessary for performance measures to be weighted to take account of legitimate factors outside the provider's control, so that it is the performance of the provider that is actually measured against its potential. In the above example, there needs to be a weighting developed to reflect the social background of pupils at a school so that the league tables reflect only the effective value added by the school's efforts and to enable judgements to be made about the relative performance of schools.

A second way of making comparisons of performance is by comparing performance in one year with the previous year or years. At least this approach should ensure that the figures are of a comparable order, even if they might be distorted by unusual occurrences such as where a prolonged period of hot weather increases leisure facility admissions. Such occurrences can usually easily be identified and allowed for in interpreting the comparison. A rather more serious defect is that this kind of information does not involve a comparison to any planned activity level or the organization's objectives and so is of limited use. It may be that the number of qualified nurses at a hospital may rise, indicating lower staff turnover and more effective recruitment and training, but the figures do not indicate whether this is consistent with the numbers that the hospital needs or has planned for.

Probably the most useful comparative measure is where actual performance is compared to an intended standard or target. The organization concerned is obliged to express its aims in terms of a stated set of targets. Examples include:

For a National Health Service (NHS) hospital trust:

- Percentage cost reduction with reference to economy targets.
- Target percentage bed occupancy rates.

For a passenger transport undertaking:

- Target number of passengers in a transport undertaking (an output or volume target).
- Percentage reduction in compensation payments made to dissatisfied customers (an efficiency target).

The difficulty is in developing tangible targets from the more general objectives of the organization. There is a tendency for those that can be developed more easily to dominate the less easily quantifiable ones, distorting management's priorities and actions. For example, school university admission targets might squeeze out measures of social education in a school. Jackson and Palmer (1988) classified performance measures into those that are:

- Prescriptive, linked to particular objectives (most unpublished measures for internal management).
- Proscriptive (negative indicators that show when performance is unacceptable).
- Descriptive (multiple statistics showing what an organization does, i.e. activities and throughput).

Performance measures should be seen as 'mirrors' reflecting various aspects of an organization's activities. Box 8.1 shows a set of qualities that Jackson (1988) identified for an ideal set of performance indicators.

Types of measure

Having considered the basis for comparing performance measures, it is now appropriate to examine the types of measure that have been developed to meet the need for demonstrating achievement of the '3 Es'.

Rouse (1993) groups economy and efficiency measures together to demonstrate that a defined volume and quality of service is provided with the minimum consumption of resources. He identifies four measures which meet this requirement:

1 Workload and productivity ratios.
2 Time targets.
3 Utilization rates.
4 Unit cost indicators.

Box 8.1 Ideal performance indicators

Performance indicators should be:

- Consistent: definitions used to produce the indicators should be consistent over time and between units.
- Comparable: following from consistency it is only reasonable to compare like with like.
- Clear: performance indicators should be simple, well-defined and understood.
- Controllable: the manager's performance should only be measured for those areas that she or he has control over.
- Contingent: performance is not independent of the environment in which decisions are made, including the organization structure, the management style adopted and the uncertainty and complexity of the external environment.
- Comprehensive: do indicators reflect those aspects of behaviour which are important to management decision making?
- Bounded: concentrate on a limited number of key indices of performance, e.g. those which are most likely to give the biggest pay-off.
- Relevant: many applications require specific performance indicators relevant to their special needs and conditions. Do the indicators service these needs?
- Feasible: are the targets based on unrealistic expectations? Can the targets be reached through reasonable actions?

Source: After Jackson (1988: 12).

Workload and productivity ratios are used to measure the quantity of useful work performed by employees over a prescribed period of time. Examples might be: the number of outpatient cases seen per hour; or the number of emergency fire call-outs attended per week.

Time targets are used to measure the average amount of time taken to complete or undertake a defined quantity of work. Examples here might be: time taken by an ambulance to reach the scene of a distress call; or time taken to install a window frame of a defined size.

Utilization rates measure how much a service is used. Occupancy rates are the clearest illustrations of these, as applied to hospital beds, or school places.

Unit cost indicators measure the actual cost of delivering a defined unit of service. This is usually compared with a standard or target figure from another providing authority or over time within the same authority, or with planned unit costs. Examples are: cost per school place, cost per 1000 population of the fire service, cost per house completed, cost per 10 km. of cable. They are used to highlight activities or service elements where costs are unusually high or low, as a means of identifying areas where investigation of the cause of the rogue cost might be fruitful in generating recommendations which could bring about savings or better service.

However, Rouse (1993) is critical of the use of unit cost measures because:

- They do not show a great deal about performance; they only flag differences and as such are of little use for policy planning and control.
- They are measures of average cost, which rarely reflects marginal cost (the cost of an extra unit). This is vital information in deciding whether to vary the level of service provision. Managers need to know what the cost of reducing the service by 5 per cent might be, rather than the average cost of the service. Basing decisions on unit or average costs might result in likely savings being overestimated (ignoring the effect of continuing fixed costs) and wrong decisions being made. Furthermore, unit costs only measure financial costs, not opportunity cost (the cost to society as a whole). They would not recognize the cost or benefit to society in terms of congestion, pollution, property values, environment etc. of a new road development. They would only reflect construction costs, and may again lead to wrong decisions being made.

Rouse (1993) next goes on to look at effectiveness measures which are concerned with the extent to which the right services are provided. They measure outcomes in terms of organizational objectives and/or clients' changed welfare. The Audit Commission (1988) introduced the concept of 'service effectiveness' – a way of measuring the extent to which a service does what it sets out to do. It recommended that organizations ask 'Is the service getting to the right customers, in the right way with the right service, in keeping with stated policies?' It advocated using measures such as the amount and level of service delivered, opening hours and response times – very closely related to efficiency measures.

This interpretation of effectiveness contrasts sharply with the concept of user effectiveness propounded by Henkel (1992). This is a much more demanding measure which considers how far a service achieves what consumers want. It is concerned with notions of quality of service and has an output focus, based on consumer-determined standards (Thomson 1992). It seeks to measure the change in the customer's welfare state as a result of consuming the service. It judges a service in terms of the extent it meets customer expectations, not the extent to which it satisfies managerial or professional standards. It is very difficult to measure. In 1992 the Audit Commission argued that measuring cost and efficiency is relatively easy, but measuring quality and efficiency is much more difficult. According to Henkel, it may challenge resource allocation decisions and the distribution of power in designing and operating services, and hence may encounter some resistance.

The Citizen's Charter is based on the notion of customer-determined services, i.e. user effectiveness-driven services. According to Thomson (1992), its intent is:

- An overt and articulated commitment to quality, measured by clear and agreed criteria in standards of service delivery.
- An increase in the public visibility of people involved in public service provision.
- A commitment to continuous improvement in public services.
- An intention that PSO workers will aim for the best standards in delivering public services. PSOs will be changed into learning organizations, seeking continuous improvement.

Despite the difficulty in developing user effectiveness measures because of problems in establishing causal relationships between outputs and outcomes, when a range of influences can affect ultimate outcomes, several measures have been suggested:

- Throughput of clients.
- Level of customer complaints.
- Measures of added value.
- Measures of customer's willingness to pay.

Throughput of clients has been advanced, for example, in the number of housing repairs completed, or number of school meals provided. However, this is a crude measure of work performed which provides little direct indication of improved customer welfare. In order to measure welfare, greater ingenuity is needed. Such an approach might be to look at the level of customer complaints. This however necessitates the use of systematic market research into customer satisfaction levels in order to put complaints into the context of overall satisfaction. These are now being used increasingly by PSOs.

A further approach might be to conduct consumer satisfaction surveys designed to measure added value generated by a service in terms of changed welfare state. Experimental work is being carried out centrally by the Department for Education into value added in schools, though it is still at a very early stage. Finally, economists are looking at measures based on customer's willingness to pay as a proxy for customer satisfaction.

The Audit Commission has been very active in promoting VFM auditing and in developing performance measures and indicators for local government services. Since the 1992 Local Government Act, local authorities are required to do this to comply with the demands of *The Citizen's Charter*. The Commission publishes a number of profiles of local authority activities across a wide range of dimensions, including comparative costing profiles in which the cost of purchasing a well-defined item or cost of providing a specific activity is measured and compared for all local authorities in England and Wales. The Accounts Commission in Scotland performs similar work. Since December 1994, local authorities are legally required to publish performance data in accordance with the model format developed by the Audit Commission.

Box 8.2 VFM framework for a hospital building programme: an illustration of the way in which performance measures aimed at each of the '3 Es' might be integrated

Economy
The tendering, contract and project control procedures to establish how far the hospital and associated facilities has been built to specification, on time and at the lowest achievable cost or within approved cost limits.

Efficiency
Utilization of wards, beds, theatres and equipment; medical and administrative staff allocations and mix; integration of services; maintenance; management and resource allocation systems etc.

Effectiveness
Results in terms of, for example, reductions in patient waiting lists, increases in operations performed, improved diagnostic and treatment rates and (ultimately), improvements in health and quality of life, reduced mortality rates etc.

Source: After National Audit Office (1988) in Jackson (1988: 13).

Box 8.2 provides an early illustration from the National Audit Office of the way in which performance measures orientated towards effectiveness (service effectiveness in this case) might be dovetailed with those measuring economy and efficiency into a single integrated package.

Using performance measures: a methodology for internal and external use

Having considered the nature of performance measures or indicators, it is now appropriate to examine how they might be used. The methodology for their use will be discussed in turn from the standpoint of their use by:

- Internal management.
- Stakeholders/external users, in particular the general public.
- Internal and external auditors, acting on behalf of stakeholders.

The first category of user is the organization's internal manager. A variety of models have been put forward to explain how performance measures might fit into organizations' internal management processes. One, based on the Audit Commission's approach for local authorities, is elaborated upon below as a typical approach, although a simple 'input-output' model after Rouse (1993) has already been alluded to in defining the '3 Es' in the section 'performance measurement rationale' (see page 170) part of this chapter. It is a small step from this model to appreciate how performance measures of the kind considered earlier might be of value at each stage in the management process.

The Audit Commission's methodology (explained in Venables and Impey 1996: 409–10) starts with the organization defining its goals or vision in the form of a corporate statement of policy aims – a mission statement. Goals or aims are then disaggregated and cascaded down to managers at all levels to form a hierarchy of objectives. In undertaking this work of defining objectives, managers should be involved in a participative process of refinement. This is necessary for them to develop ownership of their individual strategic objectives by analysing the organization's mission and identifying the parts to which they might contribute effectively. They should learn from the organization's history of achievement as indicated by past performance measures.

The next step is to formulate a strategic plan to coordinate the achievement of the policy objectives. It should first involve the establishment of a suitable structure orientated to making management accountable. In a local authority, this should involve:

- Establishing the right committee structure.
- Defining the roles of the chief officers and the chief executive.
- Establishing a performance review committee.
- Making managers in each department responsible for each activity.

Performance measures or indicators should be structured in such a way as to facilitate this process of managerial accountability. Systems should be devised, making optimal use of available information technology (IT), to provide information to managers. Information should be relevant to the needs of services and departments. Other organizations' methods should be considered in arriving at an appropriate approach. Arrangements should be built in for generating performance measurement information regularly and in a way which best meets the needs of managers who have to demonstrate performance against objectives.

The organization's style or culture should be fully considered, and should be regularly reviewed by the organization's political and managerial leadership who should consult during this process. Questions to consider might be:

- Is delegation of decision making and problem solving carried out as far as possible ?
- Are steps taken to encourage continuous improvement? Is there a contingency reserve for initiatives?
- Are standing orders sufficiently flexible to allow for virements?
- Is there a system of rewards/encouragements for staff suggestions?
- Is there a process of consultation/participation with managers, supervisors and staff, especially over performance indicators?

- Are steps taken by line managers to reinforce the organization's commitment to serving the public well?
- Are there steps being taken to increase community involvement?

The strategic plan should ensure effective supervision, suitable staffing and adequate skills. In addition:

- Individual responsibilities should be clearly defined for all managers.
- There should be effective control systems.
- There should be the right staff in place to manage performance measurement.
- Supervisors should be trained.
- The performance of managers should be regularly assessed against agreed goals.
- Training and development needs should be identified and acted upon.
- There should be a system for rewarding exceptional performance, though difficulties in identifying an individual's contribution to improved delivery of a public service may militate against this. The risks of demotivating managers with a scheme which is divisive in its inability to separate individuals' contributions in a generally accepted way may be judged to be too great.
- Active consideration should be given to whether the organization recruits middle managers or trains its own. A responsible senior officer should review staff vacancies before posts are filled.

The strategic plan should be translated into regular operational plans. There should be an annual action plan for each major activity and each manager, drawing from experience of past performance as evidenced by performance measures. An annual budget should be produced and monitored, based on responsibility centres. The integration of performance measures or indicators into the budgetary process should be considered, and additional measures developed where appropriate.

Steps should be taken to monitor progress and performance against targets. Regular reports such as monthly budgetary control statements, staffing level reports, and overall performance measures should be produced. Variances should be identified and managers required to explain them and propose and take remedial action. A detailed analysis of trends and variations should be produced for the organization as a whole.

Finally, there should be a formal review process. An annual review of performance against plans should be carried out at all levels and performance reports should be produced. At an organizational level, the results should be available to the public. The review of the information generated by this process should form an essential part of the forward planning process both in terms of producing annual plans and in terms of the continual revision of the organization's long-term strategic goals.

The legacy of under-performance in public sector organisations today is widespread – frustrated staff, disgruntled stakeholders and a poor track record of fundamental improvements. Conversely, those who have unlocked the potential of performance measurement will attest to the benefits – motivated staff, satisfied stakeholders, and a demonstrable track record of continuous improvement. Indeed, the benefits can be far greater than most managers would believe without direct personal experience. A framework of objective-setting and review against visible indicators, and prioritised improvement initiatives effectively pulls-through everything else needed to achieve radical performance improvement. It enables people to create, rather than to react, and injects pace and method in the delivery of an organisation's strategic objectives.

(Meekings 1995: 12)

Meekings clearly endorsed the Audit Commission's model as a vehicle for using performance measurement to improve overall service delivery in public service organizations. However, research conducted by McKevitt and Lawton (1996) suggests that there is: '. . . a lack of attention paid to middle and junior management in the development and implementation of performance measurement systems and hence the lack of embeddedness of systems throughout the organisation' (p. 52). It appears that: '. . . performance measurement has been used as a top-down instrument of senior management control in both central and local government' (p. 51).

Unless issues of consultation, communication, information and feedback with those below the senior management level are addressed, the chances of performance measurement succeeding in improving organizational performance are severely impaired. McKevitt and Lawton (1996: 52) go on to say:

Top down implementation, combined with middle-manager disenchantment with the process, can mean that organisations show consistent inattention to the users of the services . . . Senior managers and politicians must seek active dialogue with the operating core of managers and professionals if effective and responsive performance measurement systems are to be designed and implemented.

The second category of user is the stakeholder or external user. The role of the external user of performance measures is typically defined by *The Citizens' Charter*, published by the then Conservative government in 1991 (Cmnd. 1599 1991), though it drew from earlier ideas in local government in the 1980s. It now represents a whole raft of accountability measures, extending across most public services, to which the Labour government would appear to be strongly committed. It sets out, service by service, to produce nationally-defined standards of performance (some require local standards too). Service providers are required to publish performance against them. The aim is to empower the consumer, by requiring publication of reports on achievement and using the power of publicity to focus public critical attention on the poor achievers. Public response and pressure through the media should serve to focus the minds of managers to seek ways of bringing about improvement. Additionally, in some services, the public are given the right of redress. For example, the *Passenger's Charter* provides for compensation to be paid to the customer if trains are significantly late. In principle, this should act as a financial stimulus for managers to get it right, provided that target times are not set excessively leniently so that they could be met without managers extending themselves (Wilson 1996).

The Citizens' Charter is in fact a large collection of charters, one for each service. In September 1995, there were 40 separate charters, for example: a *Patient's Charter*; *Parent's Charter*; *Jobseeker's Charter*; and a *Tenant's Charter*. See Box 8.3.

As an extension to *The Citizen's Charter*, the 1992 Local Government Act provided statutory powers for the *Charter* to operate in local government. The Act charged the Audit Commission with the task of developing a set of performance indicators which would 'facilitate the making of appropriate comparisons (by reference to the criteria of cost, economy, efficiency and effectiveness) between standards of performance achieved by different authorities and standards of performance achieved in different years' (Bowerman 1995: 173–4). It also gave to the Audit Commission the duty to require local authorities to publish such information and for the Audit Commission to make comparisons between local authorities and different years. In other words, they were to define the information needed to fulfil the public accountability role, to audit the information provided, to publish comparative information and to provide support and guidance to local authorities.

A draft list of indicators was produced for consultation in September 1992, and a definitive list of 77 indicators was published in December 1992. Additions were made in December 1993 bringing the total to 90 indicators requiring answers to 275 questions. Every local authority in England and Wales (a parallel arrangement was developed for Scotland) was required to measure its performance against the appropriate indicators and to publish details annually from 31 December 1994, together with explanations when needed. An illustration of the flavour of the published indicators is reproduced in Table 8.1.

The principles behind the local government indicators are:

- They should cover all areas perceived to be of interest to citizens.
- They should deal with cost, economy, efficiency, quality and effectiveness.
- They should lend themselves to comparison between local authorities.
- They should cover all the main services.
- There should be a degree of acceptance by citizens and service professionals that they represent a valid assessment of service standards.

Box 8.3 Published charters as at September 1995

England:

- Passenger's Charter
- Taxpayer's Charter (Inland Revenue)
- Traveller's Charter
- Parent's Charter
- Redundancy Payments Service Charter
- Jobseeker's Charter
- Tenant's Charter
- Patient's Charter
- Taxpayer's Charter (Customs and Excise)
- Courts Charter
- London Underground Customer's Charter
- Benefits Agency Customer's Charter
- Contributor's Charter
- Employer's Charter
- Child Support Agency Charter
- Charter for Further Education
- Charter for Higher Education
- Road User's Charter
- The London Bus Passenger's Charter

Scotland:

- Justice Charter
- Parent's Charter
- Patient's Charter
- Tenant's Charter
- Further and Higher Education Charter

Wales:

- Parent's Charter
- Patient's Charter
- Tenant's Charter
- Charter for Further Education
- Charter for Higher Education

Northern Ireland (NI):

- NI Charter
- Parent's Charter
- Charter for Patients and Clients
- NI Tenant's Charter
- Railway Passenger's Charter
- Charter for Social Security Agency Clients
- Training and Employment Agency Customer's Charter
- Royal Ulster Constabulary (RUC) Charter
- Bus Passenger's Charter
- Child Support Agency Charter
- NI Courts Charter

Source: After Citizen's Charter Unit, Office of Public Service and Science, in Wilson (1996: 46).

Table 8.1 Extracts from the Audit Commission's performance indicators, Wyre Borough Council, Lancashire, 1995–6

Collection of council tax	1994–5	1995–6
Net amount of council tax which Wyre should have received during year, excluding reliefs and rebates	£20,069,370	£20,522,545
Percentage of this that was received during the year	97.12%	97.13%
Net cost of collecting council tax per chargeable dwelling	£17.50	£17.00

Paying of housing benefit and council tax benefit	1994–5	1995–6
New claims for council tax benefit	3,033	2,933
Percentage of such claims processed in 14 days	94%	92%
New claims for housing benefit from local authority tenants	495	442
Percentage of such claims processed in 14 days	98%	92%
Successful new claims for rent allowance	1,456	1,469
Percentage of such claims paid in 14 days	98%	87%
Total number of benefit claimants	12,110	12,228
Gross cost of administration per claimant	£61.69	£54.37

Provision of services generally: net expenditure per head of population	1994–5	1995–6
Highways	£3.06	£3.00
Public transport	£3.46	£3.76
Environmental health	£5.59	£5.92
Planning and economic development	£4.83	£6.11
Refuse collection and disposal	£10.51	£9.82
Street cleansing	£3.79	£3.90
Sport and recreation	£13.67	£15.27
Administration of housing and Council Tax benefit	£7.19	£6.38
Collection of council tax	£7.53	£7.15
Other costs and services	£28.32	£30.02
Capital charges	£0.78	£3.03
Interest receipts	Inc £0.86	Inc £1.43
Government grants	Inc £2.65	Inc £2.77
Movements in reserves and balances	£5.83	Inc £0.13
Net expenditure	£91.05	£90.03

Percentage of net expenditure financed from:	1994–5	1995–6
Block grant and non-domestic rates	70.8%	69.8%
Council tax/precepts	29.2%	30.2%

Leisure and recreation	1994–5	1995–6
Net expenditure per head of population on swimming pools and sports centres	£1.88	£2.86

Table 8.1 Cont'd

Number of swims	298,839	313,499
Number of other visits	259,145	241,738
Net cost per swim/visit	£0.35	£0.54
Number of playgrounds which reach minimum standards	33	37
Number of sports pitches available to the public	31	27
Hectares of parks and open spaces provided or managed by Wyre	100.55	100.55
Net expenditure per head of population on parks and open spaces	n/a	£10.47

Refuse collection	*1994–5*	*1995–6*
Is household waste collected from back door of domestic properties?	Yes	Yes
Is garden waste collected free of charge?	No	No
Are appointments given for the collection of bulky waste?	No	No
Is bulky waste collected free of charge?	Yes	Yes
Are recyclable materials collected separately from household waste?	No	No
Is a direct line telephone service available eight hours per working day and is there an answerphone service which takes messages of complaint at all other times?	Yes	Yes
Are special arrangements made on request to help disabled people?	Yes	Yes

Reliability	*1994–5*	*1995–6*
The number of household waste collections which were missed per hundred thousand collections	n/a	79
The percentage of missed collections which were put right by the end of the next working day	99%	99%

Recycling	*1994–5*	*1995–6*
Tonnes of household waste collected	33,400	31,150
Percentage of household waste recycled	5.2%	6.38%

Expenditure	*1994–5*	*1995–6*
Number of households	44,701	45,062
Net cost per household	£24.44	£22.73

Inc: Income
n/a: Not applicable
NB Performance indicators still to be subject to external audit verification.

Source: Wyre Voice, Autumn 1996, Wyre Borough Council.

Up to November 1996, two sets of local authority indicators had been published together with comparative data by the Audit Commission covering all local authorities in England and Wales (and by the Accounts Commission in Scotland). Despite the enthusiasm of the Audit Commission for this task of informing the public, it is apparent that the reception of this information has been somewhat lukewarm. According to Vevers (1995: 17), the Commission's associate director responsible for their publication: 'The overall message from the public is that they are often initially reluctant to look at performance information. But when the individual indicators are brought to their attention, they begin to get interested'.

Langham (1996: 10), Camden London Borough Council's head of communication observed: 'If local interest in performance indicators was measured in terms of press coverage, it would rank somewhere between cats stuck up trees and mayors kissing babies. But it's not lack of effort by local authorities that gives them so little pride of place. Officers are hard at it for months before PI day'.

By way of illustration, she reported of the experience of Lewes District Council which had set up a special hotline when it published its performance indicators. It received six phone calls and five letters. The council's publicity and marketing officer was not impressed, especially since 89,000 people live in the district.

However, Langham also observed that a more important audience existed, namely council members. The performance indicator supplement in the *Local Government Chronicle* for 1996 points out that some improvements had been observed among those authorities which had returned below average performance in the 1995 performance indicators. However, there was concern that councils, through their members, were forming the view that 'maintaining an average performance indicates an acceptable standard of service' (*Local Government Chronicle* 1996: 1), and that significant numbers of authorities with performance indicators around the average were not actively seeking to improve.

It is clear from Vevers (1996) that some authorities have reacted very positively in incorporating published performance indicators into their internal processes for performance management, and in the setting of more detailed measures for internal use as in the Audit Commission's management model considered earlier in this chapter. Cambridge City Council provides a good example of how this might be developed: 'using them constructively, incorporating published PIs into quality management systems, seeing them as a starting point . . . using them to add to its management processes and service delivery' (Egan 1996: 8).

The development and bedding-in of such systems takes time and a commitment to changing the organisation's culture. To achieve a corporate approach we have involved staff in developing a quality management structure and holding workshops to arrive at a consensus. A PIs working group with representatives from each department meets regularly to exchange information and explore any problems that might have arisen. We hold regular training sessions for officers and members to ensure that everyone is clear about the objectives and processes of performance management.

(Egan 1996: 8)

The final model for utilization of performance measures is one developed for the use of internal and external auditors in seeking to protect the public interest. The National Audit Act 1983 and the Local Government Finance Act 1982 both require internal and external auditors (in central and local government) to consider the provision of VFM when conducting their regular audits. The local authority external auditor is required to report on the extent to which the authority has made safe and efficient arrangements for the achievement of VFM in the spending of public money. This responsibility is quite distinct from the organization's strategy for achieving the '3 Es'. The Audit Commission's Code of Local Government Audit Practice (Venables and Impey 1996: 409–10) states: 'The achievement of economy, efficiency and effectiveness depends on the existence of sound arrangements for planning, appraisal, authorisation and control of the use of resources. It is management's responsibility to establish these arrangements and to ensure that they are working properly'. From this, internal auditors are obliged to review these arrangements on management's behalf.

A typical programme for a VFM audit by a local authority external auditor might be as follows (after Venables and Impey 1996: 409–10):

1 Identify the organization's policy objectives.
2 Establish that the organization structure is appropriate to its activities: responsibilities, authority and accountability are codified.
3 Establish that line managers understand and implement policy as defined and intended by senior managers; that they plan, budget and control income and expenditure and are able to react to performance indicator information.
4 Review effectiveness of performance measures or indicators.
5 Examine the performance of each section of the organization against the organization's objectives.
6 Ensure that information reaching managers is reliable and adequate for monitoring results against performance objectives and standards to ensure that outstanding performance is encouraged and unacceptable performance is corrected.
7 Ensure monitoring of cost is effective.

The auditor's report should normally go to a performance review committee, an audit committee, or directly to the chief executive.

Performance indicators: problems in their design and use

It is clear that there are benefits to a PSO if it adopts an approach akin to the Audit Commission model with its management committed to a performance measurement-driven culture. However, going down this road is not without its difficulties, so it is useful now to consider some of the problems that have arisen in organizations that have adopted this approach to date.

- Performance indicators can distort an individual's motivation and behaviour if they are applied mechanically without considering the consequences. An example might be where a police force is motivated by a measure of the number of arrests per month. It might be expected that this could lead to an increase in the number of wrongful arrests.
- There is a serious risk that if only a narrow range of performance targets is set, managers will seek to achieve the target measures at the expense of wider aspects of service delivery, a process referred to by Rouse (1993: 73) as 'targetology'. A good example of this is where a hospital is required to achieve shorter waiting lists for defined operations and diverts resources from other aspects of service delivery to reach the target. There is also the risk that politically motivated targets might be set which distract managers from overall service delivery quality. The police, for example, might be given targets to address burglaries at the expense of child molesting or domestic violence, because doing so renders it easier to achieve an improvement in a headline-grabbing detection rate (Wilson 1995).
- A consequence of targetology is a tendency for decision makers to give priority to decisions aimed at short-term results at the expense of long-term issues: 'short-termism'. This might be particularly noticeable when a manager's career depends on short-term performance. The effect is likely to be underinvestment in innovation and quality.
- A further effect is that techniques become ends in themselves, in that achievement is measured in terms of the techniques used and not the results produced.
- Performance measurement depends on accurate and current information. A possible problem might be that information systems are not up to delivering what is required. In addition, an organization might not be prepared to meet the unavoidable extra cost of adding to information systems to generate the extra data, or greater accuracy or timeliness needed for performance measurement. Information needs to be relevant, simply presented and directly focused on the appropriate measures. It should avoid swamping managers with detail that is not required.
- A difficulty arises where a non-measurable performance area is deemed to be more important that measurable ones. An effect might be the oversimplification of the non-measurable area in order to devise something that is measurable to demonstrate attainment.

- VFM auditing can omit the customer/client perspective. It is necessary to be clear whose values should influence decisions: the organization, the user or the taxpayer. Performance measures satisfying the needs of the organization may be wholly inadequate in demonstrating that society's needs are being met. However, it is often very difficult to identify precisely who a public service organization's customers are, and what they want. Consider the prison service – does it serve the prisoner, the criminal's victim, the police or society as a whole? A private sector organization is much less likely to experience this difficulty.

- There is a very strong risk that political considerations might overturn a decision based on the logical, performance measurement-based evidence. 'Even if an optimal location algorithm tells you that the best place for a garbage dump is across the street from a congressman's house, I can assure you that it isn't going to be built there' (Savas 1972:). Nevertheless, politics does allow decisions to take on board the views of users and others with relevant opinions. Cold performance data should not be the only input into the decision-making process.

- A common weakness is that a performance measurement-based management system can be subverted by internal organizational politics. It is vital that such a system is fully integrated into the existing relationships in an organization, that the right climate exists with top management commitment to the principle, and a fully participative style accepted throughout the organization.

- One final problem area is the fact that over time, managers become more skilled in 'working the system' in terms of agreeing soft targets and being able to achieve them without extending themselves, resulting in a lower that expected improvement in performance. Pollitt (1989) called this 'gaming'. To overcome this requires the progressive development of training, and the performance information database, to supplement and develop the organization's culture.

Box 8.4 contains advice provided by Likierman (1993) on ways in which these pitfalls might be overcome in order that the benefits to be derived from making use of performance measurement might be felt.

Conclusion

Stewart and Walsh (1994: 45) provided an excellent summing-up of the fundamental problems in performance measurement in public service organizations and a pointer to the way forward:

> The development of performance-based management poses special difficulties for the public service. There is a tendency to focus on measurement, but that ignores the way quality needs to be judged in

---

Box 8.4 Performance indicators: early lessons from managerial use

Concept

1 Include all elements integrated into what is being measured.
2 Choose a number of measures appropriate to the organization and its diversity.
3 Provide safeguards for 'soft' indicators, e.g. quality.
4 Take account of accountability and politics.

Preparation

5 Ownership is vital: devise measures with people on the ground.
6 Build in counters to short-termism.
7 Ensure that measures fairly reflect the efforts of managers – precision is vital
8 Allow for uncontrollable items and perceived injustices.
9 Use the experience of other organizations.
10 Establish realistic levels of attainment.

Implementation

11 Provide for development time and for revision of indicators.
12 Link indicators to existing systems.
13 Measures must be easily understandable by those whose performance is being measured.
14 Choose proxy measures with caution, e.g. HM Customs and Excise use the street price of drugs as a proxy for their success.
15 Reassess internal and external relationships during introduction.

Use

16 Data must be trusted and correct.
17 Results should be used as guidance: interpretation is the key.
18 Feedback and follow-up are vital for credibility.
19 Trade-offs and complex interactions must be recognized.
20 Results must be user friendly.

Source: After Likierman (1993).

---

the public realm. The assessment of performance, when values can conflict, is necessarily a matter of judgement. Fully satisfactory measures of performance will shift as political debate develops. There is a need to recognise the imperfections and limitations of measures, and to use them as a means of supporting politically informed judgement.

It is very evident that a well-founded system of performance measurement, fully integrated into the management processes of a public service organization, and to which management at all levels are committed, can, in principle, provide a considerable stimulus to improved performance and service delivery. The practical pitfalls identified must first be addressed and overcome, but, if they are, such a scheme is to be commended. However, there must be serious doubts over the effectiveness and objectivity of schemes of externally developed and imposed performance measures and indicators as management tools. It would appear to be all too easy for them to be subverted for political ends, and used as devices for presenting a politically motivated picture, rather than serving as a means of demonstrating improved service performance, providing the stakeholder with a means of monitoring performance and taking action if it falls short of what the public might expect. In spite of this, the experience of local authorities such as Cambridge City Council (Egan 1996) demonstrates that such a system can be made to work.

References

Audit Commission (1988) *Performance Review in Local Government: A Handbook for Auditors and Local Authorities.* London: HMSO.

Audit Commission (1992) *Citizen's Charter Performance Indicators.* London: Audit Commission.

Bovaird, T., Gregory, D. and Martin, S. (1988) Performance measurement in urban economic development. *Public Money & Management*, 8 (4): 17–22.

Bowerman, M. (1995) Auditing performance indicators – the role of the Audit Commission in the Citizen's Charter Initiative. *Financial Accountability and Management*, 11 (2): 173–85.

Burningham, D. (1990) Performance indicators and the management of professionals in local government, in M. Cave, M. Kogan and R. Smith (eds) *Output and Performance Measurement in Government: The State of the Art*, pp. 124–42.

Burningham, D. (1992) An overview of the use of performance indicators in local government, in C. Pollitt and S. Harrison (eds) *Handbook of Public Service Management*, pp. 86–100. Oxford: Blackwell.

Butt, H. and Palmer, R. (1985) *Value for Money in the Public Sector: The Decision Maker's Guide.* Oxford: Blackwell.

Cmnd. 1599 (1991) *The Citizen's Charter: Raising the Standard.* London: Cabinet Office.

Day, P. and Klein, R. (1987) *Accountabilities: Five Public Services.* London: Tavistock.

Drucker, P. (1974) *Management: Tasks, Responsibilities and Practices.* New York: Harper & Row.

Egan, C. (1996) Fixing a course by flexible landmarks. *Local Government Chronicle Performance Indicators Supplement*, 22 March: 8.

Fulton Committee (1968) *The Civil Service*, vol 1: Report of the committee, Cmnd. 3638. London: HMSO.

Gould, M. and Campbell, A. (1987) *Strategies and Styles.* Oxford: Blackwell.

Henkel, M. (1992) The Audit Commission, in C. Pollitt and S. Harrison (eds) *Handbook of Public Service Management*, pp. 72–85. Oxford: Blackwell.

Hinton, P. and Wilson, E. (1993) Accountability, in J. Wilson and P. Hinton (eds) *Public Services and the 1990s: Issues in Public Service Finance and Management*, pp. 123–42. Eastham: Tudor.

Jackson, P. (1988) The management of performance in the public sector. *Public Money & Management*, 8 (4): 11–16.

Jackson, P. M. and Palmer, A. J. (1988) The economics of internal organization: the efficiency of parastatals in LDCs, in P. Cook and C. Kirkpatrick *Privatisation in Less Developed Countries*. London: Wheatsheaf.

Langham, L. (1996) An uphill battle to stimulate interest. *Local Government Chronicle Performance Indicators Supplement*, 22 March: 10–11.

Likierman, A. (1993) Performance indicators: 20 early lessons from managerial use. *Public Money & Management*, 13 (4): 15–22.

Local Government Chronicle (1996) Performance Indicator Supplement, introductory editorial comment.

McKevitt, D. and Lawton, A. (1996) The manager, the citizen, the politician and performance measures. *Public Money & Management*, 16 (3): 49–54.

Meekings, A. (1995) Unlocking the potential of performance measurement: a practical implementation guide. *Public Money & Management*, 15 (4): 5–12.

Pollitt, C. (1989) Performance indicators in the longer term. *Public Money & Management*, 9 (3): 51–5.

Pollitt, C. and Harrison, S. (1992) Introduction, in C. Pollitt and S. Harrison (eds) *Handbook of Public Service Management*, pp. 1–22. Oxford: Blackwell.

Rouse, J. (1993) Resource and performance management in public service organisations, in K. Isaac-Henry, C. Painter and C. Barnes (eds) *Management in the Public Sector*, pp. 59–76. London: Chapman & Hall.

Savas, E. S. (1972) How to make operations research fail in government without really trying. *Interfaces*, 4, August.

Stewart, J. and Walsh, K. (1994) Performance measurement: when performance can never be finally defined. *Public Money & Management*, 14 (2): 45–9.

Thomson, P. (1992) Public management in a period of radical change: 1979–1992. *Public Money & Management*, 12 (3): 33–41.

Venables, J. S. R. and Impey, K. W. (1996) *Internal Auditing* (4th edn). London: Butterworth.

Vevers, P. (1995) Have we got news for you. *Local Government Chronicle*, 23 June: 16–17.

Vevers, P. (1996) Aim to hit the service target bullseye. *Local Government Chronicle Performance Indicators Supplement*, 22 March: 4–5.

Wilson, J. (1995) Charters and public service performance, in J. Wilson (ed.) *Managing Public Services: Dealing with Dogma*, pp. 91–108. Eastham: Tudor.

Wilson, J. (1996) Citizen Major? The rationale and impact of *The Citizen's Charter*. *Public Policy and Administration*, 11 (1): 45–61.

Further reading

Frequent articles dealing with new developments in the design and use of performance measures or indicators can be found in *Public Finance* and *Local Government Chronicle* (weekly), and *Public Money & Management* (quarterly). For the most recent detailed analysis of local government performance indicators, the *Performance Indicators Supplements* issued with *Public Finance* and *Local Government Chronicle* are extremely useful.

part four

Key sectors

nine

Local government financial management

Christopher J. Pyke

Key learning objectives

After reading this chapter you should be able to:

1 Understand the scale and significance of the resources under the control of local government.
2 Explain the objectives and process of budget preparation in local government.
3 Understand how budgetary control is exercised in local government.
4 Explain the accounting framework within which a local authority prepares its financial accounts.
5 Explain the scope and content of a local authority's statements of accounts.

Introduction

During the last two decades local government has experienced unprecedented levels of change as successive Conservative governments sought to remould the role and scope of the public sector. Many of the policy initiatives from central government have been directed towards limiting and controlling the level of local government expenditure and taxation. In addition, there has been legislation forcing councils to expose services to private sector competition.

Local government has adapted by introducing new organizational structures for service delivery often based on market or quasi-market trading relationships. More 'business like' techniques and methods have been adopted, not least in the field of financial management. In addition the need for more financial information about the efficiency and effectiveness of local government has led to increased external reporting requirements and will become more important under the 'best value' regime (see DETR 1998).

This chapter examines how local authorities plan and control their financial resources internally and how financial performance is reported externally. The chapter begins with some background information which helps to define the scale and significance of the resources under local government control.

Background

The functions and structure of local government

All areas of Britain are divided into local authorities which are responsible for planning and delivering a wide range of local public services, including: education; personal social services; housing; highways; police; fire; museums and art galleries; libraries; planning; economic development; refuse collection; waste disposal; trading standards; and recreational facilities. Consequently, the management of local government is complex, not just because of the diverse nature of the services provided, but also because of the interaction with central government, the need to reconcile limited resources with local needs and the influences of party political organizations.

In April 1991 central government announced its intention to review the structure of local government in England, Wales and Scotland. The then Conservative government's stated preference was for more unitary (i.e. single tier) authorities to be created. In England, a local government commission was set up in 1992 to carry out the review on an area by area basis and to make recommendations for reorganization. However, in Wales and Scotland the government resolved to impose a structure of unitary authorities. As a consequence of the review the number of local authorities in the United Kingdom (UK) was reduced from 540 in 1994 to 482 in 1998 (Barnett and Carmichael 1997). The current structure now comprises the following:

- Unitary authorities: 32 Scottish districts, 22 Welsh districts, 26 Northern Ireland districts, 69 metropolitan districts and 46 English unitary authorities. This type of authority provides the majority of local services for its area. However, some services such as police, fire and transport coordination may be provided by joint boards.
- Two-tier authorities: these are predominantly in rural areas, and constitute 34 counties and 253 non-metropolitan districts which provide services between them. For example, responsibility for environmental planning is split between the tiers, with strategic planning such as the siting of a new

waste disposal facility being determined at county council level while the responsibility for the collection of waste rests at district council level.

Internal management

The internal management of local government is controlled by democratically-elected councillors, who represent the interests of local people on the council. The council will meet on a regular basis to consider recommendations from its committees (and sub-committees). Committees are at the centre of the decision-making process; they are where officers present their reports and give verbal advice to councillors, and where the detail of policy is debated.

The committee structure varies between local authorities, but they are usually organized around the major services, with a policy and resources committee responsible for coordinating policy-making and allocating resources (Mallabar 1991). The Local Government Housing Act 1989 established the principles for allocating committee and sub-committee places. The principles are that:

- not all seats should be allocated to the same political group;
- the majority of seats should be allocated to the majority party;
- the number of seats on ordinary committees which are allocated to each political group should be in proportion to the number of members of each group on the council;
- on outside bodies the council's representation should reflect the party balance of the council.

In addition to the elected political committee structure, a local authority will also have an officer management structure which will usually mirror the committee structure. At the highest level, a management board chaired by the chief executive will be responsible for the strategic management of the authority, reporting to the policy and resources committee. At departmental level, senior officers will form management teams to manage departments, implement service policy and advise councillors.

Local authority expenditure and financing

Local authorities, like most other large organizations, account for their use of resources through two separate financial accounts: a revenue account, which records the cost of running services, e.g. salaries and wages paid; and a capital account which records investment expenditure, i.e. expenditure which provides a long term benefit to the authority, such as the building of new school premises.

In 1996–7 local government was responsible for spending an estimated £75.8bn, rising to £76.1bn in 1997–8 (Ernst & Young *et al.* 1996). This is nearly a quarter of general government expenditure (GGE) and just over

Table 9.1 Local authority service revenue expenditure in 1996–7 (outturn prices)

Service	Revenue, provisional outturn 1997–8 (£m)	Analysis of service expenditure (%)
Education	17,976	40
Personal social services	8,385	18
Police	6,619	14
Fire	1,358	3
Other Home Office	879	2
Highways and transportation	2,084	5
Libraries, museums and art galleries	789	2
Parks and recreation	1,156	3
Planning and economic development	703	1
Waste management	1,146	3
Other services	4,306	9
Total service expenditure	45,401	100

Source: *Financial and General Statistics 1996/97*, CIPFA (1996a).

10 per cent of the gross domestic product (GDP) (estimated at £746bn for 1996–7). Just over 9 per cent (£7.3bn 1996–7) will be spent on capital investment, the remainder being revenue expenditure (Ernst & Young *et al.* 1996). Table 9.1 shows an analysis of local authority 1996–7 service revenue expenditure. It can be seen that the majority of expenditure is on the provision of school education (40 per cent), personal social services (18 per cent) and police (14 per cent).

Local authority expenditure is financed from three main sources which are:

1 Central government.
2 Council tax.
3 Sales, fees and charges.

Funding from central government accounts for nearly 83 per cent (CIPFA 1996a) of local government financing. The majority of this funding, 65 per cent (CIPFA 1996a), is in the form of grants, of which there are two main types:

1 The revenue support grant (RSG): this amounted to £20bn in 1996–7, equivalent to 40 per cent of total central government support for local authorities. This grant may be spent at the discretion of the local authority and is distributed by central government on the basis of assumed local service needs and taxable capacities. Those local authorities which have a high demand for their services are compensated with more RSG.
2 Specific grants: which the local authority must spend on specified government projects or services, e.g. magistrate's courts. In 1996–7 they amounted to £14.6bn. These grants account for approximately 30 per

cent of central government support for local authorities. They are paid as proportion of the total cost of the project or service. Local authority expenditure which attracts a specific grant is strictly defined and grant claims are usually subject to scrutiny by the external auditor.

The other main source of central government funding to local authorities comes from national non-domestic rates (NNDR). This income is collected by central government and then distributed to each local authority based on their local populations. The Labour government is committed to returning this source of funding back to local government control.

The council tax was introduced in 1993 to replace the discredited community charge (poll tax). It is a local tax based on the capital value of domestic properties with every domestic property allocated to one of eight bands A–H (see Midwinter and Monaghan 1995). The tax is collected by the unitary and non-metropolitan district councils (billing authorities), which also collect on behalf of the shire and police authorities (precepting authorities). In 1996–7 the overall average council tax demand on band D dwellings (the bench mark tax band) in England and Wales was £636.60, an increase of 6.7 per cent over the previous year. The average household payment in 1996–7 was £510.66, an increase of 6.8 per cent. This amount is less than the benchmark tax (band D) because more than two thirds of dwellings are in the lower bands A, B and C (CIPFA 1996a).

The proportion of local authority expenditure financed from local taxation has declined from 55 per cent in 1989–90 to less than 15 per cent in 1995–6. This decline is mainly as a result of the transfer of non-domestic rates income to central government control. Consequently the level of council tax is more highly geared to increases in expenditure beyond those allowed for in the government's grant settlement and the redistribution of national non-domestic rates. As a result, relatively small increases in a local authority's expenditure will be reflected by a greater proportionate increase in their council tax. For example a 1 per cent increase in expenditure by a local authority (above that allowed for by central government) would increase a council tax requirement by approximately 7 per cent.

Sales, fees and charges are another independent source of income for local authorities. They arise from providing services such as home helps, car parking and leisure facilities. Most charges are discretionary, i.e. local authorities are able to decide the level of charge locally. Wilson and Game (1994) identify four main types of charge:

1 Social: made when a council wishes to encourage the use of a service, for example adult education. A social charge is set below the full cost of provision, so the service is subsidized.
2 Means-related: based on a service user's ability to pay and may be used, for example, when deciding how much a client should pay for staying in a residential home.

3 Market rate: based on what the market will bear and set at a level which maximizes profit, e.g. the hire of a squash court.
4 Deterrent: these charges are used to try and limit the amount of service or facility used, e.g. city-centre car park charges and cemetery burials as opposed to cremations.

The decisions whether to subsidize a particular service, by how much and in what way present some of the most fundamental political decisions taken at a local level. Such decisions are usually discussed at length during council meetings. As a consequence, service users can pay different charges for the same service, depending upon in which local authority area they reside.

Local authority financing is an important aspect of local government management, as it affects everyone. Without effective financial planning and management systems it would not be possible to deliver services efficiently and effectively. In the rest of this chapter the techniques of financial management in the context of local government are examined.

Financial management in local government

The function of financial management is broad and encompasses nearly every aspect of a council's activities. Tongue and Horton (1996: 74) define financial management as: 'the process and techniques linking: delegated financial responsibility with financial accountability; resource inputs with service outputs; and planning and control of the management process and operational providers with financial providers'.

Financial management in local authorities has traditionally been based upon the notion of financial stewardship, with financial responsibility for the authority's affairs being entrusted to the chief officers who manage service departments. The chief financial officer (CFO), however, has a specific legal responsibility for ensuring there are 'proper arrangements' for the financial administration of the council's affairs under section 151 of the Local Government Act 1972.

Chief officers, who are accountable to service committees, delegate their responsibility for service delivery to operational managers and hold them accountable for discharging those responsibilities. The primary role of a chief officer, therefore, is to translate organizational goals and objectives into service-specific objectives for their subordinate managers to achieve. Finance provides a common basis into which the organization's objectives and activities can be translated. It allows managers, at all levels, to produce quantifiable measures, e.g. targets and budgets, against which performance can be assessed and reported. However, to ensure the highest quality of information for decision making it is essential to have effective financial planning and control. A key financial tool that aids planning and control in local government is the annual budget.

The annual budget

Every local authority produces an annual budget which comprises both capital and revenue. The fundamental reasons for preparing an annual budget are to:

- Determine the level of local spending on individual services: despite the tight financial control of total local authority expenditure by central government, local authorities are still able to determine their own service priorities and to allocate resources accordingly.
- Coordinate the expenditure plans of different service departments within the authority: the policy and expenditure decisions of one service can affect the level of service expenditure in another department. For example, transferring a service to the private sector will reduce the demand for other internal support services like payroll, income and payments.
- Satisfy statutory requirements: local authorities are required by statute to set a balanced budget prior to the financial year which begins on 1 April. A balanced budget is one where the estimated revenue expenditure can be met from estimated income from all sources, including contributions from reserves. It is illegal for a local authority to levy a supplementary council tax part way through the year to cover any overspends, whether the overspends were intentional or not.
- Establish the level of council tax that will need to be levied that year: by constructing the annual budget the level of revenue expenditure and income can be calculated. Councillors can then assess the political acceptability of the proposed council tax for that year and assess whether central government expenditure control limits will be exceeded.
- Provide a framework for the councillors to authorize expenditure: the process of preparing a budget gives members an opportunity to compare and evaluate alternative service management initiatives. By accepting a course of action and incorporating it into the budget, councillors are giving managers the authority to proceed with a particular course of action.
- Provide a basis for controlling expenditure: the budget provides the benchmark against which actual expenditure can be compared. If variances are identified then these can be investigated by managers and, where appropriate, reported to councillors.

The budgetary process

The different theoretical approaches to budgeting were discussed in Chapter 3. In local government the most common budget preparation method is the incremental approach, as the majority of its services are either mandatory or are fundamental to meeting organizational goals and will continue in future years (Jones and Pendlebury 1992), e.g. education, community care, domestic refuse collection etc. This approach to budgeting is also pragmatic as it focuses both councillors and managers on the activities at the margin which can be controlled.

With incremental budgeting, the current year's budget is used as the base budget for the following year to which is added commitments, the impact of proposed policy changes, the revenue expenditure consequences of the draft capital programme (e.g. the costs of staffing a new school) and the expected impact of price and wage inflation. See Figure 9.1.

Commitments would normally include the following:

- The full year effect of policy changes agreed by the council but not wholly included in the previous year's budget.
- Annual salary increments for staff and estimates of nationally and locally agreed pay awards.
- Debt repayments arising from capital expenditure incurred in the previous year.
- Any superannuation fund deficiencies which need to be made good in this budget period.

Most local authorities prepare their budgets at the 'November price base' prior to the budget year. This ensures there is a consistent approach to income and expenditure budgets and allows for yearly comparisons to be made. Contingency budgets for pay and price inflation will also be agreed and added to the budget if necessary (see Coombs and Jenkins 1994). Alternatively, budgets may be inflated to outturn prices (i.e. 31 March prices) for the financial year under consideration prior to becoming an operational budget. Budgets presented at outturn prices avoid the need to make in-year budget adjustments and therefore eliminate any uncertainty regarding the level of budget available to the budget holder for the year.

Incremental budgeting is often criticized because there is no detailed analysis of the base budget during the preparation process. Consequently, if services are being delivered inefficiently then those costs are permanently built into the base budget requirement. However, some authorities will undertake periodic 'base budget reviews' across services. These reviews involve a detailed analysis of the volume, methods and costs of delivering a particular service. Their purpose is to establish the level of resources actually required to deliver the service. For these reviews to be successful the commitment of senior managers is essential, especially from within the service under review.

Budget preparation

Local authority budgets were traditionally demand-led, with service departments and committees preparing their individual budget estimates based on an assessment of the resources required to meet expected service demands. These budget estimates were then aggregated to form the total estimated budget for the authority. This total estimated budget was invariably too

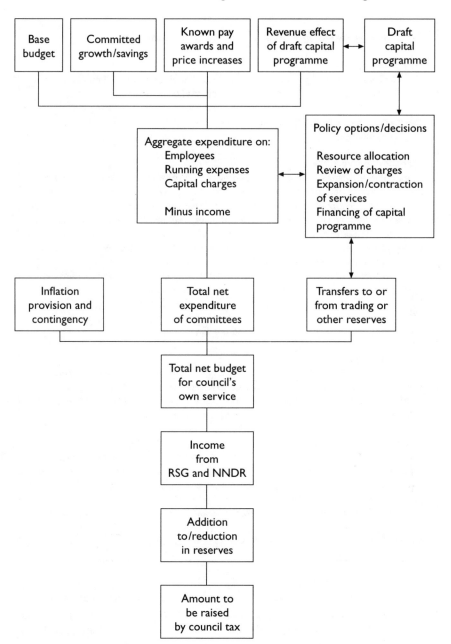

Figure 9.1 Local authority annual budget preparation
Source: *Councillors Guide to Local Government Finance*, CIPFA (1995).

Box 9.1 Key stages in annual budget preparation

April–September
The CFO will produce guidelines for each spending department which explain the basis on which they should compile the basic budget estimates for the following year (beginning 1 April). The guidelines will take account of current council policy, the medium term financial strategy of the council and assumptions to be made regarding inflation.

October–November
The budget estimates will be scrutinized by the CFO. Additional information from the mid-year review of expenditure for the current year will help to determine whether the proposed budget estimates are realistic. A report will be made to the policy and resources committee outlining the implications of the budget estimates on services and the implied level of council tax (or precept for non-billing authorities, i.e. shire and police authorities). If there is a risk of exceeding the government's spending limits then this will also be identified, perhaps giving details of some of the options available to the council. Service departments will also report to their own committees on the proposed budget and its implications for service delivery. At this stage the authority will usually consult representatives of non-domestic rate-payers on its proposed expenditure plans, as required under Section 65 of the Local Government Finance Act 1992.

December–January
Fine tuning of the budget as government grant figures are confirmed and the provisional criteria for capping local authority spending is made known. A provisional outturn of the current year's expenditure may also now be available which will help to identify carry-forward expenditure commitments.

February–March
Adjustments for contingencies and planned reserves etc. are made before presenting the budget to the full council for approval. Once agreed, the council can publish its council tax level or precept. Precepting authorities must issue precepts to billing authorities before 1 March. Billing authorities must set the level of council tax before 11 March prior to the financial year to which the tax applies.

Source: Based on Henley *et al.* (1992) and CIPFA (1995).

---

high and had to be reduced in order to keep increases in local taxes (the then rates) to a politically acceptable level. However, since 1976 and the beginning of tighter local government financial control by central government, budget preparation has become increasingly centralized, with the CFO and the policy and resources committee controlling the process. While in practice every local authority will prepare its budget in a slightly different way, they all tend to follow a similar annual cycle. Box 9.1 describes the four key stages to budget preparation during the year.

The preparation of the budget can be a highly political activity as the politicians seek to produce a budget which reflects their priorities. In authorities where no political party has overall control negotiation and compromise will be necessary. The agreed final annual budget will usually be published as a formal financial document of the authority. This document may contain additional information, such as an outline of the major issues which influenced the setting of the budget, for example: the financial environment; council policy changes; inflation assumptions; any necessary contingencies. Although there is no statutory requirement concerning the distribution of the published budget, copies are usually made available to councillors of the authority, members of the press, other local authorities and local libraries.

Budgetary control

Budgetary control is the process of monitoring actual expenditure and income against the approved budget. It is a fundamental financial management tool and is used in assessing the ongoing performance of the local authority against its agreed objectives. Once a local authority has agreed its annual budget the responsibility for budgetary control will normally become that of the chief officers who will, in turn, devolve responsibility to individual officers (budget managers).

The philosophy of devolved budget responsibility is now firmly established in local government. Specific legislation such as the Education Reform Act 1988 which requires responsibility for school budgets to be delegated to the headteacher (and governors) of schools, and the Local Government Act 1988 which requires certain defined activities to be exposed to compulsory competitive tendering, have encouraged the development of devolved budgeting structures and the need for market-price testing.

In services other than education and direct service organizations (DSOs) the degree of budget delegation will vary between authorities. However, it is generally accepted that operational managers should be responsible and accountable for the financial consequences of their decisions. In practice, this means delegating the budget to the lowest level of management within a hierarchy of budgetary control responsibilities. Figure 9.2 shows an example of how budgets might be devolved in the operations division of a social services department to a cost centre manager.

The Audit Commission (1989) identified the need to align financial accountability and operational responsibility; it also suggested that managers should not be expected to control budgets for activities which are beyond their operational control. Another important aspect to successful devolved budgetary control is that managers accept ownership of the budget for which they are responsible. The purpose of establishing ownership is to improve the motivation and commitment of budget holders, so that they

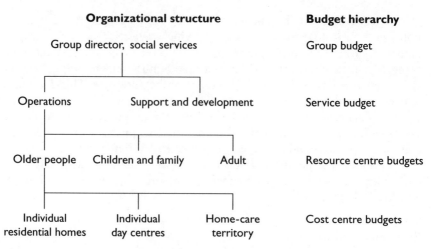

Figure 9.2 An example of a simplified hierarchy of delegated budgets within the operations division of a social services department

monitor and control their budgets more effectively. Ownership, the Audit Commission (1989) argued, could be encouraged by involving managers in the planning of their budgets. Some local authorities encourage budget ownership by naming the manager responsible for each budget in their published budget book.

Effective budgetary control requires budget managers to receive relevant, reliable and timely information on actual expenditure against their approved budgets. Budgetary control reports will usually be generated by the budgetary control system on a monthly or four-weekly basis. The format of the report will vary between authorities but it will usually compare actual expenditure to the profiled budget with an estimate of the likely year-end outturn figure. Budget variance may be highlighted with indicators which grade the level of variance, e.g. 'A' may be used to indicate a small adverse variance and 'AAA' for a major overspend.

The level of detail included in the report will depend on the position of budget manager in the budgetary control hierarchy. The lower down the hierarchy the more detailed the information. Table 9.2 shows an example of a summarized budgetary control report for a cost centre halfway through the financial year.

The quality and adequacy of budgetary control information produced by local authorities was investigated in 1983 by Pendlebury (1985). He undertook a cross-sectional survey of local authority budgeting practices and found that budgetary control information frequently suffered from lack of timeliness, the absence of budget profiling, the failure to distinguish between controllable items, and the ignoring of non-financial output measures. In 1988 Skousen (1990) replicated Pendlebury's study and found that

Table 9.2 Sports and leisure centre summarized budgetary control report, period ending September 1997

Narrative	Total budget (£000s)	Profiled budget (£000s)	Actual expenditure (£000s)	Variance (£000s)	Forecast total expenditure (£000s)	Under(−)/over(+) expenditure (£000s)	Indicator
Employees	350	175	180	+5	370	+20	A
Premises	60	30	36	+6	69	+9	A
Transport	10	5	5	0	10	0	–
Supplies and services	50	25	30	+5	46	−4	F
Gross expenditure	470	235	251	16	495	+25	A
Income	−200	−100	−120	−20	−240	−40	F
Net expenditure	270	135	131	−4	255	−15	F

A = Adverse variance
F = Favourable variance

there had been some improvements, but that many of the deficiencies identified by Pendlebury still remained.

Concerns regarding the quality of budgetary control reports were also highlighted by the Audit Commission (1989), which identified the need for local authority budgetary control reports to be well presented, designed to meet the information needs of different levels of management, to highlight significant variances and be up to date. The Audit Commission suggested that more up-to-date information could be made available by providing access to a commitment accounting system, more frequent updates of the financial ledgers, and on-line access to users.

Significant improvements in the quality of budgetary control information were, however, identified in 1994 by Pendlebury when he examined the management accounting practices of two local authorities. He attributed this improvement to the general increase in devolved budgeting and market testing in local government. However, surprisingly, Pendlebury observed that in both local authorities the budgetary control information that was available to services, outside the DSO activities, did not appear to have improved significantly. It would appear from this that local authorities have much to do if effective budgetary control is to be exercised.

Councillors and budgetary control

Members of the council will not tend to be involved in the day-to-day budgetary control of a service, but are usually consulted on an exception basis. Two situations where they may be involved are: when a budget virement is required; or if a supplementary budget is required.

Budget virement is the act of moving a budget provision from one budget head to another. Budget managers will normally be allowed to vire budgets up to a certain financial limit without consulting members. The limit will be defined in the authority's financial regulations. Virement for amounts above the limit will usually require the approval of the relevant service committee and possibly the policy and resources committee.

Supplementary budget approval may be required by members if, for example:

- A policy change is to be implemented part way through the year which was not included in the original budget.
- An unexpected budget variance arises which cannot be accommodated within existing budgets.

Budget managers will normally be required to present a report to the policy and resources committee explaining the necessity for the supplementary budget. In the report it will be necessary to identify options for funding the supplementary budget because, as noted earlier, the council is unable to issue a supplementary council tax levy during the financial year.

Most local authorities will undertake a substantial review of their budget position part way through the year: a mid-year review. The purpose of this review is to forecast the expected level of expenditure and income at the end of the financial year and to compare this against the agreed budget. Significant variances from the budget, together with explanations, will be reported to members with recommendations for any corrective action that may be required. This mid-year review also enables the CFO to fulfil the requirements of Section 114 of the Local Government Finance Act 1988 under which the auditor and members of the local authority must be notified of likely overspending.

Capital expenditure monitoring

Another key financial management function in local government is monitoring capital expenditure. Capital expenditure includes both expenditure on new assets and any capital grants made to other organizations or individuals. For example, expenditure on the construction of a new school or sports centre would be regarded as capital expenditure.

Before a capital project is started it will normally have undergone a rigorous appraisal process. This process may involve initial reports to the service committee on the viability of the scheme, cost estimates and an analysis of the revenue consequences. Alternative options may also be considered, e.g. renting or building conversion, rather than building from new.

When an authority decides to include a project in its capital programme, a suitable site may then be acquired or reserved. Detailed design and contract tenders will then be invited and considered. Once the project starts the project manager is responsible for controlling the contract costs and progress payments to contractors. A large scheme may take several years to complete.

Monitoring capital schemes is a time-consuming and complex process, as projects tend to be unique, each with their own expenditure patterns. In addition there are a number of uncertainties which could affect a project, e.g. the government not issuing sufficient annual credit approvals (i.e. approval to borrow money), inflation (cost increases) and slippage (unforeseen project delays).

Forecasts of the timing of actual spending (cash flow forecasts) are essential for effective capital programme monitoring as different projects will incur different levels and rates of expenditure. Capital estimates for each project are usually broken down into monthly or quarterly cash flows relating to each type of expenditure, e.g. land, design, construction, fees and equipment.

A formalized and regular monitoring system similar to the operational budgetary control system is essential. Comparisons between actual capital expenditure and cash flow forecasts will normally take place on a monthly basis so that problems such as overspends can be dealt with quickly. Reports will normally be compiled at three levels:

1 Detailed reports for project managers on their individual projects. These reports might include the capital budget for the scheme, broken down into types of expenditure such as land, design, construction, architects fees and so on. Control of an individual project by a project manager will not usually include information on capital financing.
2 Service capital monitoring reports which summarize all projects within a particular service, identifying overspends and circumstances where further committee approval may be required. These reports will normally be used at CFO level to monitor the progress of schemes.
3 A corporate capital monitoring report which summarizes all the authority's capital expenditure and indicates how the expenditure will be financed. This report would be used by the CFO.

After a project is completed a formal review will be undertaken to assess whether it has met its original objectives and whether the capital appraisal and monitoring process was successful. Weaknesses identified in the systems may then be rectified for future capital projects. In the future the government envisages that more local government capital schemes will be undertaken in partnership with the private sector either through the private finance initiative (PFI) or 'challenge funding' (see below).

Developments in financial management

Since 1979, there have been some fundamental changes in the way local government services are delivered and financed. Three significant developments have been the introduction of:

1 Compulsory competitive tendering (CCT).
2 The PFI.
3 Challenge funding.

These initiatives will now be discussed.

CCT

During the 1980s CCT was introduced for blue-collar workers and more recently for white-collar workers and professional services. Although the compulsory aspects of CCT will be abolished, as a result of the election of a Labour government (May 1997), the legacy of CCT will be more long-lasting and will provide a framework for demonstrating 'best value'.

As a consequence of CCT, local authorities created separate provider units, i.e. DSOs or direct labour organizations (DLOs), to compete with the private sector for the right to undertake work for the local authority. If the DSO/ DLO wins a tender, then it is monitored by the local authority (referred to as the client) for the quantity and quality of its work. The service provided has to be delivered at the agreed price, subject to any contract variations.

The DSO/DLO must recover its costs as failure to do so could result in its closure by the government. The previous government set down strict rules and regulations on the conduct of CCT to ensure a level, competitive playing field for all potential contractors. DSOs and DLOs are required to break-even, having allowed for a 6 per cent rate of return on any capital employed. In order to compete successfully for contracts DLOs and DSOs have had to reduce the costs of labour, resulting in loss of staff, reduction in terms and conditions of service and, in some instances, lower wages (Greenwood and Wilson 1989; Shaw *et al.* 1994; Cope 1995).

The process of budgeting for contracts is different from that of preparing a revenue budget. The quality level and the cost of services are clearly specified and formally agreed in a contract. The contract provides the basis for both the DLO/DSO (or private company) and the local authority to monitor performance. As many of the contracts are normally only for three years, a lot of uncertainty is built into the management process, and managers are forced to focus on the short term. Under the system of contracting there is no opportunity for cross-subsidization as each provider unit is regarded has having an independent budget and set of accounts. Failure to win a significant contract could mean the collapse of the DSO/DLO.

The PFI

A new development in local government finance has been the introduction of the PFI. It is a scheme designed to encourage the private sector to invest in public sector projects and improve the delivery of services through better value for money.

The government originally intended that private finance would be 'additional resources' (see HM Treasury 1992) to the public sector and not a substitute for public funding. However, reductions in the amount of local authority capital expenditure supported by the government contradicts the original intentions. Barnett and Carmichael (1996: 136), commenting on local authority capital funding for 1996–7, identified that: 'it is now clear that private finance is to substitute for public finance rather than represent additional funding'. The government, by using the PFI as a substitute for direct capital funding is therefore able to force the public sector into PFI arrangements and reduce pressure on the public sector borrowing requirement (PSBR).

With local authority resources tightly constrained and with almost unlimited demand for their services, the PFI does, in principle, provide an alternative approach to funding assets used by the public sector. This is achieved by the local authority transferring the risks related to the owner-ship of assets to the private sector – risks such as ownership and the responsibility for service provision. These risks are transferred at a price to the private sector who receive regular payment over the period the asset is provided. As a consequence, emphasis shifts from up-front capital invest-ment to long-term revenue expenditure by the local authority. The capital costs incurred by the private sector are recovered over the life of a contract.

An implicit feature in the PFI is that local authorities are regarded as enablers and not direct service providers. This role is consistent with pol-icies pursued by the previous government such as CCT and it is not sur-prising therefore that some commentators have referred to the PFI as 'privatization through the back door'. However, while a degree of success has been achieved in central government, the prison service and the health service, the development of suitable PFI schemes in local government has been slow. There are two reasons for this: the complexity of local govern-ment capital controls; and the additional revenue costs of servicing a PFI contract.

PFI projects, like any other proposed investment by a local authority, should be subject to a rigorous value for money (VFM) appraisal. The previous government's guidance made it clear that where the PFI approach to procurement cannot demonstrate VFM, then the PFI option should not be implemented. The following methodology was defined when appraising the VFM aspects of PFI projects:

- Competition: a PFI proposal should be exposed to competition in the market, in line with the requirements of an authority's own standing orders and European Commission procurement rules. Before proceeding to test the market, however, the authority should first satisfy itself that the project will be technically feasible and that the PFI options are likely to be financially viable, after taking into account public sector contributions.
- Comparison of options: the comparison should contrast the expected outcome of all realistic options in terms of their forecast whole-life costs and benefits, using common financial measures. This should include the effect of any contributions by the authority.
- The public sector comparator: the appraisal should include a public sector comparator if there is a reasonable prospect of capital funding becoming available for the project in the foreseeable future. In other cases, the financial appraisal should normally compare competing PFI proposals only. Where a public sector comparator is required, it should centre on the costs of a realistic public sector solution for delivering the same outputs as the PFI option.
- Transfer of assets to the private sector: PFI options are likely to include the transfer to the private sector operator of land, buildings or other assets and such transfers should be appraised. In many cases, the value

to a local authority from such disposals will not come in the form of capital receipts, either up front or later, but in the form of lower annual payments throughout the period of the contract. If the asset transfer is integral to the project in either a physical or logistical sense, then the value for money appraisal should focus on the PFI transaction as a whole.

Local authorities have naturally been cautious about transferring assets and the running of services to the private sector as there will be a loss of direct public control and accountability. There are also inevitable concerns about individual contractors going out of business or failing to deliver the service. If this happens the public will perceive this as the local authority failing in its duty to supply services.

In an effort to try and make the PFI work the local authority associations have set up the Public Private Partnership Programme Ltd (4 Ps), a company limited by guarantee and financed by top-slicing the RSG. Its aims are to deliver greater investment in local services with enhanced cost effectiveness, through increased partnerships between the public and private sectors.

The PFI offers the opportunity for local authorities and the private sector to work in partnership to mutual benefit. However, the fundamentally different objectives of each party should not be ignored. The only incentive for the private sector to enter into a PFI arrangement with a local authority is to make a profit. Therefore, it is likely that the more socially desirable projects, which tend to be unprofitable, will at best be given a lower priority in capital programmes, and at worst never be developed.

Challenge funding

Challenge funding was another initiative developed by the previous government which complements the PFI. This initiative requires local authorities in partnership with the private sector to bid for additional funding from the government for jointly financed schemes. Local authorities are effectively in competition with other authorities for government grants. Various funds exist, e.g. the single regeneration budget challenge fund, the capital challenge and the estates renewal challenge fund. This method of funding is seen by the government as a means of encouraging the private sector to become more involved with the delivery of public services, by matching public and private funds pound for pound.

Financial accounting and reporting

Financial accounting is concerned with recording monetary transactions and reporting financial performance externally. There are two basic concepts of financial accounting which have traditionally underpinned local authority accounts: stewardship and accountability. Stewardship refers to the holding of someone else's assets and demonstrating they have not been misused. Accountability refers to answering for ones actions to someone else (Jones and Pendlebury 1992)

The overall objective of financial reporting is to provide relevant information to the users of the financial statements. However, fundamental questions need to be answered, e.g. who are the users of local authority financial statements and what are their information needs? Drebin *et al.* (1981) identified four main user groups of local authority financial statements:

1 Resource providers (of finance, labour, materials).
2 Resource allocation decision makers (e.g. management, central government).
3 Elected officials and the electorate.
4 External parties in transactions with local government.

Each user group will have its own specific financial information needs. Anthony (1979) classified users' information needs into four main categories:

1 Financial viability: does the authority have the resources to continue in its present or planned form?
2 Fiscal compliance: has the organization complied with the conditions laid down in its authority to spend?
3 Management performance: has the money been spent wisely?
4 Cost of services provided.

Local authority financial statements are used by a wide range of different interest groups with different information needs. In the rest of this chapter the financial statements of local authorities are reviewed and their relevance and appropriateness to user needs are examined.

The financial framework

The local government financial accounting framework is influenced by two main factors:

1 Statute and regulations.
2 Professional accounting standards and guidelines (i.e. Statement of Standard Accounting Practice (SSAP), Financial Reporting Statement (FRS), and Statement of Recommended Practice (SORP).

Statutes only usually define accounting requirements in broad terms, professional accounting standards and guidelines provide the detail. The most important professional guidelines covering local authority financial accounting are found in the *Code of Practice of Local Authority Accounting in Great Britain* (CIPFA 1996b) prepared by the Chartered Institute of Public Finance and Accountancy (CIPFA) and the Local Authority (Scotland)

Accounts Advisory Committee (LASAAC) joint committee. The code is formally recognized as a SORP by the Accounting Standards Board (ASB).

The *Code of Practice* was first issued in 1987 and has been revised regularly to take account of new accounting developments. It is a compilation of legal requirements, best accounting practice as determined by CIPFA/ LASAAC, and pronouncements from the AS Board. For the CFO it provides a single comprehensive point of reference (Layton 1996). See the Appendix (page 223) for the objectives and fundamental requirements of the *Code of Practice*.

The statement of accounts

The *Code of Practice* is prescriptive regarding the content of a local authority's statement of accounts. A brief description of the contents of each statement is given in Box 9.2.

There follows an overview of the main accounting statements.

Box 9.2 Statements to be included in the annual statement of accounts

An explanatory foreword: the foreword explains any significant financial matters which are presented in the accounts. It is intended to assist the reader in interpreting the accounting statements and provide a commentary on the major influences affecting the authority's income, expenditure and cash flow.

A statement of accounting policies: this statement explains the basis upon which the accounts have been prepared. The statement should clearly disclose the policies adopted, any changes in accounting policy, and identify where fundamental accounting concepts have not been followed.

The accounting statements: these will comprise the following statements as appropriate to the authority's functions.

- Consolidated revenue account: this statement reports the net cost for the year of all the authority's functions and shows how that cost has been financed.
- Housing revenue account: the Local Government and Housing Act 1989 (schedule 4) requires local authorities to account separately for their housing provision. This statement brings together all housing revenue expenditure and shows how it has been met by rents, subsidy and other income.
- Summary of direct service organization (DSO) revenue and appropriation account: local authorities have a statutory obligation to account separately for direct service organizations. This statement summarizes these activities and would normally show the turnover, total expenditure and surplus/deficit for each DSO. This statement should be prepared in accordance with the CIPFA code of practice for compulsory competition.
- Collection fund (England and Wales): billing authorities have a statutory obligation to maintain a separate collection fund which shows how income from non-domestic rates and the council tax has been distributed to preceptors and the general fund.

- Council tax and non-domestic rate income accounts (Scotland): these are two separate accounts and show the net income raised from council taxes and from non-domestic property.
- Consolidated balance sheet: this statement shows the financial position of the authority at the end of the financial year. It shows the assets and liabilities of all activities, excluding the superannuation funds and other trust funds.
- Statement of total movements in reserves: all recognized gains and losses of the authority during the period are brought together in this statement. Movements on revenue and capital reserves are shown separately.
- The cash flow statement: this statement summarizes the revenue and capital inflows and outflows of cash from the authority.
- Group accounts: those authorities with material interests in subsidiary and associated companies are required to prepare group accounts. These comprise a group revenue account and a group balance sheet. A group cash-flow statement and group statement of total reserves may also be provided in summary form.

Notes to the accounts: notes will be included for each of the above accounting statements. These should add to and help interpret their contents, where matters of financial significance cannot adequately be treated in the statements themselves.

Statement of responsibilities for the statement of accounts: this statement sets out the respective responsibilities of the authority and the chief finance officer (CFO) for the accounts.

The superannuation fund accounts: the detailed financial statements for the superannuation fund are presented in a separate annual report. The information presented in the final accounts of the authority is merely a summarized statement of these activities. The statement should show the revenue income and expenditure of the fund and the market value of assets under the fund manager's control.

Source: Code of Practice of Local Authority Accounting in Great Britain, CIPFA (1996b).

Consolidated revenue account

The consolidated revenue account brings together the income and expenditure of all the authority's functions into one statement. It includes services provided under the general fund and the housing revenue account. The consolidated revenue account has four main sections:

1 Net cost of services.
2 Corporate income and expenditure.
3 Appropriations.
4 Sources of finance.

Notes to the consolidated revenue account provide additional detailed information on, for example: any prior-year adjustments; exceptional or extraordinary items; income from providing services to other public bodies;

effect of leases on the revenue account; the nature, turnover and profit/loss of any trading undertakings.

Consolidated balance sheet

This statement is fundamental to understanding a local authority's financial position. It is similar to a commercial balance sheet in that it includes all the assets and liabilities of all activities of the authority excluding separate funds, i.e. the superannuation fund and trust funds. The main sections of the balance sheet are:

- Fixed assets.
- Other long-term assets.
- Current assets.
- Current liabilities.
- Long-term liabilities.
- Fund balances and reserves.

The balance sheet is supported by a number of notes which give more information and explain the figures on the balance sheet. The level of detail provided will vary between authorities depending on their accounting policies and the nature of the transaction. However, sufficient detail should always be provided to enable the reader of the accounts to gain a good idea of the financial position of the authority.

Cashflow statement

This statement identifies the movement of cash into and out of the authority. The statement is based on the presentation laid down in an FRS, but is amended to reflect the different nature of the activities of local authorities.

There are four main sections shown on the statement:

1 Revenue activities: cash income and expenditure on the day-to-day activities of the authority.
2 Servicing of financing: the revenue elements of financing, e.g. interest received or paid.
3 Capital activities: the purchase and sale of assets.
4 Financing: the principal elements of external financing.

In the notes to the statement there will be a reconciliation between the net surplus or deficit on the income and expenditure account and the revenue activities net cash flow.

Publication of financial statements

In England and Wales local authorities are required to prepare their accounts by 30 September and to publish them by 31 December. In Scotland the accounts must be prepared by 31 August. All councils are obliged to publicize their accounts and the public have a right to inspect them.

The financial statements and accounts are subject to independent scrutiny by an external auditor as appointed by the Audit Commission. The Audit Commission was established under the Local Government Finance Act 1982 to be responsible for monitoring the financial and managerial competence and probity of local government. The Audit Commission scrutinizes local authority accounts and reports on their legality and accuracy. If an authority is thought to have acted unlawfully or fraudulently then an Audit Commission investigation may be initiated and could lead to the prosecution of officers and councillors.

Local authorities expend considerable time end effort producing the above financial statements. However, there is some evidence to suggest that the intended users of the statements do not understand the information presented. Research by Butterworth *et al.* (1989) into the use made of local authority accounts by the general public found the level of interest almost insignificant. They used two methods:

1 A straw poll of 100 residents in one town: 97 per cent of those polled had not looked at the county council's annual report and were unaware of its existence.
2 A questionnaire inserted into each of the annual reports, budget books and the minute books lodged in the three main libraries: no responses were received from any of the sites.

A later study by Collins *et al.* (1991) looked at the use made of local authority financial accounts by external and internal user groups. They found a wide range in the level of understanding within user groups. Lack of financial experience and suitable training tended to be the main barrier to understanding the financial information. These findings support the idea of varying the style and content of financial reports, particularly by the introduction of simplified financial statements.

It would be inappropriate to draw general conclusions about the usefulness of local authority financial statements from these two studies. In fairness, many local authorities produce interesting and readable annual reports which attempt to explain, in lay person's terms, how resources have been used.

Conclusion

Throughout the last two decades local government has had to adapt to a new regime of financial stringency with the levels of service provision being determined by available finance, rather than service needs. Consequently, the budgeting process has become more centralized with the policy and re-sources committee (through the CFO) setting expenditure guidelines for indi-vidual service departments. Service committees are now required to manage their limited resources more effectively, by prioritizing service objectives and controlling costs.

The devolving of budgets to operational managers has helped to improve efficiency as managers have become directly responsible and accountable for the financial consequence of their decisions. Resource usage has become more closely scrutinized with managers identifying new and innovative methods of service delivery while at the same time releasing resources for other projects.

The development of the internal market, as a forerunner to introducing white-collar CCT, has sharpened up support-service providers, e.g. legal, information technology (IT), and finance. These services have become more customer orientated, identifying and quantifying customer needs, reducing costs and improving productivity. Many authorities have adopted formal service level agreements (SLAs) between support service providers and users. Financial management has been central in facilitating these changes in the management and delivery of services.

Improvements have also been made in local authority external financial reporting by introducing a formal code of practice. This has attempted to enhance the usefulness of the local authority final accounts by narrowing the accounting treatments available and defining clearly the contents of each statement. However, their usefulness is perhaps limited to the small user-group of accounting professionals; for the lay person the financial statements can still present a real barrier to understanding the finances of a local authority.

Appendix

The Code of Practice on Local Authority Accounting in Great Britain

The objectives of the *Code of Practice* are to:

- Specify the principles and practices of accounting required to prepare a statement of accounts which present fairly the financial position and transactions of a local authority.
- Set out the proper accounting practices required for statements of accounts prepared in accordance with the statutory framework.

The *Code of Practice* has been prepared on the basis that a local author-ity's published statement of accounts should provide clear financial informa-tion to the users of the accounts and should identify:

- The cost of services provided.
- How the expenditure was financed.
- The assets and liabilities of the authority at the end of the year.

The *Code of Practice* requires that local authority accounting statements are prepared in accordance with fundamental accounting concepts. The code identifies the following six concepts:

1 *Going Concern*: a local authority's statement of accounts should be prepared on a going concern basis, i.e. that the authority will continue to exist next year. However, if certain operations are being terminated, e.g. a DSO, it may be necessary for stocks to be written down and provisions to be made for redundancy costs. If a local authority is being reorganized and its assets are being redistributed to successor authorities then the going concern concept should still be applied to the provision of services, even though the authority itself may cease to exist.

2 *Materiality*: whether or not an item is material depends on the amounts concerned and the areas in which it occurs. Strict compliance with the code is not necessary if the amounts involved are not material to the fair presentation of the financial position.

3 *Matching*: income and expenditure should be matched to the services provided in the same accounting period. This requires compliance with the concept of accruals for revenue and capital income and expenditure, except where the concept of prudence dictates otherwise.

4 *Consistency*: consistent policies should be applied both within the accounts for the year and between years. A change in accounting policy should not be made unless it can be justified on the grounds that the new policy is preferable to the one it replaces, because it will give a fairer presentation of the transactions and the financial position. This concept particularly applies to:

- Valuation of fixed assets.
- Write-off period for assets.
- Valuation of stocks and work in progress.
- Bad debt provision.
- Allocation of overheads.

5 *Prudence*: the accounts should be prepared in accordance with the prudence concept. Income should only be included to the extent that it can be realized with reasonable certainty, and proper allowance should be made for all known and foreseeable losses and liabilities.

6 *Substance over form*: the accounting statement should be prepared so as to reflect the reality or substance of the transactions and activities underlying them rather than only their formal legal character. In determining the substance of a transaction, it is necessary to identify all of the transaction's aspects and implications.

Where a local authority decides not to prepare its financial statements in accordance with the above concepts then full disclosure is required as part of the accounts.

References

Anthony R. N. (1979) *Financial Accounting in Nonbusiness Organisations.* Stamford, CT: Financial Accounting Standards Board.

Audit Commission (1989) *Better Financial Management*, management paper no. 3. London: HMSO.

Barnett, R. R. and Carmichael, P. (1996) Local government, in P. Jackson and M. Lavender (eds) *Public Services Yearbook 1996–97*, pp. 131–44. London: Pitman Publishing.

Barnett, R. R. and Carmichael, P. (1997) Local government, in P. Jackson and M. Lavender (eds) *Public Services Yearbook 1997–98*, pp. 101–14. London: Pitman Publishing.

Butterworth, P., Gray, R. and Haslem, J. (1989) The local authority report in the UK: an exploratory study of accounting communication and democracy. *Financial Accountability & Management*, 5 (2): 73–87.

CIPFA (Chartered Institute of Public Finance and Accountancy) (1995) *Councillors' Guide to Local Government.* London: CIPFA.

CIPFA (Chartered Institute of Public Finance and Accountancy) (1996a) *Financial and General Statistics 1996/97.* London: CIPFA.

CIPFA (Chartered Institute of Public Finance and Accountancy) (1996b) *Code of Practice of Local Authority Accounting in Great Britain.* London: CIPFA.

Collins, W., Keen, D. and Lapsley, I. (1991) *Local Authority Financial Reporting: Communication, Sophistry or Obfuscation.* London: CIPFA.

Coombs, H. M. and Jenkins, D. E. (1994) *Public Sector Financial Management* (2nd edn). London: Chapman & Hall.

Cope, S. (1995) Contracting out in local government: cutting by privatizing. *Public Policy and Administration*, 10 (3): 29–44.

DETR (Department of the Environment, Transport and the Regions) (1998) *Modernising Local Government: Improving Local Services through Best Value.* London: HMSO.

Drebin, A., Chan, J. and Ferguson, L. (1981) *Objectives of Accounting and Financial Reporting for Governmental Units: A Research Study.* London: National Council on Governmental Accounting.

Ernst & Young, CIPFA and Ernst & Young ITEM Club (1996) *Corporate Strategy 97.* London: Ernst & Young.

Greenwood, J. and Wilson, D. (1989) *Public Administration in Britain Today.* London: Unwin Hyman.

Henley, D., Likierman, A., Perrin, J., Evans, M., Lapsley, I. and Whiteoak, J. (1992) *Public Sector Accounting and Financial Control* (4th edn). London: Chapman & Hall.

HM Treasury (1992) *Private Finance.* London: HM Treasury.

Jones, R. and Pendlebury, M. (1992) *Public Sector Accounting.* London: Pitman Publishing.

Layton, J. (1996) Cracking the code. *Public Finance*, 16 February: 18–19.

Mallabar, N. (1991) *Local government administration – in a time of change.* London: Business Education Publishers Limited.

Midwinter, A. and Monaghan, C. (1995) The new centralism: local government finance in the 1990s. *Financial Accountability & Management*, 11 (2): 141–51.

Pendlebury, M. (1985) *Management Accounting in Local Government.* London: CIMA.

Pendlebury, M. (1994) Management accounting in local government. *Financial Accountability & Management*, 10 (2): 117–29.

Shaw, K., Fenwick, J. and Foreman, A. (1994) Competitive tendering for local government services in the United Kingdom: a case of market rhetoric and camouflaged centralism. *Public Policy and Administration*, 10 (1): 63–75.

Skousen, C. R. (1990) Budgeting practices in local government in England and Wales. *Financial Accountability & Management*, 6 (3): 191–208.

Tongue, R. and Horton, S. (1996) Financial management and quality, in D. Farnham and S. Horton *Managing the New Public Services* (2nd edn), pp. 71–93. London: Macmillan.

Wilson, D. and Game, C. (1994) *Local Government in the United Kingdom.* London: Macmillian.

Further reading

One of the problems with studying local government financial management is that it becomes factually dated very quickly. To keep up-to-date with local government issues the following weekly publications are recommended: *Public Finance* and *Local Government Chronicle*. The techniques of financial management are considered in Coombs, H.M. and Jenkins, D.E. (1994) *Public Sector Financial Management* (2nd edn) (London: Chapman & Hall). For a critique of changes in local government refer to Wilson, J. and Hinton, P. (eds) (1993) *Public Services and the 1990s: Issues in Public Service Finance and Management* (Eastham: Tudor).

ten

National Health Service financial management

George Foster and John Wilson

Key learning objectives

After reading this chapter you should be able to:

1 Appreciate the scale, significance and utilization of resources devoted to the National Health Service.
2 Understand and evaluate the main issues within the provision of healthcare in the United Kingdom.
3 Evaluate how financial management is exercised and demonstrated.

Introduction

The 50th anniversary of the National Health Service (NHS) (5 July 1998) can be regarded as a milestone in the history of public service provision in the United Kingdom (UK). The NHS has become, in many respects, a key service in the lives of UK citizens. Not only does it provide expert care when needed but, importantly, its very existence provides a sense of security and peace of mind. A former Chancellor, Nigel Lawson, may have exaggerated when he claimed that the NHS is like a religion to the British people (complete with priests, i.e. clinicians, whose 'teachings' cannot be questioned nor understood by the laity, and worshippers, i.e. the public), but the view reflects the deep affection, loyalty and sense of comfort which the NHS inspires. Being seen to undermine the 'religion', to question its central 'doctrines', can prove to be a minefield for politicians. Perhaps because of this, the structure of the NHS and the nature of service delivery remained largely unchanged for most of its life, even though it grew at a rate which would have been considered inconceivable and unaffordable when it was established in 1948. However, throughout the 1980s and 1990s, the NHS has experienced a period of fundamental change, key features of which are now, it would appear, accepted by Labour. This chapter considers the nature of these changes and, in so doing, focuses on the significance and nature of financial management in the NHS.

The NHS: background

Domestically and internationally, largely through the work of the World Health Organization (WHO), attempts are being made to encourage healthier living. In the UK, the Department of Health (DoH) published, in 1992, *Health of the Nation*, which emphasized disease prevention and health promotion and established targets for improving health in five key areas:

1 Coronary heart disease and stroke.
2 Cancers.
3 Mental illness.
4 HIV/AIDS and sexually-transmitted diseases.
5 Accidental deaths.

It must be noted that the key areas given above are not exclusively a matter of health spending. They embrace education, social services, housing and wider socio-economic considerations. However, the NHS has a key role to play and, in order to achieve the targets, the NHS has six medium-term priorities to take it to the end of the 1990s:

1 Developing a primary-care led NHS.
2 Improving mental health services.
3 Clinical effectiveness.
4 Patient partnership.
5 Continuing care.
6 Being a good employer.

To meet its objectives, the NHS is allocated significant resources on an annual basis. For illustration, NHS expenditure figures for 1996–7 are given in Table 10.1.

Expenditure on the NHS in England in 1997–8 was estimated to be £34.4bn (November 1996 budget), and approximately £43bn for the UK as a whole (note: the DoH funds only England, with the Welsh, Scottish and Northern Ireland offices responsible for their own programmes). Total health expenditure in the UK 1997–8 represents 5.5 per cent of gross domestic product (GDP) (excluding personal social services).

Given the scale of the activity, effective management, not least financial management, is essential, but the Conservatives, throughout the 1980s,

Table 10.1 NHS expenditure 1996–7 (estimates)

	£bn	%
NHS		
Hospitals	21.7	51.1
Family health services	9.9	23.5
Community health	5.1	12.1
Training, research etc.	3.0	7.1
Central services	1.1	2.6
Administration	1.0	2.4
Loans to NHS trusts	0.5	1.2
Total	42.3	100
Hospitals		
Acute	13.1	60.4
Geriatric	2.1	9.7
Mental health	1.5	6.9
Maternity	1.1	5.1
Learning disability	1.1	5.1
Administration	1.4	6.4
Other	1.4	6.4
Sub-total	21.7	100
Family health services		
Pharmaceutical services	4.9	49.5
General practice	3.5	35.4
Dental services	1.2	12.1
Ophthalmic services	0.3	3.0
Sub-total	9.9	100

Source: Cocks and Bentley (1996).

believed that this was not being demonstrated. They embarked upon a series of changes which, though not intended at the outset, have brought about the most radical overhaul of the NHS since its inception. (For a summary of developments in the NHS 1948–96 see Powell 1997: 63–88.)

NHS structure

1973–90

The first major structural change to the NHS was implemented in 1974 by means of the NHS Reorganization Act 1973. This brought together hospital and community health services which were to be provided by area health authorities (AHAs) directly or through their districts where appropriate. Regional health authorities (RHAs) were also established with responsibility for regional planning and monitoring as well as for the provision of certain central services. In addition, family practitioner committees (FPCs) were established to administer general practitioner (GP) services and, although they operated autonomously, each was linked with an AHA sharing the same boundaries. Finally, community health councils (CHCs) were created, one for each district, in order to represent the views of the consumer and act as a local pressure group.

The aims of the Reorganization Act 1973 were commendable in that the Act sought to integrate more fully healthcare provision by bringing together the hospital and community health sectors and by promoting comprehensive strategic planning in preference to disaggregated hospital planning. This restructuring was quickly followed by the constitution of a Resource Allocation Working Party (RAWP) in 1975 to address the issue of inequalities in the system for distributing health resources throughout the country.

However, despite these developments, critics of the reorganization argued that there were too many tiers of management for efficient decision making and the report of the Royal Commission on the NHS (Cm. 7615 1979) accepted the need to eradicate one tier. In addition, the Conservative election victory in 1979 meant that attention would be focused on levels of public expenditure. For the NHS, this meant assessing the use to which resources were put and how they might be supplemented. The Conservatives stated they would 'make better use of what resources are available' and would 'simplify and decentralise the service and cut back bureaucracy' (Conservative Party 1979: 26); intentions not dissimilar to those made by the Labour Party in its manifesto in 1997 (Labour Party 1997: 20–1).

The Health Services Act 1980 eliminated the AHAs and their functions were transferred to newly-established district health authorities (DHAs). These were held accountable for managing their own hospital and community health services and encouraged to delegate responsibility for decision making to units of management, usually hospitals, wherever possible. The Act sought to encourage private sector health care provision by reducing restrictions on private medicine, and also legalized lotteries and voluntary fund-raising by health authorities.

During the early 1980s central government placed the emphasis on accountability and value for money. This led to the introduction of annual performance reviews supported by the publication of the first set of performance indicators for the NHS in 1983, and initiatives were launched aimed at securing the most efficient utilization of scarce resources.

In 1983 the Griffiths Inquiry was commissioned and the subsequent report (Griffiths 1983) proposed another restructuring of the NHS to promote speedier decision making and enhanced accountability. Consensus decision making at unit, district and regional level was to be abolished and replaced by general managers at all levels who were to be given clear responsibility for implementing policy directives and meeting targets. This also marked the beginning of a period in which attempts have been made to place clinicians into senior managerial positions, where 'They are expected to take a more corporate view and to tackle strategic issues of service configuration, finance and human resource management' (Ferlie *et al.* 1996: 84). Inevitably, this raises issues as to the power relationship between clinical professionals and managers. For an excellent discussion of this issue, placed also within the context of new public management (NPM) see Ferlie *et al.* (1996).

The management structure of the NHS was revised and two boards were established: a health services supervisory board, chaired by the secretary of state, with responsibility, *inter alia*, for formulating strategic objectives; second, a management board, chaired by a chief executive responsible for the execution of policy decisions and the control of strategic performance. Tangentially, the idea of delegation to the lowest practical level was developed through the introduction of management budgeting, a concept whereby individual responsibility for the consumption of resources is identified and incorporated into the budgeting process. This meant clinicians became budget holders thereby making them more accountable for their decisions.

This focus on accountability and control of resources was reinforced throughout the 1980s with initiatives such as the contracting-out of support services, the introduction of limited prescription lists for GPs, the establishment of cost improvement programmes (CIPs) (see 'Budgeting', page 243) for health authorities and new income generation plans for the NHS. At the same time a debate arose about the government's alleged underfunding of the service.

This debate continued until the launch of the NHS Review, announced in 1988, culminating in the publication of the White Papers *Working for Patients* (Cm. 555 1989) and *Caring for People: Community Care in the Next Decade and Beyond* (Cm. 849 1989). The proposals contained in these reports were embodied in the NHS and Community Care Act 1990.

1991–97

The NHS and Community Care Act 1990 was followed by *Health of the Nation* (DoH 1992), proposing a long-term strategy to bring the best balance of health benefits to the nation, *The Patient's Charter* (DoH 1991, 1995) which sets out the key rights every citizen has in respect of the NHS, and is also used as the basis for compiling league tables of performance, and the formulation of national Charter standards which the NHS is expected to achieve.

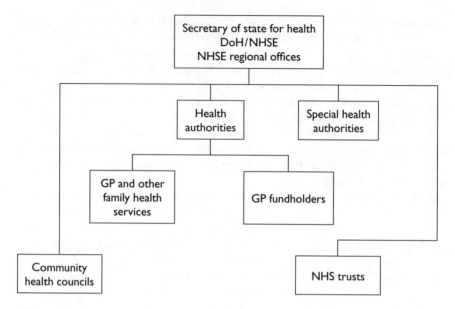

Figure 10.1 Structure of the NHS in England
Source: Prowle and Jones (1997).

The NHS and Community Care Act 1990 affected both the NHS and local authorities and represents a watershed in the history of healthcare in the UK. The main thrust of the reforms rests on the introduction of an internal market, a phrase usually attributed to Enthoven (1985), which involves the separation of the purchasing of healthcare from its provision. The internal market as a concept is based on the establishment of competition at the provider level while health authorities as purchasers continue to be financed from the DoH but in their new role have a duty to enter into contracts with a range of providers to secure the best and most efficient services possible for their resident populations. This distinction between purchasers and providers is central to the measures introduced.

The structure of the NHS changed again in April 1996 in that the RHAs, which had been reduced from 14 to 8 in April 1994, became regional offices of the NHS Executive (NHSE). In addition, DHAs merged with family health service authorities (FHSAs) to create single new health authorities (or health commissions) at local level accountable to the Secretary of State through the NHSE regional offices (see Figure 10.1). The FHSAs previously managed non-fundholding GPs (see below), general dental practitioners, retail pharmacists and opticians. This change was part of a wider strategy for the development of purchasing and the creation of a primary care-led NHS, in which decisions about the purchasing and provision of health care are taken as close to patients as possible. The role of the GP in this is pivotal.

Box 10.1 Intended benefits of GP fundholding

- **Closer focus on individual needs:** waiting lists managed with more sensitivity to individual patient's needs.
- **Better quality service:** more responsive providers producing tangible improvements in care according to GPs' wishes.
- **More effective healthcare:** self-audit by GPs of referral and prescribing differences leading to internal guidelines and shared-care agreements with consultants.
- **Increased efficiency:** managing the contract portfolio to purchase more activity at less cost, e.g. by reducing inappropriate outpatient appointments, more day surgery, using cheaper providers, better prescribing.
- **Wider choice for patients:** freedom to refer where the GP and patients wish.
- **Development of services nearer to patients:** introducing therapeutic services (e.g. physiotherapy or counselling) and consultant outpatient clinics into the practice, community hospitals or other sites nearer to where patients live.

Source: Audit Commission (1966: 4–6).

Within the market, and below the level of the NHSE, the purchasers are the health commissions, GP fundholders and private patients. The providers are mainly trusts, private hospitals and voluntary bodies. However, it is important to note that GP fundholders are also providers in that they can use funds to provide services directly in their own surgeries (e.g. physiotherapy, ultrasound scanning). Prowle and Jones (1997: 19) state: 'In fact this is probably one of the most fluid aspects of the NHS internal market and in future years it may well be that a much wider range of health services are provided in the GP surgery than is currently the case'.

With regard to providers, the policy, as introduced by the 1990 Act, has been most significant in that hospital and community units have become NHS trusts, competing with each other, and thereby self-governing. With regard to purchasers, the introduction of GP fundholding reflected a recognition of the fundamental importance of the GP as the gatekeeper to healthcare for the majority of patients. No detailed objectives of fundholding were established by the NHSE, however Box 10.1 lists the intended benefits as identified by the Audit Commission.

The initiative was designed to complement the other reforms in *Working for Patients* (Cm. 555 1989) and to give GPs an incentive to improve the services they offer and enable money to follow the patient from the GP practice itself. GP fundholding grew dramatically from its inception and now covers about half of the population and accounts for 20 per cent of patients' hospital and community care (Audit Commission 1996). However, the success of GP fundholding is open to serious doubt, as evidenced by the Audit Commission (1996) report. Though it indicated that some

---

Box 10.2 GP fundholding: conclusions reached by the Audit Commission

- Most fundholders had introduced some improvements, *viz.* improved communications with hospitals and more cost-effective prescribing, but only the best-managed practices had a major impact on services.
- Criteria for entry to the scheme should be reviewed and action taken when required standards are not met.
- Consideration should be given to other policy options, including strengthening the accountability framework and introducing accreditation for purchasers.
- Budget setting needs streamlining and standardizing.
- Most fundholders rate training as less than adequate.
- Basic financial monitoring is satisfactory but systems are needed to measure fundholders' purchasing performance.
- Commissioning strategies rarely take account of fundholders' intentions.

Source: Audit Commission (1996: 1).

---

fundholding practices are well managed and at the leading edge of purchasing, the majority have not realized the purported benefits of the scheme. The Audit Commission has called for GP fundholders to invest in top quality management expertise and to be supported by the newly-created health authorities in areas such as public health and information technology (see Box 10.2).

In addition, there have been serious criticisms concerning the creation of two tiers of health care, with preferential treatment given to the patients of fundholding practices over those from non-fundholding practices (Wilson 1995). These criticisms were acknowledged in July 1997 when the government announced that fundholding GPs would no longer be able to buy care for their patients ahead of equally sick patients from non-fundholding GPs (see *the Guardian*, 17 July). However, the Labour government published its proposals in December 1997 (DoH 1997) and intends to abolish GP fundholding in its current form. Labour proposes that teams of up to 50 GPs will hold a single budget to serve a population of about 100,000 patients. The intention is for GPs and community nurses to form primary care groups, to control a unified budget and to have responsibility for commissioning local health services. These commissioning groups will gradually replace individual GP fundholders.

In considering the structure of the market and the participants within it, it is important to highlight a further and fundamental element of change, i.e. that relating to community care. The cost of community care combined with the number of organizations involved in its provision led to a review being instigated, the results of which (Griffiths 1988) led to the White Paper *Caring for People* (Cm. 849 1989). Initially, Griffiths' recommendations were unpopular with the government as they involved an enhanced role for local authorities. Despite central government's political objections to this, it was eventually decided that local authority social services departments would have responsibility for assessing needs and ensuring they were met, but their role would primarily be that of enabler rather than provider: 'In other words, social service managers are expected to demonstrate value for money in the purchase of services from competing bodies in the public, private and voluntary sectors' (Carroll and Wilson 1993: 196).

The structural changes to the NHS were designed to ensure more effective use of resources through competition and improved management. However, as Moran (1995: 22) has highlighted, they 'have one unifying characteristic: they are all concerned with the resource allocation process in the health care system'. He says three aspects of change stand out. First, increases (e.g. prescriptions) and extensions (e.g. eye tests) to charges represent a significant modification of the 1948 reforms, which were intended to provide a comprehensive service free of charge, and 'are attempts to influence the allocation process by charging at the point of delivery' (p. 22). Second, changes have been introduced to limit the degree of medical autonomy (see Griffiths 1983, above) or to alter the balance of power within the medical profession (away from consultants towards GPs). Third, the resource allocation model has itself been changed from one of command and control to one based on market principles. All these changes raised the importance of, and had implications for, financial management in the NHS.

This chapter will now discuss the following areas of financial management:

- Funding.
- Resource allocation.
- Contracting, costing and pricing.
- Budgeting.
- Capital financing and business cases.
- Financial reporting.

Funding

In his November 1996 budget speech, the then Chancellor, Kenneth Clarke, stated that health expenditure had increased in real terms by 75 per cent since 1979, more than 3 per cent a year. The problem, however, is that healthcare output has not increased by such an amount and the expression 'real terms' can be misleading, particularly in the case of the health service. In the NHS, inflation tends to be higher than that experienced in the economy as a whole, so a 'real terms' increase as measured by the retail price index (RPI) or the GDP deflator, another measure of inflation, is unlikely, in practice, to represent an actual and equivalent increase in resources (see Chapter 1). There are three important reasons for this. First, wages and salaries, which consume more than 70 per cent of NHS resources, may increase by more than the rate of price inflation, so a 'real terms' increase may be insufficient to meet increased wage costs. Second,

Table 10.2 Estimated healthcare expenditure in 21 OECD countries

Country	% of GDP	Per capita health spending (£ sterling)
Greece	5.4	295
Portugal	5.8	337
Denmark	6.4	1249
Spain	6.7	643
Ireland	6.8	659
UK	6.8	814
Japan	6.9	1650
New Zealand	7.3	659
Norway	7.8	1367
Belgium	8.1	1214
Australia	8.2	949
Sweden	8.2	1317
Finland	8.3	1001
The Netherlands	8.4	1234
Italy	8.5	1122
Germany	8.5	1677
Austria	8.8	1513
Switzerland	9.1	2176
France	9.2	1435
Canada	9.9	1447
United States	15.7	2816
OECD average	**10.4**	**1663**

Source: Holliday (1995), Table 4.1, p. 39.

technological and medical advances in healthcare lead to greater demands upon the service, but such advances tend to be very expensive and much more so than can be accommodated within 'real terms' increases. Third, the elderly constitute an increasing proportion of the population and this trend exerts more pressure on the NHS in that total demand for healthcare rises as the population ages. This demographic trend is itself influenced by the NHS, the existence of which has contributed to greater life expectancy.

The above factors mean it is very difficult to discern precisely what is happening with regard to provision of healthcare and the level of resources devoted to it. Given the political significance of perceptions of quality and levels of healthcare, it is perhaps unsurprising that there are claims and counter-claims. However, it is possible to place the issue into a wider context by considering international comparisons. Here, the NHS would appear to perform reasonably well. According to Holliday (1995: 38), commenting on a study conducted by the OECD (Organization for Economic Cooperation and Development) published in 1995, into health-care expenditures in 21 member countries: 'All international comparisons demonstrate that one of the most striking aspects of the NHS is the small amount of resources it consumes' (see Table 10.2). The figures also illustrate the way the United States dramatically outspends all other countries. Relating the figures to health outcomes, again the UK compares favourably. Holliday states:

> A simple comparison of UK health outcome statistics with those of the same 21 OECD countries already used for cost comparison indicates that UK figures are at the very least good, and often better than that. Where the UK does slip below the OECD average – in female life expectancy at birth – it is only by a very marginal amount. In passing it might be noted that the United States, for all its massive spending on health care, registers mainly average health outcomes.
>
> (1995: 41–2)

Such favourable international comparisons, combined with periodic crises in the NHS, particularly in the winter months when demand for hospital places traditionally increases through weather-related illnesses, have led to accusations of underfunding. However, the demands upon the NHS, combined with technological and demographic factors, mean that it is unlikely, given the needs of other services including education, defence, etc. and the implications for taxation, that any government would be able to ensure levels of funding commensurate with service needs and public preference.

In June 1997, Timmins reported that, as part of a wider Treasury review of charges for all types of public services, the DoH is to consider 'pressing for a tax for the National Health Service'. The idea of a 'hypothecated' tax (i.e. one from which the revenue is earmarked for a specific purpose) for health is not new (it was actually favoured by the former Labour leader, Neil Kinnock, prior to the 1992 general election) but the fact that it remains as a serious idea illustrates the fundamental importance of healthcare funding. This was reinforced by the furore which followed an answer given to journalists, in June 1997, by Frank Dobson, secretary of state for health, relating to the Labour government's wide-ranging review of the NHS. In his answer he refused to rule out the possibility of certain charges being introduced, e.g. for visits to the GP, 'hotel' charges relating to hospital stays, etc. Though the Prime Minister, Tony Blair, subsequently attempted to defuse the row by insisting that manifesto promises would not be broken, the issue highlighted the sensitivity of the debate around charges. Despite a substantial increase in health fees and charges since the early 1980s, as a proportion of NHS finance they have actually fallen from 4.5 per cent in the late 1980s to 2.4 per cent today (Timmins 1997). The NHS remains almost wholly funded from general taxation (including national insurance, which is simply another name for, albeit a regressive form of, direct taxation). This means that the total level of resources devoted to the NHS, determined by the government each year as part of the public expenditure planning process, is cash limited and announced in the annual budget statement. This key decision remains a political one and is unaffected by the introduction of market principles, no matter how extensive their application.

Given that responsibility for the overall level of resources devoted to the NHS is a political one, and cannot be deflected elsewhere, there is every possibility that the Labour government will face a crisis over the NHS given its acceptance of the spending plans of the previous Conservative government. Despite the fact that, under the Conservatives, from 1979 to 1996, spending grew in 'real terms' by 3 per cent, Labour initially pledged to preside over cumulative growth of less than 1 per cent in the next four years, compared with 15 per cent in the last four years. Although an extra £1.2bn was allocated to the NHS by Chancellor Gordon Brown in the July 1997 budget, this still left 'real terms' growth at 2.25 per cent for 1998–9, below the average of 3 per cent achieved by the Conservatives. The consequences of this below-trend funding are likely to be exacerbated by the financial deficits many health authorities carried forward from 1996–7 into 1997–8, and possibly into 1998–9 (see *Financial Times*, 18 March 1997). The escalating financial problems within the NHS were highlighted by the National Audit Office (NAO) in July 1997 (NAO 1997; see also *Financial Times*, 18 July 1997), which reported that, at the end of the third quarter of 1996–7, the number of NHS trusts in financial difficulty was 168 compared with 95 at the end of April 1996, with 47 (more than 10 per cent of the 433 trusts) judged to be in serious difficulty against 26 nine months earlier. In the case of 23 of the 47, their main purchaser was also facing financial difficulties. Similarly, 36 out of 100 health authorities in England were forecasting deficits in excess of £1m, compared with 15 reported to be in a similar position at the end of 1995–6. Despite these problems, Labour is pledged to reducing the waiting list by 100,000 (it stood at 1.1m at the end of December 1996, see *Financial Times*, 20 February 1997), though this is meant to be achieved by reducing the costs of administration by £100m. Achieving this target will be made even more difficult given the apparent acute shortage of beds and the unexplained increases in emergency admissions in the last two years.

The reality is that the expenditure plans are unachievable. In an organization the size of the NHS there will always be scope for improved efficiency, though this may also require investment (e.g. in information technology). However, the scope for efficiency gains is not infinite and a more likely consequence of the extremely tight spending limits is the increased use of rationing (or 'priority-setting') (see Harrison 1997). It is certainly the case that, in the longer term, the issues of what the NHS is there to do, and should do, need to be debated. The former may involve the drawing-up of a 'restricted menu' of services, i.e. certain services may not be provided free or at all by the NHS, including fertility treatment, cosmetic surgery and treatment of lifestyle-related illnesses, such as those caused through smoking etc. The latter involves much greater consideration of available medical evidence, involving clinical audit and evidence-based medicine. Moves in this direction were announced in July 1997 (see *The Guardian*, 10 July 1997), whereby the government is to phase out medical treatments considered ineffective or unnecessary (for instance, one goal is to reduce the number of Caesarean births) by making hospitals report how often they are used. To this end, 15 indicators, agreed with doctor's leaders, are being pilot-tested. They include deaths in hospital within 30 days of surgery and emergency readmission within 28 days of discharge. However, though such monitoring may be sensible, medically and financially, it is hardly likely to assist Labour to stay within the spending plans in the short term.

In addition, even in the longer term, it needs to be appreciated that while it makes sense to establish priorities, gaining consensus on what the priorities are will prove to be extremely difficult. In a survey of NHS managers (see *Financial Times*, 11 June 1997) three-quarters believed that the NHS will be forced through financial pressures into defining a 'core' service, with other services excluded, charged for or rationed (fewer than two-thirds believed this *should* happen). The Dutch government has gone down this route (excluding adult dental care and homeopathic treatment from their health benefits package) but, as Dilnot (1997) and Ham (1997) have separately reported, a recent exercise in New Zealand designed to define a reduced core group of treatments ended up with a decision being made that everything that had been done in the past was a core treatment.

It also needs to be appreciated that rationing does not solve the problem of inadequate funding, but possibly exacerbates it by making the priorities that much more difficult to choose. *De facto* rationing, through the use of charging, is also problematic in that it still requires decisions as to the services to be subject to a charge and the level of charge. It is also regressive in that poorer people will be unable to afford the charge, and can also be said to be dishonest, as Hattersley (1997) argues: 'Health service charges . . . are not alternatives to tax increases. They *are* tax increases' (original emphasis). In addition, charging need not necessarily help in controlling healthcare costs, in that decreased demand from one group of patients (e.g. the poor) may lead to more services being offered to, and, therefore, demanded by, those groups most able to pay (e.g. the rich). The experience of the United States shows how health costs can continue to rise (see Table 10.2) despite the widespread use of charging (Donaldson *et al.* 1996). Charging, however, is only one means of rationing services; there are other, less explicit, techniques which, according to Stephen Thornton, speaking as chief executive of Cambridge and Huntingdon Health Authority, are used by health authorities throughout Britain. The techniques are: denial; deterrence; delay; deflection; and dilution (the 5 'Ds': see Box 10.3) (see also Harrison 1997).

Box 10.3 Techniques to ration NHS services: the '5 Ds'

'It gives me no pleasure at all to have to say this, but in Cambridge and Huntingdon, in order to pay for the growth in emergency care and mental health needs, we have *denied* women access to infertility treatment; we have *deterred* people accessing out-patient services at their local community hospital by centralising them on the district general hospital site; we have deliberately induced treatment *delays* by lengthening waiting times; we have *deflected* costs on to other public agencies and the private individual by continuing to disinvest in long-term NHS care; and we have witnessed a continued *dilution* in the quality of services as local hospitals cut nurse staffing levels to cope . . . Admit that service rationing is already happening; admit it's necessary if your financial projections are to be realised; and give us support for what we have to do as a result, even if that means public backing for our unpalatable decisions' (original emphasis).

Source: Stephen Thornton, chief executive of Cambridge and Huntingdon Health Authority, addressing the Annual Conference of the NHS Confederation, June 1997, as reported in *The Guardian*, 2 July 1997.

In all of this, the fundamental principles of the NHS – universal, comprehensive health care free at the point of delivery – are clearly being eroded. It may be that this is inevitable, but this is difficult to justify when the obvious remedies – of raising taxes and switching priorities between expenditure programmes – are ruled out.

Resource allocation

Each year a political decision is made as to the total level of resources to be devoted to healthcare. Once the political decision has been made, resources are allocated under two main headings: hospitals and community health services (HCHS) and family health services (FHS), each of which is sub-divided into revenue and capital.

With regard to revenue allocations, Rogers (1995: 209) identifies four distinct periods of change since the NHS was created. During the first period (1948–70) allocations were simply based on existing services. In the second period (1971–6) the 'Crossman formula' (named after a former secretary of state) was introduced, which based allocations on populations served, adjusted for age and sex, beds and caseload. In the third period (1977–89) the RAWP (established in 1975) formula was used, designed to equalize resources across the regions by giving proportionately more each year to the under-provided regions. Finally, in the fourth period, (1990–present) resident/capitation-based funding has been introduced. Each region's population is 'weighted' to reflect the demands placed on health services by different age groups (the weights are also refined to reflect certain geographical dissimilarities, e.g. in the case of London a specific allowance is added).

Revenue allocations are initially distributed to the NHSE regional offices and, on a weighted capitation basis, are then distributed to health authorities, as purchasers within the internal market; they then acquire healthcare for that part of the population for which they are responsible. GP fundholder budgets are calculated differently but are essentially determined by activity levels and treatment costs at the hospitals used. However, there is strong pressure to allocate GP fundholder's budgets on a weighted capitation basis and thus improve equity in the funding process. With regard to providers, viz. NHS Trusts, they earn money through the provision of healthcare; the total income they are able to generate is not cash limited but is largely determined by the volume of treatment they are capable of delivering. However, it is important to appreciate that, unlike a true market, the total level of activity *is* cash limited: 'In a "proper" market, excess demand initially gives rise to higher profits which attract additional suppliers until demand is satisfied at a price providing an adequate profit. In a cash limited market, where the accumulation of surpluses is explicitly forbidden, excess demand gives rise to waiting lists' (Mellett *et al.* 1993: 19).

With regard to capital, the basic rule is that expenditure on an individual item exceeding £5000 is capital expenditure; where an item costs less than £5000 it is revenue expenditure. The DoH agrees capital expenditure plans directly with NHS trusts. This then enables an adjustment to be made to the funds made available to the regions, which are allocated on the basis of weighted population and are distributed by NHSE regional offices to health authorities on the basis of their approved capital programmes (see 'Capital financing and business cases', page 246).

Contracting, costing and pricing (see also Chapter 4)

Operationally, the market requires providers to enter into contracts with purchasers in which the volume, quality and cost of services are specified. Contracts may be one of three types:

1 Block.
2 Cost per case.
3 Cost and volume.

In a block contract, the provider is paid an annual sum in return for which the purchaser's residents gain access to a defined range of services. The opposite of a block contract is a cost per case contract, where reimbursement will equal the price of each item or service multiplied by the volume of items or service provided. A cost and volume contract requires the purchaser to pay for the treatment of a specified number of cases. The purchaser pays the full price for a set number of cases and above this level a price equal to marginal cost is paid. In practice, the prevalent contract has been that which was envisaged: the block contract. However, there are strong moves being made by the NHSE to develop more sophisticated contracts.

In part, however, the development of more sophisticated contracts depends on the accurate determination of price. In theory, in a perfectly competitive market, managers would have little influence on price as it is determined by the interaction of all buyers and sellers. However, in 1990, the NHS, after many years of central planning, was characterized by monopolistic provision of healthcare, i.e. there was often only one major acute hospital in each geographical area. In this situation, in a free market, there is an incentive to raise prices and earn monopoly (super normal) profits. To avoid such abuse, the DoH issued guidance in 1990 on how prices used in healthcare contracts were to be constructed. They stipulated that prices are to be based on full-cost recovery, with marginal costing (see Chapter 4) only being the basis of price where there is spare capacity for a short period. In addition, there should be no cross-subsidization between services. However, towards the end of 1994, a review was established by the NHSE finance director into all aspects of the NHS financial regime and it is possible that some key aspects may be relaxed, notably those restrictions relating to cross-subsidization and pricing (see Brown 1996). There may also be a relaxation, or modification, of the three financial targets set for trusts, i.e. to break even; to achieve a 6 per cent return on capital; to stay within their external financing limit (EFL) (the EFL, in effect, is a limit set by the government on the net borrowing which a trust can undertake to finance the approved capital investment).

It was initially anticipated that comparative prices, fairly reflecting resource usage, would emerge and that purchasers would be guided by price to the most 'efficient' provider. However, there is little evidence nationally that this has happened, for which there are two main reasons. First, the predominance of block contracts does not promote the development of procedures for costing and pricing; it is a simplistic approach to contracting that adds little value to the process of price determination. Second, though it is possible to calculate average costs for various specialist treatments (i.e. average speciality costs), they are not exhaustive and exclude a wide range of treatments which are available.

The problems of costing and pricing were highlighted when, in preparation for the introduction of GP fundholding, some 113 individual procedures were costed. Despite the expectancy of comparative prices, vast variations in prices emerged. In April 1993, the then NHSME issued guidance on costing for contracting to avoid differences in reputed costs for the same patient treatment caused by unnecessary differences in cost allocation and apportionment between different providers. The guidance establishes:

- A minimum level of identification of costs by type: direct, indirect and overheads.
- A more standardized approach to methods of apportionment for indirect and overhead costs.
- A minimum level of sophistication for identifying costs as variable, semi-fixed and fixed.

Despite this guidance, variations in costing and pricing have persisted. These variations, combined with the monopolistic nature of health provision, represent a fundamental problem for the advocates of the application of market principles to the NHS. The internal market was established to improve efficiency but, without accurate prices and a reasonable degree of competition, purchasers are unable to place contracts with the most efficient providers. In theory, the cost-based pricing regime relates to a model where purchasers assess the prices charged and select the provider with the lowest price. In reality, because of the unreliability of price as a measure of efficiency and the lack of competition in many parts of the country, contracts are negotiated and long-term relationships developed almost independently of considerations of price and alternative suppliers.

None the less, provider units earn the vast majority of their income via healthcare contracts and this income needs to be translated into operational budgets, so that the organization can manage and monitor activities and ensure its objectives are met.

Budgeting

Budgeting is a key component of effective financial management, and this is particularly true in an organization the size of the NHS. It is essential to ensure that resource allocation (i.e. budgeting) is appropriate and expenditure profiles (i.e. budgetary control) are within established limits. However, budgeting is not simply an instrument of financial control. In the NHS, budgeting helps ensure that resources are utilized in a way which enables the NHS to achieve its aims and objectives, which are ultimately related to maximizing the health gains of the population. To this end, budgeting is also an instrument of performance measurement and evaluation.

There are, however, more precise legislative and non-legislative reasons for NHS bodies to prepare budgets. With regard to the former, the NHS and Community Care Act 1990 requires budgets to be produced as part of the financial control framework. The non-legislative reasons for NHS bodies to produce budgets include the following (see also Chapter 3):

- Satisfying the external environment: external groups, ranging from central government and local government, to local pressure groups and individuals, may have an interest in the budgetary information.
- Assisting in policy making and planning: the budget process allows policy makers to compose different options and resource requirements.
- Aiding policy implementation and control: the budget is the basic means of controlling resources with different emphasis at different management levels.
- Providing a basis for controlling income and investment: the budget is a management tool that assists in achieving planned levels of service and expenditure.
- Motivating managers and employees: good budgeting control systems can motivate budget holders to achieve better management performance.

Within the NHS, each organization will have its own arrangements for setting, controlling and reporting upon budgets. However, each will have to quantify the size of the budget on an annual basis. In the case of an NHS trust, estimates will need to be made of anticipated income, which will in turn depend on the contracts made with purchasers. Expenditure budgets can then be established, some of which will be retained centrally, some will be allocated to a reserve (as a contingency against unforeseen events), and the remainder will be delegated to budget holders.

Methods of budgeting (viz. incremental and zero-based) have been discussed in Chapter 3. In the NHS, the approach is an incremental one in that the starting point in determining next year's budget will be the current year's budget, which constitutes the 'base budget'. Adjustments will then be made to the base budget to reflect wage and price inflation and any efficiency gains, or cost improvement targets, which need to be made to meet unavoidable pressures. With regard to cost improvements, trusts have been required to make these on an annual basis, giving rise to CIPs. There are two types of CIP:

1 Cash-releasing: involving the provision of the same level of service at a lower cost, thereby lowering prices and producing cash savings for the purchaser.
2 Productivity-gaining: involving the provision of a greater volume of service at the same level of cost, thereby lowering prices, but the trust retains the same level of income.

The scope for cost improvements is not infinite, nor is it uniform. In reality, however, a blanket approach tends to be adopted, which penalizes the most efficient trusts and services as they will have less scope for improvement.

Once established and delegated, budgets need to be controlled and, to achieve this, budgetary information must be appropriate for any particular

Table 10.3 Flexible budgeting

Budget report: ward-based catering costs			
	Budgeted	*Actual*	*Variance Favourable (adverse)*
Patient days[1]	6,935	6,570	365
Catering cost per patient day (£)	20	21	
Total catering cost – unflexed budget (£)	138,700	137,970	730
Flexed budget (£)	131,400	137,970	(6,570)

1 Estimated patient days based on a 20-bed ward occupied for 365 days at 95% occupancy.

budget-holder (it is important to recognize that there are many different users of NHS budget information, all requiring different versions of the budget statement in varying levels of detail). Budgetary control information, as with all financial information, must be useful and therefore must be:

- relevant: the right information must be provided to the right person(s);
- accurate: it must ensure that the right decisions are made;
- comprehensive: the level of detail must be tailored to the requirements of the users;
- timely: it must be current and updated frequently;
- understandable: it must be capable of interpretation.

In controlling budgets, it is necessary to relate the budget and expenditure incurred to date to some measure of output, i.e. resources are aggregated into a budget and allocated in order to achieve specific objectives, and these objectives need to be considered when exercising budgetary control. An evaluation of budgetary performance which does not take account of the volume of activity achieved can produce misleading information. Attention needs to be paid to volume variance when evaluating budgetary control information; in other words budgets need to be flexed and variances (which may be price variances or volume variances) from budgeted activity need to be quantified. The application of flexible budgeting can lead to a more accurate interpretation of budgetary performance and, potentially, a more effective use of resources.

This is illustrated by the example given in Table 10.3 where it first appears that the catering manager has achieved an underspend of £730 for the period in question. However, since the number of patient days has been 365 less than expected, the budget should be reduced by £7300 (365 patient days × £20 per day). This flexed budget now reveals an overspend of £6570, i.e. an overspend of £1 for each of the 6570 patient days.

This raises numerous questions which, in reality, would require investigation (e.g. the cost of purchases, waste in food preparation, the appropriateness of the initial estimates, etc.). However, the point to note is that what may appear prima facie to be a good performance in that expenditure has remained within budget is in fact no such thing. It is necessary to analyse the figures further. Presenting information in a way which highlights variances facilitates budgetary control in that an analysis of the differences between budgeted and actual data enables the budget holder to decide on corrective action where necessary.

Within the NHS, budget statements tend to include information on direct costs only (as illustrated in Table 10.3). A budgetary control system which includes indirect costs and overhead costs has not, in the main, been developed. These costs are still budgeted for and managed separately from the patient-related budgets. However, service level agreements (SLAs), are being increasingly introduced in recognition of the relationship between indirect costs, overheads and patient-related activity. In exercising budgetary control, there is also a need to provide contractual activity statements, given that NHS providers earn the vast majority of their income from healthcare contracts which include activity targets.

In conclusion, the creation of the internal market, the introduction of healthcare contracts, and the resultant changes to income streams, have led to a more complex and sophisticated budgetary control system being required than was previously the case.

Capital financing and business cases

In the NHS, prior to April 1991, capital was provided by central government as a 'free good', without any interest charge, depreciation charge or repayment of principal. However, on the assumption that such a non-commercial approach did little to encourage efficiency in the use of capital, development of capital accounting/charging had been advocated by various bodies since the late 1970s and early 1980s. The NHS system of charging for the use of capital assets began in April 1991:

> This initiative was partly to encourage greater efficiency and accountability in the use of the NHS estate, whose gross value at the higher of market value or replacement cost could be upwards of £40 billion, and partly to provide relevant capital use costs for inclusion in the pricing of hospital and other NHS services, to ensure fair competition in internal market trading within the NHS and also between the NHS and the private sector.
>
> (Perrin 1992: 233)

The introduction of capital charges and their equivalents for NHS trusts, i.e. the inclusion of depreciation into revenue costs and the requirement to achieve a 6 per cent rate of return on net relevant assets, reflected increasing concern by the NHSE that capital investment should not be seen as a free good. In addition, in view of the scandals of the Wessex and West Midlands Regional Health Authorities referred to in Chapter 7, the NHSE issued, in 1994, their Capital Investment Manual (CIM).

The introduction of capital charges has meant that a more commercial approach needs to be adopted in choosing between capital investment options. The traditional methods for evaluating capital projects (including discounted cash flow, cost benefit analysis, etc., described in Chapter 5) now need to be placed within a more business-oriented context. To this end, the CIM sets out the capital appraisal process and provides a blueprint for management to follow to ensure that all investment benefits are identified, realized and evaluated. The CIM emphasizes three key points. For each capital scheme, it must be demonstrated that:

1 The business case is economically sound and financially viable.
2 Private finance alternatives have been explored and tested.
3 Effective project management is in place.

Point 2 refers to the need to explore private finance options. Today, there are three main ways by which trusts (most NHS capital expenditure is undertaken by NHS trusts, as health authorities have limited needs for capital expenditure) may finance capital expenditure:

1 Internally-generated funds (accumulated depreciation, retained surpluses, sales of fixed assets).
2 External funds (e.g. additional borrowing from the NHSE).
3 Private finance initiative (PFI).

With regard to PFI, the complexities associated with it are not discussed here but it is important to note that an NHS trust wishing to undertake a major capital investment must first demonstrate that it has attempted to obtain funding from the private sector before applying for public funding. The way in which this is demonstrated is by means of the process of business case preparation.

In preparing plans for capital investment, a trust must prepare a business case, one purpose of which is to minimize abortive effort in the presentation of capital projects for approval. It consists of three stages:

1 The strategic context: the relative demand for healthcare, the case for investment, and its relative affordability are first established from the trust's strategic direction and business plan.
2 The outline business case (OBC): this involves the identification of objectives and benefit criteria; generation of options; identification and, where

possible, quantification of benefits and costs; assessment of sensitivity to risk; identification of the preferred option.

3 The full business case (FBC): should not be commenced until the NHSE has approved the outline business case. It involves the development of the preferred option and further review and refinement of the work already done.

Recently, the transition from OBC to FBC has involved the use of the PFI to search for private sector funding.

There are a number of mandatory requirements within the various stages of the business case development including:

- The trust must take full responsibility for each project and not cede responsibility to external contractors.
- There must be a formal professional certification of the accuracy of the costs within the business case by the director of finance.
- It is mandatory for all schemes in excess of £1m to be subject to post-project evaluation.

The CIM and the business case process have established a thorough and professional framework for evaluating options and ensuring that any preferred scheme is capable of delivering the benefits identified.

Financial reporting

The financial framework and reporting requirements to which the NHS is subjected are matters of considerable importance given the proportion of public expenditure accounted for by the NHS. Internally, each health authority and NHS trust will have its own standing orders (e.g. conduct of board meetings, arrangements for delegation to officers, tendering and contracting arrangements, etc.), standing financial instructions (e.g. security of assets, internal audit arrangements, delegated spending limits, etc.) and financial procedures (e.g. ordering of goods and services, payment of creditors, collection of income, stock control, etc.).

With regard to external reporting, the NHS, as with all public service organizations, needs to be able to demonstrate that the resources which have been allocated to it are accounted for and been used for the purposes intended. In other words, there is a need for accountability. This is addressed by the annual publication of accounts which, in purpose if not in content, are similar to those for any other organization. In the case of an NHS trust, there is a need to demonstrate that the three key financial targets have been achieved (i.e. break-even, 6 per cent rate of return on capital, EFL not exceeded; see 'Contracting, costing and pricing', page 241).

The main accounts comprise:

- Income and expenditure account.
- Balance sheet.
- Cash flow statement.

Examples of each of the above are given in the Appendix at the end of the chapter, taken from the published annual report of a health authority for the year ended 31 March 1997. The examples are provided simply for illustration; detailed comments on each line of the examples are not given here, but please refer to Prowle and Jones, (1997: 96–121) for a general discussion of the nature of NHS financial reporting.

The accounts must be accompanied by a statement of accounting practice and certified by the director of finance and acknowledged by the chair of the health authority or NHS trusts prior to audit.

The Treasury requires the format of the annual accounts to follow that of the private sector, as far as possible. The accounts should be prepared in accordance with the relevant accounting standards issued or adopted by the Accounting Standards Board (ASB). In addition, NHS trusts and health authorities publish annual reports, aimed at the general public. The minimum contents of the report are specified by the NHSE and include summarized financial information which must be consistent with that shown in the statutory accounts, as confirmed by a statement from the external auditor which is also included. In the event of the accounts being qualified, a full report must be included in the annual report together with any further material needed to understand the qualification.

The information in the annual report should, among other issues, relate to:

- Principal activities.
- A review of the developments over the year.
- Important events occurring after the year-end.
- Significant changes in fixed assets.

The NHS codes of conduct and accountability also require the inclusion of information about the remuneration of directors.

Conclusion

The debate concerning the level of resources to be devoted to the NHS continues. Similarly, there are disagreements concerning: which services the NHS should offer; rationing; pricing; charging; the structure of the NHS (see Harrison 1997); the relationship with the private sector, etc. These are all key issues. Central, however, to all such discussions is the issue of financial management and control.

The need for effective financial management is perhaps uniquely important in the case of the NHS, for two main reasons. First, the demands which it seeks to meet will always exceed its ability to do so. Second, it is a high profile service which affects all of us, either directly (as a user) or indirectly (as a taxpayer, potential user, relative or friend of a user, etc.). These points may apply to other public services, notably education, but not to the same extent in that, in the case of the NHS, life and death issues are literally, and often, involved.

The radical changes introduced by previous Conservative governments may or may not be dismantled. The Labour government is committed to abolishing the NHS internal market (Labour Party 1997: 20) but shows little rush or determination to do so. There would appear to be similar ambiguity over GP fundholding. However, there is likely to be less emphasis on competition and more emphasis on partnerships in the delivery of healthcare. In June 1997 Frank Dobson announced that 'partnership and cooperation' were 'making a comeback' in the NHS, and called for the creation of 'health action zones' to give the NHS access to local authority funds and the £3.4bn single regeneration budget. The action zones, possibly between eight and ten, would bring together all health interests in partnership with local authorities, community groups, the voluntary sector and local business to agree a health strategy aimed at delivering 'integrated arrangements for treatment and care' (see *Financial Times*, 26 June 1997).

Whatever the structure of the NHS, however, and even though 'the NHS remains a bargain for UK taxpayers' (*Financial Times*, editorial, 21 February 1997), it is likely to experience extreme pressures unless more resources are devoted to it. This is a reflection of socio-economic and technological trends rather than a criticism of the policies which have been pursued since 1991. However, the extent to which these policies have achieved their objectives is open to serious doubt. The themes which have been identified in other chapters, i.e. competition (internal market, including purchasers and providers), decentralization (e.g. GP fundholding), customer-focus (*The Patient's Charter*) and performance measurement (league tables) have all been evident in the NHS. The importation of private sector personnel and techniques have also been evident, sometimes at considerable cost (see Chapter 7). However, perhaps in one key area much more needs to be done, and that is the area of performance measurement. This is problematic in the public services (see Chapter 8) and perhaps nowhere more so than in healthcare. None the less, there is a real need to ensure that scarce resources are being allocated in the most cost-effective manner, and this requires much more work on clinical audit and evidence-based medicine.

In short, despite the election of a Labour government, the financial management issues are likely to remain largely unchanged. A health service funded almost wholly from general taxation, free at the point of entry, in tandem with ever-increasing demands for its services, will ensure that financial tensions within the system are likely to be a permanent fixture.

It is likely that, in the future, the boundaries between public and private healthcare may become increasingly blurred. This may be exemplified in the case of GP fundholders using their budgets to purchase private treatment; it is also interesting to note that the largest provider of private patient services in the UK is the NHS (see *Financial Times*, 30 September 1996). 'The main impact of all of this . . . has been to redefine what we mean by the NHS – it has moved from being a national service towards a national insurance service. It still largely guarantees free care but it does not necessarily provide it' (Dixon 1996).

Fifty years on, the scale of the NHS is considerably different to that envisaged in 1948. It seems reasonable to assume that the nature and scale of the NHS in 2048 will be different to anything we may predict today. There is, however, likely to be a crucial distinction between the last and the next half-centuries. The distinction is that between expansion and contraction, or universalism and exclusion. The period 1948–98 has been characterized by dramatic and unanticipated growth, whereas the next 50 years may be characterized by unprecedented contraction as the NHS pulls away from the principles upon which it was founded. Should this prove to be the case, it will be so not for reasons of economic unaffordability but rather of political preference.

Appendix

Income and expenditure account

For the year ended 31 March 1997

	1996/97	1995/96
	£'000	£'000
Income		
Income from activities	58,082	55,248
Other operating income	12,957	15,366
Total income	71,039	70,614
Expenditure		
Operating expenses	(67,500)	(68,098)
Operating surplus	3,539	2,516
Loss on disposal of fixed assets	(2)	(33)
Surplus before interest	3,537	2,483
Interest receivable	158	233
Interest payable	(1,897)	(1,859)
Surplus for the financial year	1,798	857
Public Dividends Capital dividends payable	(833)	(328)
Retained surplus for the year	965	529
Return on relevant net assets	6.0%	4.5%

Cash flow statement

For the year ended 31 March 1997

	1996/97		1995/96	
	£'000	£'000	£'000	£'000
Net cash inflow from operating activities		6,166		5,126
Returns on investments and servicing				
of finance				
Interest received	174		226	
Interest paid	(1,881)		(1,862)	
Interest element of finance lease rentals	(10)		–	
Net cash outflow returns on investments				
and servicing of finance		(1,717)		(1,636)
Capital expenditure				
Payments to acquire fixed assets	(5,122)		(4,032)	
Receipts from sale of fixed assets	70		–	
Net cash outflow from capital expenditure		(5,052)		(4,032)
Public dividends paid		(833)		(328)
Net cash outflow before financing		(1,436)		(870)
Financing				
New long term loans (Government)	2,509		500	
Repayment of long term loans				
(Government)	(957)		(946)	
Other capital receipts	70		110	
Capital element of finance lease rental				
payments	(13)		–	
Net cash inflow from financing		1,609		(336)
Increase/decrease in cash		173		(1,206)

Balance sheet

As at 31 March 1997

	31 March 1997		31 March 1996	
	£'000	£'000	£'000	£'000
Fixed assets		67,245		62,709
Current assets				
Stocks	746		751	
Debtors – Amounts falling due				
after one year	480		410	
– Amounts falling due within				
one year	1,455		2,250	
Cash at bank and in hand	282		108	

	31 March 1997		31 March 1996	
	£'000	£'000	£'000	£'000
Total current assets	2,963		3,519	
Less current liabilities				
Creditors – Amounts falling due within one year	(5,629)		(6,509)	
Net current liabilities		(2,666)		(2,990)
Creditors – Amounts falling due after one year		(23,363)		(21,938)
Provisions for liabilities and charges		(774)		(633)
Total assets		40,442		37,148
Financed by capital and reserves				
Public Dividend Capital		23,617		23,619
Revaluation reserve		12,292		10,088
Donation reserve		713		587
Income and expenditure reserve		3,820		2,854
Total capital and reserves		40,442		37,148

References

Audit Commission (1996) *What the doctor ordered?* London: HMSO.

Brown, S. (1996) Beefing up the market. *Public Finance*, 4 October.

Carroll, A. and Wilson, J. (1993) National Health Service, in J. Wilson and P. Hinton (eds) *Public Services & the 1990s: Issues in Public Service Finance and Management*, pp. 190–207. Eastham: Tudor.

Cm. 7615 (1979) *Report of the Royal Commission on the National Health Service*. London: HMSO.

Cm. 555 (1989) *Working for Patients*. London: HMSO.

Cm. 849 (1989) *Caring for People: Community Care in the Next Decade and Beyond*. London: HMSO.

Cocks, R. and Bentley, R. (1996) *£300 Billion Government Spending: The Facts*. Reading: Databooks.

Conservative Party (1979) *The Conservative Manifesto*. London: Conservative Central Office.

Dilnot, A. (1997) Magic required, *Guardian*, 23 January.

Dixon, N. (1996) Blood, sweat and tiers, *Guardian*, 11 September.

DoH (Department of Health) (1991) *The Patient's Charter*. London: DoH.

DoH (Department of Health) (1992) *Health of the Nation*. London: HMSO.

DoH (Department of Health) (1995) *The Patient's Charter*. London: DoH.

DoH (Department of Health) (1997) *The New NHS*. London: The Stationery Office.

Donaldson, C., Scott, T. and Wordsworth, S. (1996) Operating Costs, *Guardian*, 4 September.

Enthoven, A. (1985) *Reflections on the Management of the NHS*, occasional paper 5, Nuffield Provincial Hospitals Trust.

Ferlie, E., Pettigrew, A., Ashburner, L. and Fitzgerald, L. (1996) *The New Public Management In Action*. Oxford: Oxford University Press.

Griffiths, R. (1983) *Report of the NHS Management Enquiry*. London: DHSS.

Griffiths, R. (1988) *Community Care: Agenda for Action*. London: HMSO.

Ham, C. (1997) Free-for-all flight, *Guardian*, 25 June.

Harrison, S. (1997) Health – the agenda for an incoming government. *Public Money & Management*, 17 (2): 27–31.

Hattersley, R. (1997) Just one per cent on top tax wouldn't hurt, *Guardian*, 24 June.

Holliday, I. (1995) *The NHS Transformed* (2nd edn). Manchester: Baseline Books.

Labour Party (1997) *New Labour Because Britain Deserves Better*. London: Labour Party.

Mellett, H., Marriott, N. and Harries, S. (1993) *Financial Management In The NHS: A Manager's Handbook*. London: Chapman & Hall.

Moran, M. (1995) Explaining change in the National Health Service: corporatism, closure and democratic capitalism. *Public Policy and Administration*, 10 (2): 21–33.

National Audit Office (NAO) (1997) *NHS Summarised Accounts 1995–96, England and Wales*. London: Stationery Office.

Perrin, J. (1992) The National Health Service, in D. Henley, A. Likierman, J. Perrin *et al. Public Sector Accounting and Financial Control* (4th edn), pp. 215–47. London: Chapman & Hall.

Powell, M. A. (1997) *Evaluating the National Health Service*. Buckingham: Open University Press.

Prowle, M. and Jones, T. (1997) *Health Service Finance: An Introduction* (4th edn). Glasgow: Certified Accountants Educational Trust.

Rogers, M. (1995) *Public Sector Accounting*. Cheltenham: Stanley Thornes Publishers.

Timmins, N. (1997) Spending review may lead to NHS tax, *Financial Times*, 9 June.

Wilson, J. (1995) Dealing with dogma: the National Health Service, in J. Wilson (ed.) (1995) *Managing Public Services: Dealing With Dogma*, pp. 155–70. Eastham: Tudor.

Further reading

News coverage of developments in the NHS is best obtained from specialist journals, including *Public Finance* and *Health Service Journal*. Academic journals also regularly feature articles on the NHS and you are advised to consult *Financial Accountability and Management* and *Public Money & Management*. Newspapers, notably *The Guardian* and the *Financial Times* are also a very good source of up-to-date information and analysis.

part five

Towards the future

eleven

Financial management: an overview

John Wilson

Key learning objectives

After reading this chapter you should be able to:

1 Appreciate the changed nature of public service management.
2 Evaluate the impact, actual and potential, of change on financial resource management within the public services.
3 Discuss possible future developments in public service management in general and financial resource management in particular.

Introduction

Financial resource management in the public sector represents an enormous challenge. It is technically demanding, practised in a high-profile environment and entails accountability, in a variety of ways, to senior managers, politicians, 'consumers' and the public. The resultant pressures are compounded by intense resource constraints and the need to assimilate and apply private sector financial management practices in the delivery of services for which they were not strictly intended. This chapter summarizes these issues and, in doing so, considers the current and likely nature of financial resource management in the public sector.

The nature of financial management

For nearly two decades the public sector was regarded as being not only inherently inferior to the private sector but, in fact, injurious to it. It became fashionable to believe that the scale of its activity represented an increasing deadweight on the economy and that the public sector was the enemy of enterprise. Public sector activity involved the use of finite resources which, it became increasingly popular to believe, could have been more productively utilized by the private sector. In addition, activity had to be financed and this led to levels of taxation of individuals and enterprises which were greater than those which would have been necessary had the public sector been smaller and/or more efficient. Neither reductions in scale of activity nor improvements in efficiency were likely to occur given the power of those with a vested interest either in preserving the status quo or in achieving public sector expansion such as politicians, bureaucrats, professions and trade unions.

Economic decline, it was believed, could only be arrested and reversed by reducing the size of the public sector and, in so doing, facilitating the growth of the private sector. Where possible, services should be transferred to or replaced by the private sector and all services remaining in the public sector should be subject to competition, where appropriate, and the management of them should be reformed so as to reflect private sector best practice. In effect, not only was the sharp public/private distinction to be ended, it was to be replaced by the creation of sectors which could perhaps best be described as quasi-market, and market.

The creation of a new quasi-market public sector involved the introduction of structural changes, including internal markets, purchaser/provider splits etc., which, in effect, institutionalized the Conservatives' enthusiasm for and belief in the efficacy of competition and the supremacy of private sector approaches to management. Private sector managerial practice was to be integral to the delivery of public services and, to this end, traditional public administration was replaced by 'new public management' (NPM), the main themes of which have been identified throughout this book as:

- Competition.
- Decentralization (involving freedom to manage).
- Customer focus.
- Performance measurement ('more for less').

The above themes have posed certain threats, in addition to the fundamental threat posed to job security by privatization and resource constraints for public sector personnel in general and financial managers in particular.

There are three main and related reasons for suggesting that financial managers have been disproportionately affected by the changes. These are:

1 Compulsory competitive tendering (CCT).
2 Accountability.
3 Organizational restructuring.

CCT has had a significant effect on finance departments. To take the example of local government, while the election of a Labour government in May 1997 means that a proportion of financial services activity will not have to be exposed to competition, some authorities would have already expended considerable effort in preparing for CCT as a result of Conservative policy, and possibly exposed some activities to voluntary competitive tendering. In addition, an increased workload would have resulted from the need to assist other departments to prepare for competition.

More significantly, however, the need to subject blue-collar and certain white-collar services to CCT meant that the costs of the finance department, as a key support service, came under much greater scrutiny than was ever previously the case. There was always a need to recharge to front-line services the costs of central support services, but the introduction of CCT meant that recharges now had a significant effect on the competitiveness of the departments which were receiving the recharges. Inevitably, this led departments to question, with even more force than previously, the level, accuracy, basis and timing (which were often determined at year-end rather than the beginning of the year) of the recharges they were having to absorb. Competition, therefore, led to demands for greater accountability which, in turn, is linked to the issue of performance measurement.

Finance departments, and central departments generally, were now being held accountable for their actions and, as a result, there was a shift in the balance of power from support services in favour of front-line services. In addition, to some extent, service departments would be free to decide not to use central support services but to acquire the expertise they needed from elsewhere. This put greater pressure on support services to provide the level and type of service which the customer actually wanted and for which the front-line department was prepared to pay. In short, support services needed to demonstrate responsiveness and value for money (VFM).

In order to ensure support services were being delivered in a manner which was cost-effective and consistent with customer preferences, central departments were restructured and tended to become flatter and decentralized. In the case of finance, for instance, more responsibility now rests with the financial staff located within direct service organizations (DSOs) or other support services. More significantly, however, financial responsibility has been devolved from, for instance, county hall to the local headteacher under the local management of schools (LMS) initiative, from the National Health Service (NHS) regional office to the general practitioner (GP) etc.

These developments represent a shift of managerial responsibility from 'the centre' to the point of delivery, with a concomitant dilution of longer-term centralized planning in the delivery of public services. They have affected all support services, as summarized by the Audit Commission (1994: 6):

It was common that departmental staffing establishments could not be changed, even in a minor way, without the approval of the Director of Personnel and the appropriate personnel sub-committee; IT [information technology] applications were allowed only on the central mainframe and had to compete for priority in the demands of the IT department; the Director of Finance prepared departmental budgets and had the power of virement, and spending decisions became tightly controlled . . . Furthermore, the cost of central departments was automatically transferred to service departments, often in an arbitrary way . . .

The 1980s and 1990s have seen increasing pressure to move away from the model of the controlling centre. The devolution of service provision, budgets and accountability to the point of delivery, eg in schools and homes for the elderly, has prompted a need for greater responsiveness to consumers and reduced the control that could be exercised from the centre. Equally, the need for DSOs to compete for work under CCT and survive in the market place has focused attention on the recharged costs of central departments, as these affect a DSO's financial viability. A combination of rising expectations from local authorities' customers, additional responsibilities for local government and increasing pressures on resources generally, have led to very difficult decisions about priorities for front line services. As a result, service deliverers now question the level of support provided by central departments, and the 'burden of overheads' imposed upon them.

These pressures, separately or in combination, provide challenges to the balance of power between the centre and service deliverers.

However, the effect on finance departments has been particularly felt given their traditional role in determining and controlling budgets and resource allocation decisions. Again, to take the example of local government:

Local governments are complex organisations and the balance between departments, professions and councillors will vary between them, but, even allowing for that variation, it is clear that finance departments play an important role in all of them, and the message which they carry with them helps to determine the ways in which decisions are made throughout the organisation.

(Clarke and Cochrane 1989: 44)

This was true in 1989 and remains, in part, true today but less so given the developments in the intervening period which have forced finance departments to respond to competition, become more accountable and to restructure and relinquish certain powers as a result.

However, although the themes identified above and throughout this book have posed certain threats to the financial manager, they have also provided certain opportunities. As the public sector was coerced into 'reinventing' itself, a key feature of the reinvention was the change in financial management, specifically management accounting (see Chapters 3, 4 and 5), rather than any variant of traditional public administration. It could, therefore, paradoxically be argued that although the role and power of the traditional finance department (professionally and organizationally dominant, traditionally structured and centrally located) have diminished, those of the financial manager have increased.

The emphasis on VFM, performance measurement, resource accounting, priority-setting, budgeting, etc. has enhanced the power of the financial manager who must now display entrepreneurial flair and demonstrate that resources have been effectively allocated and utilized. This will also particularly apply in local government given the Labour government's intention to replace CCT with 'Best Value'. The focus is no longer on inputs but rather on outputs and, increasingly, outcomes. It is no longer sufficient to say that the public sector will employ more teachers, nurses, social workers, soldiers, fire-fighters or police personnel; nor is it sufficient to say that more schools, hospitals, roads etc. will be built, or to assume that the public sector should provide any service in preference to the private sector. The key criterion is VFM, not the level of inputs or the sector which delivers. Performance needs to be quantified and 'returns' on investment demonstrated.

These developments demand technical skills and the finance manager is best placed to provide them. Gray and Jenkins (1995: 88) go so far as to claim that 'In the practice of public management, the 1980s and 1990s have become the age of the financial manager'. They go on to say:

> Accounting, budgeting and auditing have dominated the discourse about the delivery of public services and changed the language and rules of resource allocation in areas as diverse as education, health, and policing both in the UK and overseas . . . The theoretical literature used to legitimise this transformation has been drawn frequently from the fields of academic accounting and, to a lesser extent, the work of economists interested in the public sector and public management processes . . . This has also been aided by the emergence and development of bodies such as the National Audit Office in central government and the Audit Commission . . . bodies who in their staffing and focus have reached beyond the traditional role of audit to value for money studies.
>
> (Gray and Jenkins 1995: 88)

Gray and Jenkins believe that the most 'significant practical impact of these changes has been the emergence of accountable management and regimes of performance measurement' (p. 88) (see also Chapter 8).

However, as has been discussed previously (see Chapter 2), a number of the changes are of questionable merit. Competition, for example, and the creation of internal markets, can create their own bureaucracy, inefficiency and transaction costs. Decentralization can lead to a dilution of the role of finance as an impartial central department capable of arbitrating between the rival claims of service departments for increased resources. Similarly, the fragmentation of the finance department and the emphasis on key aspects of NPM, including competition, entrepreneurialism, risk and innovation, can undermine the stewardship function and lead to increased risk of malpractice, fraud or corruption (see Chapter 7), perhaps demanding an alternative approach to audit (see Chapter 6) or, at least, a rediscovery of the importance of probity. (It is also important to remember that, at least in local government, chief financial officers have a statutory duty to ensure audit arrangements are appropriate.) Customer focus is inherently commendable, but, in the case of public services, identification of the customer and the longer-term needs of the services are problematic (see Chapters 2 and 8). Measuring performance is also problematic (see Chapter 8) in most public services, including health, education, the police etc.

Gray and Jenkins also question the extent to which all of these developments are new. For instance (p. 89):

> The issue of performance measurement is far from new in either the theory or practice of public administration, having been central to earlier discussions of policy evaluation . . . as well as featuring in debates on successive innovations such as cost benefit analysis (CBA), planning programming budgeting (PPB), zero-based budgeting (ZBB) and management by objectives (MbO).
>
> (1995: 89)

Similarly, it is legitimate to question the extent to which public service management has actually changed.

At national level, contrary to popular thinking, the period 1979–97 under four consecutive Conservative governments was characterized by centralization of powers and nationalization of large areas of activity which considerably reduced local power and freedom to act (this was particularly true in the case of local government) (Jenkins 1995). At local level, managerial freedom to act and to make decisions on resource allocation is still constrained for those who remain in central support services, though it has increased for local managers who are now budget holders. In turn, this has led to new skills being required by those to whom financial responsibilities have been devolved. However, the degree of financial autonomy must not be exaggerated given that, across the public sector, resources are tightly controlled by central government. In addition, the proportion of any budget over which discretion can be exercised is small, mainly because of the labour-intensive nature of the public sector and the size of a budget accounted for by salaries and wages. In so far as there is enhanced managerial freedom, it is debatable as to the extent to which it has actually changed behaviour and resource allocation. Similarly, the extent to which such freedom is actually wanted (in the case of headteachers at local education authorities' schools, for instance) is also debatable.

It is true that, in the case of central support services, not least finance, there is now much greater accountability in the use of resources and the quantification and recharging of costs (see Chapter 4). The impact of competition has also been considerable. However, fundamentally, the scale and nature of change may be exaggerated; the replacement of old-style bureaucrats by new public entrepreneurs is, perhaps, more stated than observed. This scepticism as to the extent of change applies to all public services but is perhaps particularly true of those industries which have been privatized and which now regard themselves as 'businesses' in every sense, including the water companies, British Telecom, British Gas, etc. They have sought to be entrepreneurial, to diversify from core activity, to embrace private sector styles and practices, but how much has changed? Technically, they may no longer be monopolies, but in reality they are able to exploit a monopolistic position and this, in the main, provided the justification for Gordon Brown to introduce a windfall tax in his first budget (July 1997). Speaking as Labour's Paymaster General and entrepreneur, Geoffrey Robinson, actually accused some heads of privatized industries of having made risk-free fortunes just by being in the right place at the right time (see the *Observer*, 18 May 1997): '. . . these people [heading the utilities] have not taken a risk in their lives; they have inherited [their fortunes]. That is offensive to those who fought and took risks'.

This statement is quite remarkable given its source but exemplifies the point being made, which is that calling a company or an industry a 'business' does not, in itself, make it one. Changing labels does not, in itself, change market conditions. Cultural change may be brought about, and private sector attitudes and practices replace public sector ones, but such change does not occur spontaneously. In other words, real differences between public and private sectors remain. Essentially, the latter is concerned with achieving profits in competitive conditions and the former, in large part, is concerned with delivering services in non-competitive conditions. This distinction is, of course, misleading in that it ignores both the degree of cartelization which exists in the private sector and the competition which exists in the case of the public sector (this has been increased since 1979, e.g. by CCT, but, it should also be recognized, competition was in place prior to 1979, e.g. the fierce competition faced by the former nationalized industries, including steel and aerospace).

Even though in part misleading, the distinction is useful in that it reminds us that the two sectors are fundamentally different. The public sector must consider, for instance, issues such as equity, uniformity of provision and access, and these considerations, combined with the sheer cost of providing public services, financed through taxation, distinguishes it from the private sector. Appreciating this fact is sensible, not old-fashioned. Recognizing the limitations of 'profit' as a measure of private sector efficiency and its inapplicability to much public sector activity is helpful rather than unhelpful. Refusing to concede that certain roles are inherently more useful and productive than others actually reflects an open mind rather than a closed one – in the case of public services, there is no inherent merit in being an entrepreneur rather than a bureaucrat, or a manager rather than an administrator, and there is no inherent merit in being a private sector employee rather than a public sector employee. There is an overwhelming need to ensure an appropriate balance between the public and private sectors and for each to use resources efficiently and effectively, but there is also a need to recognize differences in how efficiency and effectiveness are measured. Similarly, it is important to appreciate the significance of economic criteria in assessing resource allocation and utilization; economic conclusions may not be the same as financial ones (a company may improve its financial performance through large-scale redundancy but the economic cost to the country of such action may exceed the financial gain to the company).

In other words, there is a need to challenge a number of assumptions which underpin conventional wisdom. This applies just as much now, under a Labour government, as it did in the period 1979–97.

Financial management: the future

The election of a Labour government has changed the atmosphere within which public services are provided. It remains to be seen, however, how much will actually change in practice.

Before the general election, Labour accepted the public expenditure plans for 1997–8 and 1998–9 as outlined by the then Chancellor, Kenneth Clarke, in his budget of November 1996. Irrespective of the political wisdom of this decision, the economic wisdom is extremely questionable. During the general election campaign (conducted throughout April 1997), the Institute for Fiscal Studies (IFS) (in its *Election Briefing*) claimed that the expenditure projections of both the Conservative and Labour Parties did not look credible without cuts in public services. Clarke's plans envisaged lower sustained growth in public spending than had been achieved at any time in the past three decades. In his report on the IFS figures, Timmins (1997a) states: 'Overall, spending was set to rise by an average of 0.4 per cent a year against 1.9 per cent on average over the past 18 years [i.e. since 1978–9]: a difference that would put public spending in the last year of the next parliament [i.e. 2001–2] about £24bn lower than if the previous trend was maintained'. This means that the macroeconomic environment for public services is possibly going to be worse under Labour than under the Conservatives, and this perhaps remains the case despite the selective increases in resources allocated to health and education, as announced by the chancellor in the budget of July 1997 and since (see Chapter 1). Given that sound financial management is even more important in times of relative contraction rather than expansion, with an urgent need to balance inadequate resources with the demands for services, financial managers can expect difficult times ahead. This is especially true in the NHS, for which particular problems were forecast. Timmins (1997a) states:

> Spending on the [NHS] . . . in particular was 'strikingly tight' the IFS said – in spite of both parties' commitment to real-term year-on-year increases . . . Either the plans were not feasible and would be broken, or there were likely to be 'serious implications' for the NHS as a universal provider of free health care . . . averaged over three years, health spending would rise by 0.6 per cent a year, a fifth of the level of the past 18 years, certainly the lowest sustained level for 30 years, and quite possibly the lowest since the NHS was founded.

The implications of this were reinforced by the *Financial Times*, 14 April 1997:

> The position is bad under the Conservatives and may be worse under Labour . . . Labour's claim it can meet the issue by cutting bureaucracy does not bear examination. Even on its debatable claim that the NHS market added £1.5bn to management costs, close to all of that would be required [in 1998–9] to meet spending needs. Nothing like all of it is available . . . Without more money, the choices are simple: either a dramatic decline in levels of service, or new charges – prescription payments for the elderly, a charge for hospital stays and GP visits.

These warnings retained their validity after the first Labour budget. Though the increased allocation of £1.2bn for 1998–9 meant that current health spending in England would now increase in 'real terms' by 2.25 per cent rather than 0.2 per cent, it remains below the average increase of 3 per cent which has occurred since 1979.

The choice outlined by the *Financial Times* also applies to social services, the provision of which rests with health authorities and local authorities but is increasingly falling between, rather than on, them.

A decline in the quality of service, accompanied by increases and an extension of charging, will encourage more people who can afford to do so to switch to private healthcare. This also applies to education and other key component parts of the welfare state, notably social services and pensions. Inevitably, therefore, the balance between public and private sectors is likely to tilt further in favour of the latter. This may or may not be what the country wants, but it is the most likely scenario, as stated by Timmins (1997b): '. . . without some fairly radical restructuring of government spending priorities, there is likely to be a continued shift to private provision. This will occur either by default as the better-off bail out of over-stretched health and education services, or by increased compulsion for private provision in higher education, pensions and, possibly, for long-term care'.

It is unlikely, however, that Labour will 'radically restructure' its spending priorities, though it is committed not so much to increasing public expenditure but to evaluating it so as to ensure money is well spent. Its manifesto (Labour Party 1997: 11) states that 'The level of government spending is no longer the best measure of the effectiveness of government action in the public interest' (though this ignores the fact that it never was the best measure) and goes on to say (pp. 11–12):

> It is what money is actually spent on that counts more than how money is spent . . . A new Labour government will give immediate high priority to seeing how public money can better be used. New Labour will be wise spenders not big spenders. We will work in partnership with the private sector to achieve our goals. We will ask about public spending the first question that a manager in any company would ask – can existing resources be used more effectively to meet our priorities? And because efficiency and value for money are central, ministers will be required to save before they spend. Save to invest is our approach, not tax and spend.

Labour made considerable effort, prior to the election, to convince the electorate that it would behave 'responsibly' if elected and, therefore, not all statements can be taken at face value. However, it seems reasonable to conclude that the above quote from its manifesto is a genuine one and that Labour has adopted the 'good housekeeping' approach to economic management most recently associated with Thatcher but which can perhaps be traced all the way back to Gladstone.

The implications of Labour's macroeconomic caution are quite profound. The acceptance of the previous government's expenditure plans means not only that the total level of expenditure will be extremely difficult to stay within (as indicated above) but that any increase in resources to one part of the public sector will have to be met by corresponding reductions elsewhere. This, in turn, places increased pressures on financial managers. However, the social impact should not be forgotten in the midst of public expenditure technicalities and NPM jargon.

Box 11.1 provides a case study which illustrates the:

- significance of public expenditure decisions;
- competition between services for resources;

Box 11.1 Case study: illustration of budget pressures and the inter-relationship between public services

[Gloucestershire County Council] says it will probably face a £3m shortfall in its social services budget [in 1997–8] and overall it estimates a deficit of £11.8m.

It is a familiar story. All over the country councils have cut services [in 1996–7] to avoid overspending their social services budget. It is understood that Sheffield has made cuts worth £5.6m this year, while £2m of cuts have been made by Sunderland. St Helens is believed to have cropped £7m off its social services budget [in 1996–7].

Councils say that social services funding will be £545m less [in 1997–8] than in [1996–7], before inflation, pay rises and additional service pressures. Once additional responsibilities are taken into account, the shortfall increases to £1.6bn [in 1997–8].

Social services have three options open to them to cover this shortfall . . . They can cut services, increase charges or tighten the criteria that govern who is eligible for care . . .

But where will the cuts fall? It appears that the most significant cuts will fall at the 'margins'. This means that the elderly who are largely self-sufficient but who may need a little extra help around the home, such as having their weekly shopping done, will be particularly hard hit . . . [but] this may turn out to be false economy as discharged patients who are not supported adequately are more likely to return to hospital . . .

The pressure on social services often manifests itself in bed blocking, which occurs when a patient is well enough to be discharged but there are insufficient resources to look after them in the community. According to a recent survey . . . of 69 English and Welsh councils, 75% of authorities with responsibilities for social services reported bed blocking. In all, 1365 beds were blocked . . . To ease bed blocking the health department will make £20m available [in 1997–8]. This is going to health authorities but councils hold little hope that much of this extra cash will filter through to community care. Social services directors may look jealously at the extra money their counterparts in the health service will receive [in 1997–8], but there is also genuine concern that the gap will increase pressure on community care . . . the extra money for the health service will mean greater throughput of patients, being discharged ever faster into the community. However, because social services funding has not kept pace with that of the health service, councils will not have the resources to support people in the community. Beds will be blocked or patients will be discharged and not receive adequate care, making another spell in hospital more likely.

Source: Ward 1996: 8–10.

- opportunity cost of resource allocation;
- need for 'losers' if there are to be 'gainers' when total expenditure remains 'fixed';
- impact on services (e.g. social services) following decisions made in other services (e.g. health);
- long-term cost of short-term 'savings';
- difficulty of remaining within budgets;
- scale of required budget cuts (the 1996–7 budget for personal social services was approximately £9.8bn nationally);
- choices which have to be made;
- essential service-based, as opposed to profit-based, nature of public sector activity;
- social impact of decisions taken (cuts in weekly shopping service).

Similarly, Box 11.2 illustrates the:

Box 11.2 Illustration of the relationship between central and local government

Seventeen years of – in the main – remorseless centralisation of UK local government have left local authorities and the government stuck between a rock and a hard place.

Their location is amply illustrated by [the November 1996 budget]. The government announces that it wants another £830m spent on education and adjusts councils' standard spending assessments to allow for that. Local authorities reply that they are already spending more than that sum implies – so they will have to raise the council tax to do it.

But the government, having eased the capping rules last year to allow extra education spending through, has tightened them again this – to limit the size of council tax rises ahead of the general election.

Many big authorities therefore face a 1 per cent limit on their spending, while being expected to find 3.6 per cent more for education.

The result can only be a further big squeeze on their other big budget – social services. But lack of cash there is already trapping elderly patients in hospital beds . . . This is no way to do business. No one gains from it. Government is blamed for all deficiencies. Councils lose the ability to choose, innovate and in any real sense to govern. The electorate is increasingly denied the right to decide what level of services it wishes to see locally.

The answer must be to restore local government's financial base – making its own resources more closely match the duties placed upon it.

Source: Financial Times, 2 December 1996.

- unacceptable relationship, politically and financially, between central and local government;
- constraints upon local government's freedom to manage;
- confusing claims concerning 'increases' in spending on a particular service;
- political dimension to decision making (e.g. imminence of a general election);
- interrelationship between services: 'winners' require 'losers' (e.g. education and social services; social services and the NHS).

It may be that, after the first two years in office, Labour will alter its macroeconomic priorities. It may also be the case that, throughout its period of office, it radically transforms the way in which the country is governed – for instance, returning powers to local government, pursuing devolution, establishing regional tiers of government – and the way in which public services are managed, perhaps notably the health service. However, the emphases, during the period of Conservative rule, on attempting to promote the private sector, restrain the public sector and 'privatize' public sector management, are emphases which Labour has, it seems, embraced.

For this reason, combined with the explicit acceptance of previous Conservative expenditure plans and the pledges not to raise taxation, and despite the commitments, for instance, to: prioritize in favour of education (Labour Party 1997: 6–7); abolish the internal market in the NHS (p. 20); abolish CCT (p. 34); and to lay the foundations of a modern welfare state (p. 5), it is at least questionable as to how much things will actually change for public service managers under Labour. Also important here is the question of economic and monetary union and the implications for public expenditure and public services of the requirements for membership.

VFM – 'best value' (Labour Party 1997: 34) – performance measurement etc. will continue to be stressed, as will public and private sector partnerships, specifically the private finance initiative (PFI), which Labour is committed to 'reinvigorating' (p. 16). The language has not changed and nor have the constraints. The hostility to the public sector has, it seems fair to say, been removed, but an underlying feeling of the need to justify its existence remains.

Conclusion

In achieving that which is expected of them, the public services will continue to need enthusiastic and skilful managers. The complexity of managing inadequate resources in a high-profile, political environment in order to deliver services which are of fundamental importance to each of us as individuals and to society as a whole, demands personal, inter-personal and technical skills of the highest order. Central to this is the need for effective financial management and the requirement, for all financial managers, to demonstrate – and to assist others to demonstrate – that resources have been economically, efficiently and effectively allocated and utilized in fulfilling the purposes for which they were intended. The justification, appropriateness, origin and impact of competition, decentralization, customer focus and performance measurement are all open to debate, but they are developments which represent key features of the changed public service landscape and are likely to remain so for the foreseeable future.

References

Audit Commission (1994) *Behind Closed Doors: the Revolution in Central Support Services*. London: HMSO.

Clarke, A. and Cochrane, A. (1989) Inside the machine. *Capital and Class*, 37, Spring: 35–61.

Gray, A. and Jenkins, B. (1995) From public administration to public management: reassessing a revolution? *Public Administration*, 73, Spring: 75–99.

Jenkins, S. (1995) *Accountable To None: The Tory Nationalization of Britain*. Harmondsworth: Penguin.

Labour Party (1997) *New Labour Because Britain Deserves Better*. London: Labour Party.

Timmins, N. (1997a) Parties warned welfare state faces death by a thousand cuts, *Financial Times*, 10 April.

Timmins, N. (1997b) Cut down to size, *Financial Times*, 29 April.

Ward, S. (1996) Reduced service, *Public Finance*, 20 December: 8–10.

Further reading

Please refer to texts as recommended at the end of each chapter. In addition, you are strongly recommended, not least because of the pace of change, to refer to the main public service management journals, including *Public Administration, Public Money & Management, Public Policy and Administration, Financial Accountability & Management* and the annual publication, *Public Services Yearbook* (London: Pitman). Professional journals also contain useful and topical material, including *Public Finance* and *Management Accounting*.

Index